# Advertising
# and
# Promoting
# the
# Professional
# Practice

# Advertising
## and
# Promoting
## the
# Professional
# Practice

# Morton Walker, D.P.M.

HAWTHORN BOOKS, INC.

*Publishers*/NEW YORK

*A Howard & Wyndham Company*

To the members of the
Connecticut Podiatry Association
who, by use of this book, will have come full circle

# Contents

Contents

# PART III
## Public Relations and Promotion

# Preface

In this book, I attempt to describe the practice and philosophy of advertising and promotion for the professional person who sells services to the public. It is a businesslike guide that has long been looked for and suddenly has become absolutely necessary. Changing times, altered ethical codes, new rules, and enforcement of old mandates under the Federal Trade Commission have made this book necessary reading. The United States Supreme Court, by its removal of discriminatory practices of professional associations against advertising members, has created an uproar in the learned professions. This handbook had to be published.

It has always been my belief that the public has the right to know everything there is to tell about the professional services it needs and wants to receive. People should also be informed about the practitioners who deliver these services. As a former practicing doctor of podiatric medicine for more than sixteen years, I provided the public with foot-care information. I aimed to educate them in all phases of foot health.

Over time, I discovered that this public-information practice was against the precepts of a closed professional association. Its members were antagonistic to educating people in how to help themselves.

The result was conflict over most of the sixteen years of my professional practice. Fellow podiatrists considered me an "advertiser," although I never paid a cent for any kind of commercial message. They called me a "pitchman," and in this my colleagues were correct. I pitched the message of professional podiatric care and interspersed it with helpful hints on home care of the feet.

Preface

I still believe that public information was and is the proper course to follow. Apparently, modern podiatry and its practitioners have changed their minds, too. They have adopted my original philosophy, and today they are advertising and promoting the sale of their services. Today they are hiring public relations counselors to raise the image of the profession. Old-line traditionalists are seeking new ways to popularize the treatment of foot problems. The story being told is an old one. I broadcast and published it more than twenty years ago, but now it's being presented in a more salable professional package.

The use of advertising and promotion is intrinsic to the capitalist system. The early American patriots used it to sell the Constitution to their fellow citizens. Two hundred years later, the Supreme Court has declared that under that same Constitution, the learned professional has the right to engage in advertising and promotion. I say, it's about time.

So, with encouragement from an astute editor, I have written this book on how to advertise and promote your professional practice, using the names of real people and their situations. When I've changed a name, I've made a note of it. This book is dedicated to helping you mold public opinion in your favor. It can act as the means for you to sell more professional services to greater numbers of people who require them.

My conviction is that service in the public interest is the ultimate criterion by which a person or a policy must be judged. This book will stimulate the dispensing of more professional services in the United States and Canada. Canada's restrictions in advertising and promoting professional services are, in fact, less stringent, since it has national health insurance. It will give you a greater opportunity to use your technical skills, which were developed through aptitude, training, and experience. I believe you will have your outlay for this book returned to you ten thousandfold. I wish I had owned it when I was in practice.

Good luck with your advertising and promotion!

# PART I

# Your New Right to Advertise Professional Services: Restoration of a Constitutional Freedom

# 1

# The Legalization of Professional Advertising

*The codfish lays ten thousand eggs,*
*The homely hen lays one.*
*The codfish never cackles*
*To tell you what she's done.*
*And so we scorn the codfish,*
*While the humble hen we prize,*
*Which only goes to show you*
*That it pays to advertise.*

—*Anonymous,* It Pays to Advertise

It's no longer considered illegal, unethical, or unprofessional to advertise and promote your professional practice.

The Federal Trade Commission, the Justice Department, the courts, and almost all consumer groups now encourage professionals to make known the services they offer, how much they charge, and other pertinent aspects of practice. In the past, in most parts of the country, those professionals who advertised prices and services were considered mavericks or renegades by the mainstream of the organized professions. That old attitude has changed. You can now advertise and seek publicity for the services you provide.

There are nearly 4 million practitioners governed by professional-practice acts in the fifty states. Up to now, these acts have banned the advertising and promotion of the learned professions by individuals, except in subtle ways. These professional-practice acts have protected practitioners from the competition of more ambitious colleagues. Noncompetition is supposed to have been an influence for the improvement of professional service. It was also used, however, to create monopolies that operated against the public welfare. Since early in 1974, the Federal Trade Commission (FTC) has decried these monopolistic practices. The FTC is finally getting its way. Everything relating to professional advertising and promotion is altered by a landmark June 27, 1977, ruling of the United States Supreme Court in the case of John R. Bates and Van O'Steen versus the state bar of Arizona. I shall tell you about attorneys Bates and O'Steen later in this chapter.

## LICENSURE AND THE LEARNED PROFESSIONALS

The professions are not always sharply distinguished from other vocations or occupations. They may be described as occupations that provide highly specialized intellectual services. These occupations possess three principal features:

1. A body of knowledge, a set of attitudes, and a technique of application for the service of people through an educated group
2. A standard of success measured by accomplishment in serving people rather than by personal gain
3. A system of control over the practice and education of their practitioners through associations and codes of ethics

Thus, just as architects would be considered professionals who have a body of knowledge, standards of procedure, and controls over practice, so would insurance consultants who have the same criteria under which they conduct their business. Adding up all of the people engaged in occupations governed by the aforementioned definition of a *profession,* there are probably 16 million Americans who could generally be considered "professionals."

In this country, each state regulates a number of professions through the issuance of licenses to practice. These licensees make up the four million so-called learned professionals. Licensure is for the protection of the public welfare, and the licensee's admission to practice is in the hands of the various state boards of examiners. They administer the individual state laws that provide for the licensing of a profession—the professional practice acts.

It has long been accepted practice by the organized professional associations to use the power of the state boards of examiners for their own purposes. Members of these boards are frequently appointed by the governors from lists of candidates preselected by the organized professional associations of the respective states. The board members thus take their seats with built-in prejudices in favor of rulings and requests made by the organized professional associations of which they invariably are members.

As an example, in Connecticut, the New Haven County Medical Society, (an affiliate of the Connecticut State Medical Society, which is linked to the American Medical Association), frowns on any of its physician-members advertising or promoting themselves to the public. Some participants on the board of medical examiners in Connecticut come from New Haven County and belong to the three affiliated organized medical associations. Board participants are predisposed to enforce the American Medical Association's (AMA) Principles of Medical Ethics adopted by the New Haven County Medical Society and the Connecticut Medical Society. These societies have also adopted the interpretive reports and opinions put forth by the Judicial Council of the AMA.

The code of ethics does not have the force of law. It is just a set of principles physicians are supposed to follow in order to remain in good standing with the AMA and its affiliated organizations.

As it happens, the word "advertising," does not appear anywhere in the "Principles." Section 4 admonishes physicians to "uphold the dignity and honor the profession and accept its self-imposed disciplines." Section 5 says a doctor "should not solicit patients." Organized medicine prefers to interpret these sections as forbidding advertising and promotion. If physicians disregard this general interpretation, their county society is likely to censure them or kick them out.[1]

Either of these actions is serious, for it is tantamount to branding the physician as "unethical." The medical examiners of the state of Connecticut look with jaundiced eyes on an unethical practitioner. They are likely to call him or her before their august body for a hearing. Depending on findings, the board's decision could either be a warning or a license suspension for a limited period or a license revocation altogether. Seldom does the examining board rule in favor of an individual, which might be contrary to the determinations of the local or state medical society. This is the Sword of Damocles held over the head of any erring physicians who act in a manner out of the mainstream of their fellow physicians.

While the medical profession has been criticized for being too lenient with erring physicians when they violate patients' rights, organized medicine comes down hard on doctors who infringe intraprofessionally on colleagues' rights. A medical association keeps its members in line and discourages any doctor from "soliciting business, by advertising or otherwise, engaging in price competition, and otherwise engaging in competitive practices." In fact, this was the charge made by the FTC in a 1977 official complaint that it brought against the AMA, the same Connecticut Medical Society, and the same New Haven County Medical Society—these last two simply as examples of the linkage by which organized medicine makes its influence felt on individual doctors.

The FTC further charged in its writ that as a result, "prices of physician services have been stabilized, fixed, or otherwise interfered with," while competition among M.D.s has been "hindered, restrained, forclosed, and frustrated." The complaint adds that these practices deprive consumers of the benefits of competition, including "information pertinent to the selection of a physician."

The FTC wants the AMA to change its code of ethics insofar as the code rules out advertising, and to tell M.D.s that the old interpretations no longer apply. Such a change would free doctors to advertise if they desired but would not compel them to do so. The FTC has requested that physicians have freedom of choice and not be restrained from fair trade. Until now, the Sherman Antitrust Act has been violated by organized medicine, and by most of the other learned-licensed professions.

## FTC SUPPORT OF PROFESSIONAL ADVERTISING

On May 24, 1976, the United States Supreme Court upheld a lower-court decision and said that "commercial speech" is subject to free-speech protection of the First Amendment. "Commercial speech" means paid advertising. The Court concluded that commercial speech to the effect that "I will sell you the X prescription drug at the Y price" was entitled to certain protection, and found that preferred justifications were inadequate to support the ban on price advertising. This ruling was a victory for the FTC. It meant that a Virginia law prohibiting the advertising of prescription-drug prices was unconstitutional. The professional association of pharmacists in that state could no longer prevent druggists from advertising how much they charged customers for prescribed pharmaceuticals.

Additionally, the same Supreme Court decision voided a California law that prohibited the advertising of prescription eyewear prices, because such a prohibition was now unconstitutional. Optometrists, ophthalmologists, opticians, and ocularists were suddenly freed from the limitations imposed on them by their respective professional associations. If they wanted, they could legally advertise eyeglasses, artificial eyes, and other prostheses associated with the appearance or function of the eyes.

For two years, the FTC had been trying for this kind of legal victory. The agency had previously focused its enforcement efforts on blocking mergers and acquisitions in highly concentrated industries. It attempted to protect the consumer from deceptive commodity advertising and exposed swindlers who bilked the public. Then suddenly it shifted attention from these various commercial problem areas to the services rendered by professionals.

This attitudinal change first took place in 1974 when FTC Chairman Lewis Engman suddenly pressed for a full-scale crackdown on the health-care field. Commissioner Engman, along with other commissioners, voted to authorize a closed-door investigation of state-level restrictions on the advertising of prescription-drug prices. The commission investigation centered on efforts by professional pharmacist groups to frustrate the dissemination of drug price information to the public.

But it never was Engman's intent to probe in only one area of health. He made it clear that he was even more concerned about similar "ethical" restrictions on fee disclosure by dentists, podiatrists, optometrists, physicians, osteopaths, chiropractors, physical therapists, private nurses, bioengineers, psychologists, marriage counselors, naturopaths, naprapaths, and other health professionals. Ever since Engman's retirement from the FTC, his juggernaut health-care enforcement program has been carried on. Officers in the health-care professional associations have suspected that the FTC is out to "get" them, and their speculations are correct.

The man who took over as FTC chairman, Calvin Collier, picked up the ball from Engman and ran with it. "The walls are crumbling bit by bit," said Commissioner Collier in a *Dental Management* interview near the end of his term of office, "and the sooner doctors and other professionals realize it, the healthier it will be for them."

Why does the FTC want professionals to advertise? "It's a matter of simple economics," Collier said in the same 1977 interview. "By using our resources to chase down every fly-by-night promoter, we might be able to save the consumer a few million dollars a year. But by reducing anticompetitive practices in the professional area and eliminating price fixing by professional groups, we can save the public *billions* of dollars annually. The cost-benefit ratio is tremendous!"[2]

With a bigger budget, an expanded staff, and more legal authority, the newest FTC chairman, Michael Pertschuk, as former chief counsel to the Senate Commerce Committee, contributes to strengthening the laws the agency enforces. He came into office in 1977 pledging to push to the "outer limits," the FTC's ability to stop concentrations of economic power.

Indications are that the FTC's enforcement of advertising and promotion among all the professions, but more especially among the vendors of health services, has just begun. Here's why:

- During the last year, the FTC launched probes of veterinarian licensing and restrictions on advertising.
- It is at present investigating optometry-industry restrictions on optometric practice in retail establishments.
- It is examining the California dental laboratories' prohibition against direct sales of dentures to patients.
- It has initiated a "limited" investigation of the nursing home industry. Specifically, the FTC is looking for misrepresentation in the promotion of nursing home services.

7

- It launched a nationwide study of the seventy-one Blue Shield plans to determine whether physician control of these organizations has led to M.D. fee-fixing and came to the conclusion that it had. Now, physicians cannot sit on Blue Shield boards. This latest FTC ruling is being appealed to the courts.
- It required the American Academy of Orthopedic Surgeons and the American College of Obstetricians and Gynecologists to cease and desist from developing "relative value scales" for physicians' charges. This prevents price-fixing among these specialists.
- Also in the courts is the FTC's wiping out of forty-five state laws regulating price advertising of eyeglasses. Every state except Arizona, California, Colorado, Iowa, and Maryland had these prior restrictions. So far, six states have notified federal courts that they want to appeal the eyeglass rule, and all the cases probably will be consolidated into one. The eventual ruling will not merely affect the way eyeglasses are sold. The FTC already is preparing rules for at least a dozen other industries. These would preempt hundreds of state laws.

Commissioner Pertschuk, charged with policing unfair, monopolistic, and deceptive trade practices, has staffed the FTC with aggressive lawyers eager to battle professional associations and other business groups to protect consumers. The encouragement of professional advertising and promotion are among his goals. His agency is moving on one profession after another.

## The FTC Assault on Funeral Directors
The Federal Trade Commission wants broad reform of the funeral industry. On June 19, 1978, it released a 526-page report that furnished five years of research on the National Funeral Directors Association and the business practices of its membership. This report contains proposals, now being acted on, which seek the first national regulation of funeral directors.

Arthur Angel, an FTC attorney who directed the commission investigation and the writing of its report, said that his agency's purpose was not only to curb abuses "but to sensitize funeral directors to the fact that practices they think are acceptable are perceived as abusive and exploitative by those outside the industry." The commission is quite specific about what it wishes from the funeral industry.

"There are certain options a consumer has in selecting a funeral," Angel said, "and the funeral director has an obligation to present those options openly and honestly and let him choose what he wants."

As with the medical profession, the funeral industry also uses professional licensing boards for its own ends. It makes a power play to deny mortuary practice in a state. Angel's FTC report says: "We found that funeral director trade associations exert an enormous influence on the boards and their activities. Often the professional associations and state licensing authorities are indistinguishable from one another in terms of composition, provisions on issues, and perceptions of their responsibilities."

The FTC's assault on funeral directors includes a rule mandating that undertakers provide itemized price lists to consumers, and give prices over the telephone. Reformers say that some undertakers have been charging different prices for essentially the same services under different names.

Moreover, the FTC wants civil penalties against undertakers who try to prevent other members of their industry from advertising prices or cooperating with memorial societies, which are nonprofit groups endeavoring to arrange simple, low-cost funerals for their members.

Blame for abuses by morticians and owners of funeral homes is placed by the FTC on the efforts made by "the undertaking trade to elevate itself to the status of a profession," with the result that undertakers have sought to downplay "commercial aspects of the business, particularly price advertising."

Elizabeth C. Clemmer, executive director of the Continental Association of Funeral and Memorial Societies in Washington, D.C., the national headquarters for memorial societies, has said in a *New York Times* interview, "The thousands of letters we get asking for assistance show the degree to which bereaved families have been at the mercy of the funeral industry. My group strongly supports the FTC proposals. By requiring price disclosures, the FTC will go a long way toward opening the funeral industry to competition and giving consumers a fair break."[3]

The FTC report says, "The organized industry has done everything in its power to ensure that consumers would be denied access to (1) relevant information about funeral prices and (2) alternatives to the full funeral service.

"Apparently, the industry feels that if consumers were aware of prices and options, had access to sellers of alternatives, and could plan funerals in advance of need, they would not continue to select the full funeral package."[4]

## LOWER PRICES AND MORE BUSINESS THROUGH CONSUMER EDUCATION

Communicating information to consumers through advertising is the key to lowering the prices of services while creating still more business for the vendor-professional. Services about which they lack information are utterly worthless to prospective purchasers. Like an automobile without wheels, a service offered for sale with no information attached becomes fully useful for its intended purpose only when a set of wheels (or information) is supplied in advance.

Why are new cars usually sold with a full set of wheels? If it was the accepted procedure, buyers could get wheels elsewhere, other than from the manufacturer or seller of the new car itself. The answer, of course, is that it is cheaper for the manufacturer to put wheels on the car at the plant than it is for car buyers to attend to that detail later on.

The same holds true for information supplied by professional or commercial advertisements. Information about service or product characteristics and price can invariably be provided more efficiently and less expensively by dispensers and/or manufacturers than it might be obtained by consumers on their own. The source of a service or product frequently knows more about it than anyone else.

In most commercial product transactions, there is a great deal of competition among sellers to provide information to consumers. As a result, happily, consumers do get the benefit of price and quality information. This has not been the rule in the sale of professional services. Perhaps it's because professionals are laboring under a misapprehension.

Most people believe that advertising products or services results in higher prices. It is argued that advertising costs money, that the advertiser must recover those costs somewhere, and that those costs will be reflected in higher prices for the advertised product. This view, which happens to be totally wrong, had been embraced until recently by the American Institute of Certified Public Accountants and the American Institute of Architects. Exponents of advertising in both of these professions have shown that an open presentation of hourly costs for services brings down fees by competitive bidding. The client is able to choose not only on the basis of professionals' reputation but also from their prices. I will talk more about the lowering of overhead cost through the use of advertising in chapter 2.

Proper understanding of the effect of price and quality advertising depends on an appreciation of the role that product and service information play in consumer choice. Advertising, in fact, creates more business by building demand with consumer information. Holding back information causes price elevation. While it's true that a consumer who has no basis for comparison can't complain about prices being high, that consumer is also unlikely to buy many services. An uninformed consumer will be ignorant of the usefulness and cost effectiveness of your professional services. In effect, then, hidden prices are usually *higher* prices!

Professor Lee Benham of the University of Chicago tested the belief that unadvertised professional prices are elevated ones. He compared the costs of a particular product dispensed by a service profession: optometry. Benham chose optometry because price advertising regulation has varied from state to state in this profession, and also because the tester could make a judgment on a tangible, uniform product—eyeglasses. The historical and functional distinctions between professions may require considerations of quite different factors. Physicians, lawyers, accountants, and others do not dispense standardized products; they render professional services of almost infinite variety and nature. They are individualized—tailored to the patient or client. There is always the possibility of confusion or even deception connected with such service or its advertising.

Benham found that "advertising restriction in this optometric market increased the prices paid by 25 percent to more than 100 percent." The more advertising was restricted among optometrists, the higher the cost of eyewear to the public.

He also found that prices were correlated with the proportion of optometrists who were members of the American Optometric Association (AOA). As such proportion of AOA optometrists increased from 43 percent in Illinois to 91 percent in North Dakota, the price of eyeglasses increased by $12 a pair. Benham made his evaluations in 1963. Today, all of the prices transposed into current inflated dollars have probably tripled.

The Benham survey uncovered that the average price for eyeglasses where there was no advertising restriction was $26.34. In states with ad restrictions, the average price was $33.04. In North Carolina, the most restrictive state in Benham's classification, the cost was $37.48. In Texas and the District of Columbia, the least restrictive jurisdictions, the average retail figure was $17.98.

Thus, the dispensing of eyewear accompanied by high-quality eye care rendered by skilled optometrists costs less in states that don't restrict price advertising, according to Professor Benham.[5]

The tendency for prices to be lower across the board in nonrestrictive states suggests that competition, engendered by promotional advertising and not by lower standards of care, is responsible for keeping prices down.

## PROFESSIONAL ADVERTISING AND INCREASED COMPETITION

Even if consumers bought lower-quality professional services in states where promotion and advertising are permitted, they would still be better off. At least they would have made the choice for lower quality knowingly and willingly. Not all of us can afford Lincoln Continentals. It's nice to have the information available that the Mazda GLC costs less—even if it is presumably of lesser quality. It is difficult to see how the purchase of professional services presents a different case.

The point is that in most states, government intervention and professional organization rulings have been used by established professionals to suppress competition. It is a way to keep out newly graduated architects, accountants, attorneys, and other practitioners. They cannot establish their own practices because clients don't know they exist or that they will render services inexpensively. Admittedly those services would come from a less experienced practitioner, but at least the consumer should have the chance to purchase them if he or she chooses to.

Newly graduated professionals advertising to establish themselves in practice would have the time to teach their clients the knowledge of their specialty. Advertising professionals foster client-patient-customer teaching by the information they impart in their advertisements. The whole object of advertising is to impart knowledge so that the consumer can be persuaded to purchase the services of the teaching professional. Yet eliminating professional advertisements by ruling them "unprofessional" permits the learned professions to prevent consumers from being taught about the new professional's services.

Many practitioners of these learned professions who sell their services have doctoral degrees. One of the definitions of doctor is "teacher." The doctor of education, the doctor of laws, the doctor of medicine, the doctor of dental surgery, the doctor of science, the doctor of philosophy in psychology or sociology, and the rest are all part of established institutions containing a body of knowledge needed and desired by our fellow citizens. The "future shock" predicted by Alvin Toffler lies not in the future any longer; it's with us now. There has been a tremendous rattling of the foundations of established institutions. More than ever before, we are questioning our doctors. Clients, customers, patients—consumers in general—want to know more. They want the doctors to be teachers.

Unfortunately, prior restrictions placed on advertising by professionals has made the public solely dependent on professionals for law interpretation, tax preparation, the building of edifices, health care, emotional stability, and other things. But advertising and promotion of professional services will tend to make the consumer and the learned professional partners in the application of knowledge. It will be a shared responsibility, and may lead to a reduction in the incidence of malpractice legal actions brought by disgruntled clients or patients. Professionals are less likely to be condemned for nonperformance or negligence if responsibility is shared.

12

Service advertising raises the standard of living of the entire community. It encourages healthy competition. It tends to increase a professional's productivity, to provide full value to others in return for patronage. This is good. It makes for better service and more of it. It pays to advertise. The practitioner and the consumer benefit jointly.

Besides, the practice of a profession is a business. The ban on professional advertising originated in English law as a rule of social attitude and not as a rule of ethics. Early lawyers in Britain viewed the law as a form of public service rather than as a means of earning a living, and they looked down on "trade" as unseemly. This has carried over into all of the other professions.

But habit and tradition are not in themselves an adequate answer to a constitutional challenge. In this day, we do not belittle those who earn their living by the strength of their arms or the force of their minds. Since the belief that professionals are somehow "above" trade has become an anachronism, the historical foundation for the advertising restraint has crumbled. That is why John R. Bates and Van O'Steen won their Supreme Court case against their professional association and the Supreme Court of Arizona. Advertising is now legally open to all professionals. Every one of the professional-practice acts in all fifty states is invalid, null, and void in regard to advertising and promotion.

## LANDMARK DECISION: THE BATES CASE

A U.S. Supreme Court decision has struck down the legal profession's ban on advertising, and most professional organizations agree that it applies to their members as well.

After admission to the state bar of Arizona and working as attorneys with the Maricopa County Legal Aid Society, John R. Bates and Van O'Steen left the society in March 1974 and opened a law office in Phoenix; they called it a "legal clinic." Their aim was to provide legal services at modest fees to persons of moderate means who did not qualify for governmental legal aid. They accepted only routine matters, such as uncontested divorces, uncontested adoptions, simple personal bankruptcies, and changes of name, for which costs were kept down by extensive use of paralegals, automatic typewriting equipment, and standardized forms and office procedures. The two lawyers set their prices so as to have a relatively low return on each case they handled. They depended on substantial volume to survive.

After two years, it was apparent they would not survive in private practice with the "clinic" approach unless the availability of legal services at low cost was advertised and, in particular, unless fees were advertised. Consequently, in order to attract clients, the young men on February 22, 1976, placed an advertisement in the *Arizona Republic,* a daily newspaper. The advertisement stated that the two attorneys were offering "legal services at very reasonable fees," and listed their fees for certain services.

They referred to their joint practice as a legal clinic and identified the following four legal services, indicating an exact price for each:

1. *Divorce or legal separation*—uncontested, both spouses sign papers: $175 plus $30 court filing fee, preparation of all court papers and instructions on how to do one's own simple uncontested divorce: $100.

2. *Adoption*—uncontested severance proceedings: $225 plus approximately $10 publication costs.

3. *Bankruptcy*—nonbusiness, no contested proceedings; individual: $250 plus $55 court filing fee; wife and husband: $300 plus $110 court filing fee.

4. *Change of Name*—$95 plus $20 court filing fee.

The advertisement also stated that information regarding other types of cases would be furnished on request.

Traditionalist Arizona attorneys looked with horror on this sort of public announcement. Immediately, they pointed to any deception they could find. For instance, the advertisement made reference to a "legal clinic," an undefined term, they alleged. The two young lawyers said that they offered services at "very reasonable" prices, but, at least with regard to an uncontested divorce, the establishment attorneys declared, the advertised price was not a bargain. Finally, it was noted, the ad did not inform the consumer that a name change could be obtained without the services of an attorney.

The only thing Bates and O'Steen conceded was that the advertisement constituted a clear violation of a particular disciplinary rule of the Supreme Court of Arizona. This rule provides in part: "A lawyer shall not publicize himself, or his partner, or associate, or any other lawyer affiliated with him or his firm, as a lawyer through newspaper or magazine advertisements, radio or television announcements, display advertisements in the city or telephone directories or other means of commercial publicity, nor shall he authorize or permit others to do so in his behalf."

Upon the filing of a complaint initiated by the president of the state bar, a hearing was held before a three-member special local administrative committee, as prescribed by the Arizona Supreme Court. Although the committee took the position that it could not consider an attack on the validity of the rule, it allowed Bates and O'Steen to develop a record on which such a challenge could be based. The committee recommended that Bates and O'Steen be suspended from the practice of law for not less than six months.

Upon further review by the board of governors of the state bar that board recommended only a one-week suspension for each young lawyer, the weeks to run consecutively.

Bates and O'Steen then sought review in the Supreme Court of Arizona, arguing, among other things, that the disciplinary rule violated Sections 1 and 2 of the Sherman Act because of its tendency to limit competition, and that the rule infringed on their First Amendment rights.

The Arizona court rejected both claims. However, because the court, in agreement with the board of governors, felt that the two attorneys' advertising "was done in good faith to test the constitutionality" of its own disciplinary rule, it reduced the sanction to censure only.

Of particular interest is the opinion of Justice Holohan in dissent against the Arizona court plurality. In his view, the case should have been framed in terms of "the right of the public as consumers and citizens to know about the activities of the legal profession," rather than as one involving merely the regulation of a profession. Observed in this light, Judge Holohan felt that the rule performed a substantial disservice to the public. He wrote:

"Obviously, the information of what lawyers charge is important for private economic decisions by those in need of legal services. Such information is also helpful, perhaps indispensable, to the formation of an intelligent opinion by the public on how well the legal system is working and whether it should be regulated or even altered. . . . The rule at issue prevents access to such information by the public."

Although Judge Holohan acknowledged that some types of advertising might cause confusion and deception, he felt that the remedy was to ban the form, rather than all advertising. Thus, despite Judge Holohan's "personal dislike of the concept of advertising by attorneys," he found the ban unconstitutional.

Bates and O'Steen took their suit against censure to the United States Supreme Court. The decision was handed down June 27, 1977, with Justice Blackmun delivering the opinion of the Court. Justices Brennan, White, Marshall, and Stevens joined Justice Blackmun so that by a five-to-four majority, the Court ruled that lawyers cannot constitutionally be prohibited from advertising in newspapers the fees they charge clients for routine legal services. The Court also ruled that lawyers can seek clients and compete with each other just like anyone else who is in business. The majority opinion held: "Our analysis began with the observation that our cases long have protected speech even though it is in the form of a paid advertisement . . . competing interests reinforced our view that such speech should not be withdrawn from protection merely because it proposed a mundane commercial transaction. Even though the speaker's interest is largely economic, the Court has protected such speech in certain contexts. . . . Moreover, significant societal interests are served by such speech. Advertising, though entirely commercial, may often carry information of import to significant issues of the day.

"The constitutional issue in this case," wrote Justice Blackmun for the majority, "is only whether the State may prevent the publication in a newspaper of appellants' truthful advertisement concerning the availability and terms of routine legal services. We rule simply that the flow of such information may not be restrained, and we therefore hold the present application of the disciplinary rule against appellants to be violative of the First Amendment".

## SOME RESULTS OF THE BATES DECISION

Since the U.S. Supreme Court decided that attorneys could publicize their routine fees and services, many have been cautiously experimenting with promotion techniques as a means of winning new clients.

Under the direction of its vice-president, John F. Foley, *The New York Law Journal*/Law Journal Seminars-Press presented a one-day symposium on lawyer advertising on July 21, 1978. Prominent representatives of the legal profession, the media, and the advertising industry examined the pros and cons of advertising by lawyers. They reviewed the American Bar Association Code of Professional Responsibility and the lawyer advertising guidelines of the Appellate Division of New York State (see chapter 2). Pioneer lawyers who had advertised explained the media used and the responses resulting from their efforts. The program offered vital and current information on available markets, costs, expectation, and returns.

At the same time, other professional leaders, convinced that the U.S. Supreme Court decision applies to them as well, have been reevaluating time-honored positions about the role of advertising in their professions. Within certain yet-to-be defined limits, consensus among almost all groups is that advertising by the professions is legal and here to stay, an evolutionary event for good or ill. Justice Powell had rendered the dissenting opinion: "Although the Court appears to note some reservations, it is clear that within undefined limits, today's decision will effect profound changes in the practice of law viewed for centuries as a learned profession." He is correct! The decision is also having a radical effect on the other professions.

In medicine, the right to advertise has been sanctioned by Bernard D. Hirsh, general counsel for the American Medical Association. Speaking to medical journalists he has said, "You can translate that decision to mean that under the First Amendment, neither state laws or medical societies can restrain physicians from advertising prices for routine medical services."

Also, the American Dental Association's assistant executive director for legal affairs, Bernard J. Conway, has said in interviews with writers for dental magazines and journals, "The ADA is taking the position that the Supreme Court ruling applies to dentists. But we feel that it limits dentists to certain types of advertising—the availability and costs of services. We also take the position that the Court has limited advertising to the print media. Our interpretation is that dentists cannot make claims of quality or superiority. Nor can they advertise at all on radio or television."

What would happen if various state dental societies attempted to enforce their old ban on dental advertising or even adopted the new ADA interpretation? Suppose one of the state dental societies prohibited its members from advertising in the broadcast media? The dental society is likely to be sued!

Writing in the *Association Leadership Bulletin* of the ADA, the association's executive director, G. Gordon Watson, says: "Ethical bans of dental societies on advertising, including those contained in the Principles of Ethics of the American Dental Association, if enforced, possibly would expose the societies to civil, if not criminal proceedings for violations of Federal and State anti-trust statutes."

In the spring of 1977, the attorney general of the state of Maine refused to press charges against a dentist who had advertised an $88 denture, despite the state dental society's request.

On July 28, 1977, the New York State Board of Regents enacted a rule permitting advertising among all the professions it regulates. These licensed professions include:

| | |
|---|---|
| Acupuncture | Ophthalmic dispensing |
| Animal health technology | Optometry |
| Architecture | Osteopathy |
| Audiology | Pharmacy |
| Certified public accountancy | Physical therapy |
| Certified shorthand reporting | Podiatry |
| Chiropractic | Professional engineering |
| Dental hygiene | Psychology |
| Dentistry | Public accountancy |
| Land surveying | Registered physician's assistant |
| Landscape architecture | Registered professional nurse |
| Licensed practical nurse | Registered specialist's assistant |
| Massage | Social work |
| Medicine | Speech pathology |
| Occupational therapy | Veterinary medicine |

17

Advertising and Promoting the Professional Practice

In April 1978, an ultraconservative professional association, the American Institute of Certified Public Accountants (AICPA) gave its official approval to advertising and promotion for accounting firms. Quickly, one of the "Big Eight" accounting houses, Deloitte Haskins and Sells (an international company known domestically only as Haskins and Sells), took advantage of this AICPA sanction. The firm ran an ad in approximately twenty newspapers around the country just one month later. It was a brief tombstone-type affair whose basic thrust was to familiarize people with the firm's new name. The message was understated—the company contented itself with noting that its new U.S. designation would enable it to "practice under a uniform identity everywhere our clients' needs take us."[5]

The ad presaged much advertising activity to come, however, and a very large crack has appeared in the monopolistic practices of accounting and other professional associations.

The Supreme Court decision makes a clear statement regarding professional advertising and promotion. In effect, the Court is subscribing to the radical notion that there is nothing inherently different between dispensing professional services and selling a pound of hamburger; both should be quality products, both be described, and both have a price.

# 2

# The Ethics of Professional Advertising and Promotion

*You can tell the ideals of a nation by its advertisements.*
*—George Norman Douglas,* South Wind, *1917*

Consumerists are far from being in love with Madison Avenue or any of its techniques. Still, they are outraged at the refusal of many professional vendors to quote prices over the phone or to describe their services in surveys or in any other way. The result is that consumerists support commercial advertising by professionals and have been stringent advocates of greater FTC enforcement against monopolistic practices of professional associations. Were advertising, and the resulting price competition, to raise service quality and lower markups, then consumers would benefit and purchase more professional services, say consumer advocates. Everyone would benefit with more and better use of available experts among the learned professions.

Consumerists also suggest that professionals who do a little homework on advertising and marketing techniques will soon discover effective—even free—ways to get their messages across. In this respect, they would learn from consumer groups, and from other struggling nonprofit organizations that owe their survival in part to skillful use of the media.

Consumer groups want the dispensers of professional services to declare publicly their prices and what they are offering for sale.

## ADVERTISING ETHICS AND CONSUMER FEEDBACK

In early 1976, the California Citizen Action Group (CAL-CAG) attempted to do an eye-care survey in Sacramento. Two different associations of eye-care specialists thwarted them—the California Ophthalmological Society (M.D.s) and the California Optometric Association (O.D.s). Both

19

forbade members to cooperate. The professionals' objections were that such a survey would lead to "quickie eye exams" and other lowered standards. Practitioners resented it as undignified and unprofessional.

Optometrists, in particular, feared price competition from big optical chain stores with large advertising budgets. One California doctor concluded: "If people are price-shopping, I don't want them as patients. They aren't really interested in my services, and they just mean trouble."

There is growing evidence that these fears are groundless. Feedback from the medical consumer provides a more positive response to professional disclosure of charges and maintenance of service standards.

In 1977, San Francisco Consumer Action, an affiliate of CAL-CAG, tried a small but unique experiment to assess the quality, as well as the price, of eye care in the Bay area. It was the second time that California eye-care specialists were tested. A twenty-three-year-old nearsighted woman had eleven different eye exams from three ophthalmologists and eight optometrists in two counties of the state. None knew this was a test. The young woman noted no major difference in the exams she was given. She knew what to look for, since she had worked as an eye doctor's assistant.

The patient judged that the advertising optometrist perhaps was the most thorough of the group. Certainly he was the least expensive, and he had the most patients.

A few weeks later, CAL-CAG surveyed 106 eye doctors in the Alameda-Contra Costa area of California as a follow-up. The consumer-action group found the nonadvertising ophthalmologists and optometrists averaging eye examination charges of $40 and the advertising optometrists averaging charges of $27.

Then CAL-CAG looked again at its nearsighted woman from the San Francisco group. She had received eleven different prescriptions for her myopia. Unable to decide which (if any) was "accurate," she took them to two professors of optometry at the University of California at Berkeley and Davis. Each examined her and produced his own—slightly different—prescription. All thirteen prescriptions were within the limits of normal vision. The consumer-action research team was impressed, not only with the adaptability of the human eyeball, but with the validity of the original premise: consumers can legitimately shop around for a basic eye examination. And the twenty-three-year-old myopic shopper? She adopted the prescription of the advertising optometrist. His professional image was most impressive, and her judgment of his honesty and skill was positive.

Marvin S. Belsky, M.D., in his book *How to Choose & Use Your Doctor* (Arbor House, 1975) says: "There's usually little interpersonal feedback in the day-to-day relationship between a doctor and patient. . . . The best indications of your satisfaction or feelings a doctor is likely to get is a neutral one: you keep seeing him. He submits a bill. It's paid. But even that isn't a reliable guide."

And the doctor? "The doctor rarely tells you how he feels about the way the two of you are interacting," writes Dr. Belsky.

I interviewed Marvin Belsky extensively for articles I wrote for *Practical Psychology for Physicians* magazine. Our discussions led to his rendering the opinion that "the basic need in the social area of medicine is for the patient to know more about his doctor."

How can this be accomplished? Assuredly, by communicating in broadcasts, in print, and by other commercial means. It's the way for anybody who sells health services to get feedback from patients. It's the way all business professionals can receive positive feedback from their clients. Everyone needs strokes that come from positive feedback. Advertising and promotion offer the way.

## ETHICAL GUIDELINES IN THE LEGAL PROFESSION

Yet the last thing consumers—or the professions—want is false or misleading advertising of any kind, particularly regarding quality. In their efforts to build safeguards into legislation that would remove barriers to advertising and promotion, the various professional associations are trying to include mandatory quality standards. The particular professional organization that had brought this controversy to a head, the American Bar Association (ABA), had its House of Delegates take a close look at what standards of advertising should be, at least for its own members. The association held numerous committee sessions immediately after the Bates Supreme Court decision. Then, on August 10, 1977, the House of Delegates adopted new advertising guidelines.

The ABA guidelines state that advertisements by attorneys may include the following:

- Attorney's name
- Age
- Previous public office
- Military service
- Bar association titles
- Foreign language ability
- Bank references
- Law firm's name

- Telephone numbers
- Whether credit cards are accepted
- Office hours
- Biographical information
- Fields of specialized law
- Hourly rates
- Names of clients (with their consent)
- Range of fees for services
- Fixed fees for specific services

The Appellate Division of the state of New York has also set an example for the boundaries to be drawn on professional advertising. New York lawyers have had their limits set. The appellate court has adopted rules as of March 13, 1978, which were retroactive to March 1, 1978. The appellate guidelines represent a compromise between proponents and opponents of the new opportunity for lawyers to advertise, and include the following:

- A lawyer can't claim false facts or cast aspersions on the legal profession as a whole.
- A lawyer's publicity or his ad must not contain puffery, self-laudation, the quality of legal services, or claims that cannot be measured or verified.
- The lawyer mustn't lie about his education, degrees, and distinctions.
- He is permitted to tell the truth in promotion ads only about his bar admissions, specialty of law, offices held, memberships in societies, foreign-language fluency, names of clients (if they give permission), bank references, credit arrangements accepted, group legal services participated in, legal fees and rates, and some other items.
- Advertising and publicity shall be designed to educate the public to an awareness of legal needs and to provide information relevant to the selection of the most appropriate counsel.
- Advertised fees must include the scope of services.
- Broadcast advertising must be taped and approved by the lawyer and be retained by him for at least one year following transmission.
- Charging more than the advertised fee is not allowed.
- Advertising in periodicals published daily, weekly, or monthly will bind the lawyer to his representation for at least thirty days. If his fees are advertised in a publication with no fixed date, the lawyer is bound for at least ninety days.
- Broadcasting binds him for at least thirty days from the time of the broadcast.

• The lawyer must not compensate representatives of the press, radio, television, or other media in return for publicity in a news item.

These rules are in effect right now. As I indicated already, the New York State Bar Association has conformed its ethical considerations and disciplinary rules to the Appellate Division's guidelines.

## "NEED TO KNOW" IN THE LEGAL PROFESSION

A question has been raised about the adverse economic effect of large overhead costs created by the placement of commercial announcements in the media. The American Bar Association acknowledges that most people suffer a wrong silently instead of seeking redress by legal action simply because they fear the cost of filing a claim and hiring an attorney for that purpose. The ABA, in its 1972 *Revised Handbook on Prepaid Legal Services,* states, "The middle 70 percent of our population is not being reached or served adequately by the legal profession." The bar association admits that this underutilization is definitely from fear of cost and an inability to locate a suitable lawyer.

The same ABA handbook goes on to say: "We are persuaded that the actual or feared price of such services coupled with a sense of unequal bargaining status is a significant barrier to wider utilization of legal services."

In a January 1976 survey, middle-class consumers overestimated lawyers' fees by 91 percent for the drawing of a simple will, 340 percent for reading and advising on a two-page installment sales contract, and 123 percent for thirty minutes of consultation.

Although advertising by itself is not adequate to deal with this underutilization of legal services completely, it can provide some of the information that a potential client needs to make an intelligent selection of a lawyer.

To accomplish this greater availability of legal services, the bar at both the national and state level has taken the following steps:

• Increased group legal service plans used by unions, cooperatives, and trade associations
• Operated lawyer referral plans
• Sponsored legal clinics
• Created public service law firms
• Formed group insurance or prepaid service plans
• Provided counsel for indigents charged with crime
• Sponsored the Federal Legal Services Corporation to provide counsel for indigents in civil cases

With all this, the use of legal talent by the people in the middle-income level still falls short. Commercial professional promotion could rectify that problem. Now it can be used. The Ohio Supreme Court held a hearing October 24, 1977, to consider whether the United States Supreme Court's decision allowing lawyers to advertise also allowed use of the electronic media. The State Bar Association of Ohio claimed television and radio ads are unlawyerlike and might be abused.

After the opponents to broadcast advertising had their say, attorney Joel Hyatt argued the constitutional issues in favor of ads on television. The legal stenographer's transcript of the hearing indicates that he said: "Bar associations can no longer be allowed to infringe on the constitutional rights of lawyers . . . to inform the public . . . that legal services can be provided at very reasonable fees."

*Esquire* magazine reporter Steve Brill said that Hyatt then clinched the case. "He offered to show the justices a videotape 'sample' ad he'd produced," wrote Brill. "A month later, the court ruled that only deceptive radio and TV ads or those using music or actors would be prohibited. . . . Thus, Ohio became the first state to sanction TV ads for lawyers."[5]

While individual state professional associations are now issuing their own codes, certain guidelines for advertising may be followed to prove to prospective clients the advantage of using your services. The American Bar Association offers such helpful guidelines. According to its code, an attorney may list the following in a newspaper advertisement:

| | |
|---|---|
| Name | Foreign language ability |
| Firm | Bank references |
| Address | Credit cards accepted |
| Telephone number | Names of clients (with their consent) |
| Legal specialties | Fee for initial consultation |
| Previous public office | Range of fees for various services |
| Military service | Hourly rate charge to clients |
| Bar association titles | Availability of specific fee schedule on request |

Fixed fees . . . if these fees are
not likely to be deceptive . . .
with an explanation that
actual costs may vary with
circumstances

I recommend that you acquire the legal and ethical guidelines for advertising professional services from your own state professional association or from the national association of your profession. If no new guidelines have been drawn up as yet, you may decide not to be ruled by outdated codes or old-fashioned principles. Realize that old guidelines are invalid and legally void. They are unconstitutional. But also realize that your professional peer group can make life miserable for you if they don't think you should advertise—even if you're within your legal rights. Sure, you can sue to stop harassment, but the legal process takes much money, energy, and time. And the emotional stress is hardly worth it. So get those guidelines and also get some opinions from colleagues.

The fact is that attorney Joel Hyatt did not need these cautions. He had produced his first television ad and mapped out his expansion plans long before the Ohio state court had made its decision. He was determined that if the state court ruled against him, he'd open his clinics and run the ads anyway and then appeal any possible disciplinary action to the Supreme Court. However, the dynamic young attorney didn't have to appeal at all! His advertising was declared legal, as it is for all attorneys in the state. Assuming it succeeds in Ohio, Hyatt is likely to take his advertising and clinic ideas nationwide. He has proved his ability to perform.

## BEWARE THE CONSEQUENCES OF OPPOSING YOUR PEERS ON ADVERTISING

Ethics dictate that advertisements promoting the services of learned professionals must not be false, fraudulent, deceptive, misleading, sensational, or flamboyant. The ads should be judged as being in good taste.

Who is to make this judgment? Should the involved professional organization become a watchdog? Will there be an adverse effect on professionalism? What are the penalties for violation of professionalism? Who enforces them? Are there overhead costs that would overcommercialize professional service? Is professional advertising inherently misleading? These are a few of the serious questions to be faced with the setting of new standards for professional advertising. It is uncharted territory.

# Advertising and Promoting the Professional Practice

Before progressing further, let me sound an alarm of warning and provide you with special advice.

Since ethical behavior is not found in nature and does distinguish human beings from other animals, ethics could be considered an artificial form of conduct—something synthesized by mankind to avoid anarchy, immorality, confusion, and the expression of base characteristics by people in society. In fact, ethical conduct is totally theoretical. It tries to answer what is ultimately good or worthwhile. It offers rules for moral rights and obligations and defines commendable conduct or character. *Ethics* comes from the Greek *ethikos,* having to do with conduct and from *ethos,* meaning "custom."

This theoretical basis for authority of the state, the justification of legal systems, and the moral tenability of various systems of distribution of economic goods and services plays a large role in politics, jurisprudence, and economics. Thus, if you violate what is set down as the code of ethics in your profession, you will be doing more than offending a group of your peers. There is a bigger picture you'll be defacing.

You will be placing yourself in opposition to society's declarations of the kinds of things it considers worthwhile in themselves. In its view, you'll be denying your duties and shrugging off the differences between right and wrong. And finally, you'll be acting in a manner it labels reprehensible, unadmirable, and immoral. This can all be summed up by the term *unethical.*

Shrinking the big picture down to the point of this chapter, professional ethics concerns what is *justifiably* believed or valued by your professional peers. "Justifiably" is the key to what has gone before in banning professional advertising. The Supreme Court has now ruled such restrictions as being unjustified.

So, professional associations are forced to scrap the old rules and create new ones. You, who would bring your announcements of availability of professional services to the public, are beset by two voices. One tells you that now you can advertise; the other says that your colleagues have had insufficient time to make up new rules and standards for such practice. What are you going to do?

Admittedly, new standards would solve recognized problems. They have to come from the professional association itself, whether state or national, and must be adopted by the state. What you have to do is notify the official body that represents your profession of your desire to advertise. Do it with legal instruments and give a reasonable time limit for a reply. Employ the services of counsel for this purpose—a simple document filed with the state board of examiners that administers the professional practice act should be sufficient. Simply tell the board what you want to do and ask for the standards by which you may govern your actions and advertisements. The onus will fall upon your peer reviewers and unburden your shoulders.

If you fail to receive a response within the reasonable time limit you've suggested, the way may be clear for you to move ahead on your own. Then again, maybe it would be best to query a second time. Both queries should be sent by registered mail, return receipt requested. You really do want a reply from the secretary of the board of governors who are administering the professional practice act in your state. The secretary's go-ahead will remove the greatest danger to your professional survival—loss of your state license to practice.

There is, of course, the danger of professional jealousy resulting in a series of minor attacks on your happiness as a professional person. Don't minimize these little attacks. Their cumulative effect can mean one big death-dealing attack against the health of your practice, and may eventually drive you out of your area or even your profession altogether. It happened to me. When you stand out from among your fellows and force them to question their own professional images in the eyes of the public, the response won't be inward. It will be outward against you.

Better than anyone, you know how your colleagues can get to you. There are many ways in the professions. They can cut off your organizational professional liability insurance, call you to hearings to defend yourself, warn off third-party insurance carriers who ordinarily pay for services rendered to policy holders, actually solicit public complaints to present to the state board of examiners, send in other state inspectors to judge your compliance with regulations, among other things. Peer group anger can have devastating consequences for its target.

It all comes down to economics. While you may suffer emotionally from their attacks—maybe experience psychosomatic illness as a result—the big blow will be to your pocketbook. Just the mention of your name to a professional colleague by a potential client or patient may incite a vilifying response. It doesn't even have to be verbal. A sneer, a raised eyebrow, a laugh, or some other nonverbal reaction often is enough to lose you a prospect. It's not unlikely that you've done this yourself when being approached about some colleague toward whom you felt irritation. It's the way to "get a guy," an all too common practice among petty professionals.

Make no mistake! The incitement to vilify or take stringent collective action against a professional who is advertising is strictly economical. High moral issues may be cited, but by standing above the crowd the advertiser is really hitting where it hurts the most. Pricking the pocketbook of a colleague is like pulling out his ingrown toenail without anesthetic. Do it

27

a few times and he'll do whatever is necessary to get rid of you as an irritant. Consider yourself warned!

## WHO IS TO JUDGE THE PROFESSIONALISM OF ADVERTISEMENTS?

Because the public lacks sophistication in the rendering of specialized professional services, consumers may be particularly susceptible to misleading or deceptive advertising by a few members of any of the learned professions. After-the-fact action by an abused consumer lured by false advertising may not provide a realistic restraint. There may be an inability of the lay person to assess whether the service he or she has received meets professional standards. Thus, the vigilance of a regulatory agency will be necessary. Is this another burden for the Federal Trade Commission to shoulder? There are millions of purveyors of services. Could the FTC do the job when the agency is not as effective as it should be?

A better solution is probably establishment of standards and enforcement of rules concerning advertising by each professional association involved. Yes, the association must take on the additional burden of watchdog without being overly stringent in enforcement. There would be nothing worse than a return to the old monopolistic practices of the professional associations.

Whether enforcement of professionalism is carried out or not, it is incongruous for the opponents of advertising in each profession to extol the virtues and altruism of that particular profession at one point, and, at another, to assert that its members will seize the opportunity to mislead and distort. Isn't it sensible to assume that, with promotion in any form, most professionals will behave as they always have? They will abide by the commonly accepted ethics of their field—in some cases by solemn oaths— to uphold the integrity and honor of their profession.

For every learned professional who overreaches through advertising, there will be tens of thousands of others who will be candid and honest and straightforward. Furthermore, it will be in the interest of the honest ones, as in other cases of misconduct, to assist in weeding out those few who abuse their trust.

Out of fairness to opponents of professional advertising, we must recognize that many of the problems in defining the boundary between deceptive and nondeceptive advertising remain to be resolved. There may have to be reasonable restrictions on the time, place, statements, and manner of ads. Advertising concerning transactions that are themselves illegal obviously may be suppressed. And the special problems of advertising on the electronic broadcast media will warrant special consideration. These are the sort of problems to be resolved in committee by the fifty state professional groups of each national association.

## ADVERTISING ETHICS: OVERHEAD COSTS AND MARKET ACCESSIBILITY

It bears repetition that dubious claims have been made about professional advertising increasing the overhead costs of rendering services. I pointed to this incorrect thinking in chapter 1. Promotion opponents declare that these costs then will be passed along to consumers in the form of increased fees. The additional cost of practice, it is argued, will create a substantial entry barrier, deterring or preventing new graduates from penetrating the market and reaching the position of the profession's established members.

I suggest that exactly the opposite will be the case. Research by marketing firms has proven that advertising serves to reduce, not advance, the cost of products and services to the consumer. Like the retail merchant, the professional provider can and will benefit from more sales because he or she announces lower prices and a variety of services.

Even if fees for services should drop, no loss of income will result. The increased volume of business generated by the ads will more than compensate for the reduced profit per client or patient.

As for the entry-barrier argument, in the absence of public notice of some kind, professional vendors must rely on their personal contacts with the community to generate a flow of business. In view of the time necessary to develop such contacts, an advertising ban, in fact, serves to perpetuate the market position of established professionals. Advertising and promotion would allow the new competitor to penetrate the market faster and more effectively. It's only fair for the new graduate to have this chance.

## CAN ADVERTISING BE MISCONSTRUED?

Is the commercial promotion of professional services fated to be misleading because people misconstrue the advertiser's message? Opponents shout a loud "yes" and cite three reasons. First, professional services are so individualized with regard to content and quality as to prevent informed comparison on the basis of an advertisement. Second, individual consumers are unable to determine in advance just what services they need. And last, advertising tends to highlight irrelevant factors such as price, location, and affiliations, and ignores the main factor of skill.

These are potent arguments. Advertising proponents counter them with some logical reasoning.

In reply to the first objection, it is pointed out that although many professional services are indeed unique, it is doubtful that any individual could or would announce fixed prices for services of such uniqueness. Rather, advertising is a more significant force in the selling of inexpensive and frequently used services with mass markets, than in the selling of unique services. The only services that lend themselves to public announcements are the routine ones. Certainly, there is nothing deceptive in your advertisement of the cost of an initial half-hour consultation. Even before the Bates decision, in fact, the ABA permitted the disclosure of legal-fee information in the classified section of a telephone directory. If the information is not misleading when published in a telephone directory, is it more likely to be misleading when published in a newspaper or quoted in broadcasts?

Look at the work of barbers! Rarely are two haircuts identical, but that does not mean that barbers cannot quote a standard price. While barbers are not considered professionals, they are vendors who provide their services only upon becoming certified by the state.

Learned professionals perform countless relatively standardized services that vary somewhat in complexity but not so much as to make each job unique. The professional must merely perform his or her service at the advertised price. This should be the only requirement.

In answer to the second objection made by opponents—that "advertising ignores the diagnostic role"—the same could be said about the advertising of abortion services, which is commonly accepted practice among abortion clinics. Although a woman may not know all the details of the medical procedure and may not always be able accurately to diagnose pregnancy, such advertising has certain First Amendment protection.

Indeed, the same can be said of almost any professional service. It is unlikely that many people go to an accountant merely to ascertain if they have a clean bill of financial health. Accountants are more likely to be employed to perform specific tasks. Although the client may not know the details involved, he or she, no doubt, is able to identify the service desired at the level of generality to which advertising lends itself.

The third argument raised by opponents is the strongest. They say that "commercial speech" does not provide a complete foundation on which to select a professional person. The proponents claim that at least some of the relevant information needed to reach an informed decision is given in the ad. The alternative—the prohibition of advertising—serves only to restrict this small amount. An absence of advertising promotes a disadvantageous mystique around the profession and its vendor of services. This secretiveness is unhealthy.

The third argument assumes that the public is not sophisticated enough to realize the limitations of advertising. Advertising opponents say that it is better to keep people in ignorance than to trust them with correct but incomplete information.

One may easily underestimate the public. It seems unjust to keep people ignorant. It's preferable to have more disclosure, not less, in a free, democratic society.

Finally, it might also be argued that advertising is undesirable because it permits the unthinking consumer to substitute the ad copy for the reputation of the vendor. Here, the honesty of the professional person is overlooked, and professionalism is not taken into account.

In a referral system relying on reputation, the future business of a professional is partially dependent on current performance. This is true; it is the basis of professional performance over hundreds of years. Such a system has the benefit both of providing a mechanism for disciplining misconduct and of creating an incentive for dispensers of services to do a better job for their present clients or patients.

While it was this way—referrals from performance—a half a century ago when the typical professional provider practiced in a small, homogeneous community, time has made changes. Urbanization, specialization, and other factors long since have moved the typical professional practice from its small-town setting. Information as to qualifications of vendors of service is not available to many. The city is an impersonal place. Reputation counts for less than it once did, and various techniques of promotion have been substituted. Our present world has lost some of the old values.

## HOW MUCH PROFESSIONAL ADVERTISING TO DATE?

I have pointed to the legal field as illustrating how there is underutilization of the learned professions. It is a fine example. However, more examples could be cited from every other learned profession. The public simply fails to use the services of experts because in many cases, people don't know what the provider offers. I remember an instance twenty years ago when the National Association of Chiropodists changed its name to the American Podiatry Association. I proudly changed my shingle to read "podiatrist" rather than "chiropodist." No one knew the new term. When I defined it later with an additional small shingle reading "Foot disorders," my local colleagues raised a great fuss, and I removed the sign. Apparently I had almost committed the sin of advertising.

Times have changed. *The New England Journal of Medicine,* in a September 1978 issue, recommended that local medical societies print detailed directories of physicians so patients would be able to choose the best qualified doctor for treatment. The *Journal* says this is one alternative to advertising by doctors. Professional advertising is a practice the magazine and some conservatives in organized medicine oppose.

*Journal* Editor Arnold S. Relman wrote: "At present, there are only the most perfunctory kinds of physicians' directories, which are of relatively little help to the intelligent consumer seeking specific information that will aid in the selection of a physician." Relman, who accused doctors of "clannishness," suggested that state or county medical societies print directories of the practicing physicians in each community. It is one of organized medicine's first steps toward the full acceptance of physician advertising.

Relman went on to say: "These directories would include all the factual information a consumer might want to know in selecting a physician, including date of birth, medical school, residency, and other postdoctoral education, specialty certification and recertification (with dates), hospital staff and medical school appointments, membership in certain relevant professional societies and colleges, type of practice, office hours, address, and telephone number."[1]

While this is the traditionalist's temporary response to the Bates decision, quite a few other physicians think that media advertising is not a bad idea. Their attitude toward publicizing information about themselves has changed radically. The Supreme Court now says it's okay, and many medics agree. They wanted advertising and promotion even before the Bates decision.

According to a 1976 *Medical Economics* survey about advertising among M.D.s, 14.5 percent of 434 respondents replied on their questionnaires that they would consider employing whatever ad media their colleagues used, including radio commercials, TV commercials, direct mail, newspapers, and other forms of promotion.

One Iowa urologist wrote: "I think the profession has been too coy in making doctors' qualifications available to the public."

A Connecticut internist went further: "Damn it, the public has a *right* to know who we are and what we can do," he said.

A surgeon from New York wrote: "I see no difference between advertising in a directory and in a newspaper, except that newspaper advertising would probably be more effective—especially for a young doctor just starting practice in a community."

A California surgeon: "I consider my credentials and qualifications to be tops, and I would be delighted to have them known to the public."

A New York family practitioner injected a note that was echoed by many others: "I'd be willing to go along with the idea of a directory, but only if it was approved by a responsible organization, such as a medical society."

In this survey, 55.9 percent of physicians indicated a willingness to be listed in a community health-care directory.[2]

Health-maintenance organizations (HMOs) are not holding back from advertising. They pay to have their ads spread across several columns of morning or afternoon newspapers, and they use the broadcast media quite effectively. Their aim? To gain new patients willing to invest in prepaid medical care rendered by in-house physicians. Public announcements and promotion are the main way they grow.

HMOs are not lauding individual physicians by name or particular hospitals. Instead, they describe their health-care facilities as the progressive way of taking care of one's health. Sometimes the ad will say that the HMO physicians are university affiliated and actively involved in teaching medical students, interns, residents, fellows, and physicians' associates, something that is absolutely true and impressive to prospective prepaid patients.

Approximately 1,100 dentists in California are now considering advertising. And New York State has numbers of dentists banded together in clinics. They dispense a low-priced, well-advertised, mass-produced kind of dentistry typified by The Denture Center, which announces itself in *The New York Times*. In a three-column, eleven-inch display ad, The Denture Center advertises:

| | |
|---|---|
| A full custom denture | $185 |
| Simple extractions | 9 |
| Complex extractions | 25 |
| Root canal therapy | 95 |
| Fillings | 8 per surface |
| Acrylic crowns | 165 |
| Porcelain crowns | 195 |
| Cleaning | 15 |
| X-ray series | 15 |

A survey conducted among its readers nationally by *Dental Management* magazine between November 1977 and July 1978 revealed that one hundred dentists out of one thousand respondents are actively advertising. Furthermore, in reply to the question: "If you do not plan to advertise personally, are you sympathetic towards those of your colleagues who do?" 27 percent answered "yes!" And 84 percent agreed that "location of practice" should be permitted in ads, while 77 percent wanted "hours of service." "Specialty of service" was requested by another 77 percent, as well. Just 7 percent of responding dentists would allow descriptions of

33

"superiority of service," and 14 percent stated that they would advertise their fees.*

A dentist responding to the November 1977 questionnaire wrote: "There is little wrong with a free market situation, save when there is no way to determine the quality of the product. A three-surface amalgam is almost as individual as a fingerprint."[3]

The American Academy of Podiatric Sports Medicine permitted its entire membership of approximately four hundred foot doctors to be listed across a two-page spread of the April 1978 issue of *The Jogger,* the monthly newspaper of the National Jogging Association.

Among lawyers, nine months after the Supreme Court's decision permitting them to advertise, only 3 percent had done so. This was a finding of "Law Poll," the *American Bar Association Journal's* opinion survey conducted by Kane, Parsons & Associates, a New York public opinion research firm. It was based on 599 telephone interviews conducted during late March 1978.

Amazingly, 46 percent of all attorneys polled immediately following the precedent-setting Bates decision expressed support for it, but so far, few are actually advertising. Why? Because they prefer personal solicitation. A significant 25 percent of lawyers are using earnest requests of a personal nature in seeking new business. It is another form of promotion.[4]

*The nation's dentists were freed from remaining restrictions on advertising on April 27, 1979. Final settlement of the anti-trust case will depend on the outcome of a similar suit filed against the AMA; that outcome will also apply to dentists. The case is likely to be in litigation for years, but in the meanwhile, restrictions on dentists' advertising have been barred.

# 3

# Winning the Right to Advertise

*In advertising there is a saying that if you can keep your head while all those around you are losing theirs—then you just don't understand the problem.*

*—Hugh M. Beville, Jr., Nov. 18, 1954*

The famous advertising dentist of San Francisco, Painless Parker (his legal name), employed commercial announcements long before some present dentists were born. He is the ultimate pioneer in dental advertising.

I spoke to Howard Bradfute of Stamford, Connecticut, who was a copywriter on the Painless Parker advertising agency account about ten years ago. Bradfute explained that Parker loved the exposure of his name and methods, whether that exposure was controversial or not. He used billboards, the newspapers, and the Yellow Pages for trumpeting his message: "Adequate dentistry for less."

Parker is still in practice—going strong from the time of the great depression—with nearly one hundred dentists and two hundred assistants working for him in a chain of offices running the length of California from San Francisco to San Diego.

## THE GROWTH OF MEDICAL PROMOTION

Advertising by providers of professional services has never been illegal in the eyes of the law when tested in the courts. It has only been considered a violation of canons of ethics and the codes of professionalism by professional associations and their more conservative members. Professional advertising came into conflict with former state professional-practice acts when colleagues of advertisers brought formal charges against such practice promotion.

Doctors of chiropractic have always advertised their manipulations and specific adjustments on the structures of the body, especially the spinal

35

column. Since the first movement of a vertebral articulation was given by Dr. Daniel David Palmer in 1895, it's been common practice for chiropractors to let prospective patients know what they do and how they do it. They've placed advertising in the Yellow Pages, newspapers, sent newsletters by direct mail, and done other things. The chiropractic physicians have been masters at employing promotional techniques and have watched their profession grow even in the face of stiff resistance by organized medicine. Now, the other health professions are taking a lesson from chiropractors and getting into advertising.

About ten years ago, ad practices spread to organized medicine itself. Starting at first only among medical mavericks, it made an impact on physicians in Milwaukee in 1974 and later percolated through New England, Florida, New York, Pennsylvania, and much of the South and Midwest. In 1977, physician promotional practices rolled through New Jersey, the Washington, D.C. area, and the Southwest and Far West. Currently, medical promotion is stirring things up throughout California.

Physician advertising began with Yellow Pages listings not only alphabetically, but under specialty headings as well. Osteopathic physicians and medical doctors were encouraged by the American Telephone and Telegraph Company to list themselves under breakdowns in the "Physicians & Surgeons" section by field of practice. AT & T calls this a "consumer service" that makes it easier for people to find or change specialists. More than half of Ma Bell's twenty-three phone-company affiliates throughout the country have implemented specialty listings.

The American Medical Association has elected a hands-off policy on Yellow Pages listings. The AMA was stung by the Federal Trade Commission's formal complaint in 1977 against organized medicine's advertising strictures. The AMA's policy is: "A physician may give biographical information to the telephone company, so long as it is not false or misleading." That's the new policy elected by the AMA to avoid violating the Sherman Antitrust Act.

AT & T makes two dollars per month per doctor from specialty listings. The ads pay off for both the telephone company and the osteopath or physician. Company surveys indicate that about 35 million adults use the "Physicians and Surgeons" listings each year, averaging nearly eight uses per person, or more than 270 million a year.

Most of the time, these adults call specialists, says Ma Bell, pointing out that the great majority of the nation's doctors consider themselves specialists. Incidentally, 89 percent of Milwaukee-area physicians use specialty listings.[1]

Chapter 5 supplies more detail about Yellow Pages listings and the use of other types of directories for professional advertising.

## DENTAL PROMOTION—AND OPPOSITION

The dental profession has had its share of promoters. They are best represented today by the Columbus, Ohio, dentist, Ronald F. Riviere. Any recent judicial decision regarding professional advertising is strictly academic to Dr. Riviere. He has been advertising dental services since the fall of 1975. His gross annual income is reported to be in excess of $1 million.

To attract pay-as-you-go patients, Dr. Riviere advertises in local newspapers and local radio and television. His ads are simple and to the point. They zero in on just what the dentist and his three colleagues, whose names he lists in the ads, do in routine daily practice. Among the procedures he features are one- or two-day full denture service, partial dentures, extractions, X rays, and cleaning of teeth. The ads also list Dr. Riviere's address, office hours, and phone number. Prospective patients are invited to call collect. Each ad carries the clever tag line: "You'll smile tomorrow if you take care of your teeth today."

The Ohio State Dental Board of Examiners has plainly expressed its displeasure with Dr. Riviere, although his ads were legal even before the Bates case. The board was especially disgruntled over the dentist's television advertisements and attempted to stop them. Dr. Riviere countered, however, by bringing suit against the board to allow him to run his TV messages. He won the right![2]

Another fighting dentist is Jerry Zebra (fictional character) of Caliope County, Pennsylvania. During an average eight-hour day, five days a week (in a simulated situation), Zebra gets paid for 260 patients who visit his two offices. A booklet distributed to 36,000 members of Local 92 of the Amalgamated Union of Wire Splicers advertises that Dr. Zebra offers dental bargains. His low rates are among the fringe benefits of union membership.

Whereas every other private patient pays him ten dollars for an amalgam filling, the booklet advises, in bold print: "Show your union card and pay only $6.00." Many of his routine services are listed and discounted. The families of wire splicers receive these benefits, too.

Unlike medicine, where companies can employ industrial physicians on a per-diem or hourly basis to treat any worker who needs service, this dentist is not an employee of Local 92. He retains the status of an independent contractor. Dr. Zebra bills union members just as he would other patients. His reduced rates are offered to union members, since they represent a patient volume from a central source. He has easy access to the membership by booklet advertising paid for by the union, with which he has a contract. The arrangement is quite remunerative, made so by the steady stream of patients who schedule their appointments well in advance. They are satisfied with the discounted dental care.

Dr. Zebra merely considers himself part of a closed panel of dentistry sponsored by the Amalgamated Union of Wire Splicers. No one in the union dictates the quality of professional service he might render. If this had been the case, it would violate the principles of ethics by which dentistry is practiced in every state in the country. "Nothing I do is contrary to the prevailing dental code of ethics," he says.

His district dental society took a different view. Zebra's peers were bitter about his standing out from the crowd. They had not as yet revised their policy for dental advertising in response to the Bates decision. Other dental groups such as the Board of Dentistry in the neighboring state of New Jersey have already made policy changes.

The New Jersey rules on providing information to the public by means of advertising were adopted by James F. Flood, president of the State Board of Dentistry in the Division of Consumer Affairs of the Department of Law and Public Safety. In summary, the new rules say that New Jersey dentists may provide to the public, by publication in a dignified manner in newspapers, telephone directories, comparable written publications, or by permitted signs, information concerning location, availability of services, postgraduate degrees, certificates of specialty granted by the board, years of practice, and fees for routine procedures. No broadcast media were indicated as being allowed by dentists in the state.

The New Jersey State Board of Dentistry specifically prohibits: advertising services beyond the dentist's ability to perform, the use of testimonials, discounts, gratuitous services, claims of professional superiority, guarantees of satisfaction, signs larger than two square feet, signs that use flashing lights, more than two signs, the use of novelty items, slogan words, pictorial materials, or multicolored print appearing in commercial publications.

The Caliope County Dental Society of Pennsylvania sent Dr. Zebra a letter asking that he appear before its ethics and discipline committee to explain his commercial activity. A "fishing expedition" was to be undertaken by the committee members, designed to frighten the advertising dentist.

Unfortunately, this maverick was not totally sure of his position. He felt uneasy about whether he was teetering in a borderline area of nonprofessionalism. He wondered whether professional advertising might not really be unethical, and whether what he had heard about the Supreme Court decision was possibly being ignored. Even the lawyer he had consulted didn't seem to know very much.

Zebra decided to bull ahead anyway. He is standing firm on his constitutional right to inform the public about his services and fees. There is too much of an investment at stake for him to do otherwise. He was inclined to contact Dr. Riviere for guidance, but Zebra's introverted personality held him back from asking for help from any other colleague. He feared being rejected. Now he was facing peer review alone.

"Who, me? Advertising?" Zebra asked, acting startled. "No, no, gentlemen, I'm not advertising. I just made an arrangement with a union organization, which is my right."

The ethics committee chairman, a white-haired dentist, held the green-covered union benefits booklet open to the page listing Zebra's services. "You are familiar with this booklet indicating in print the reduced prices you offer, aren't you?"

"Yes, sir, but I did not authorize the passing around of my name like that."

"Then, doctor, I think this evening's committee meeting will have functioned quite effectively if you will immediately cause the union to cease and desist dissemination of your fees and services information."

"Oh, I couldn't do that!"

"Why not?"

"Because I can't tell the union officials what to do. I did not request them to advertise my services, but I surely don't object. Besides, the union probably has a bundle of cash tied up in a large stock of those booklets for distribution. Think of its loss."

"Think of your violation of our code of professional conduct, Dr. Zebra!"

"I don't know what you're talking about."

"You are advertising dental care commercially."

"The Supreme Court ruled that it was okay to do that. The current dental-practice acts for each of the fifty states and the District of Columbia have all been rendered unconstitutional regarding dental advertising," Zebra said boldly. He hoped he was correct.

The ethics committee members sat back in frozen frustration. They knew he was on firm ground. Then one peer-review member put forth: "If you would terminate your contractual relationship with the union, our problem will be solved."

"If I canceled the contract, that's when *my* problem would first begin. Practically all of my patient income comes from union members. I'd have no volume left. I would be forced to fire three dentists who work for me in two offices. I would have to close one of them. What you require is too much. I don't want that problem, gentlemen. I don't see that there is any problem anyway."

Silence lay heavy in the room.

"There's nothing wrong with your closed-panel arrangement," the elderly chairman started again, "but the error is with the manner in which the union sends this information to its membership. By booklet, by letter —it's commercial advertising of professional services. It is a violation of the ADA's *Principles of Ethics* to which this district dental society subscribes."

Jerry Zebra sensed the strength of his stand. He certainly knew how hard he had worked to reach the secure financial position he had attained. He wasn't about to give it up. He thought he would face stiffer arguments, but there weren't any he couldn't shoot down. The FTC and the highest court in the land had bestowed on him their federal blessings. He smiled and answered, "Drop the ADA *Principles of Ethics* or write new ones."

Red face blazing in a surge of anger, and exasperation tingling on his tongue, the committee chairman let fly. "If you don't stop this advertising—taking on more patients than you're competent to handle—giving each case only about ten minutes—short-changing people by inadequate care—violating our society's ethics—opening yourself to eventual claims of malpractice—this committee will see that you are thrown out of our society!"

Dr. Zebra shrugged and said what he had rehearsed, "Expelling me will be an action that's arbitrary and illegal. You will have defamed my character, caused me public embarrassment, and been responsible for my losing income. I will sue you, all of the members of this committee, and the various component professional societies for ten million dollars. In addition, I will seek to enforce criminal proceedings against this district society, and the ADA, for violations of federal and state antitrust statutes. I will sue, as well, on your violation of my constitutional rights under the First and Fourteenth Amendments. And finally, I will form a non-ADA-affiliated dental society, here in Caliope County, composed of those many dentists who are itching to advertise but are being held back by your archaic attitude."

The hearing ended quickly.

Without Jerry Zebra in attendance, the district dental society's ethics and discipline committee conferred several times, in subsequent weeks, on the matter of advertising. They had the August 1, 1977, memo to officers and executive directors of constituent and component dental societies provided by C. Gordon Watson, the executive director of the American Dental Association. His memo stated:

1. State legislatures and state boards need to examine the dental practice acts and rules and regulations governing dental practice with an eye to all absolute prohibitions against advertising by dentists in the public press of the availability of their services and the fees which they are charging for routine dental procedures;
2. Dental societies immediately should cease initiation of disciplinary proceedings against any members who advertise in the public press regarding the availability of their services or the fees which they are charging for routine dental procedures. Further, dentists who simply advertise their services in a manner that is consistent with the Bates decision, if otherwise acceptable, should now be regarded as eligible for admission to membership;
3. State dental practice act prohibitions against routine service and fee advertising are in conflict with the First Amendment of the Constitution of the United States; [and]
4. Ethical bans of dental societies on similar advertising, including those contained in the *Principles of Ethics of the American Dental Association,* if enforced, possibly would expose the societies to civil, if not criminal, and state antitrust statutes.

Moreover, the House of Delegates of the ADA approved two resolutions in October 1977. Resolution 71 called for the cessation of any disciplinary proceedings against members who advertise the availability of routine fees and service in the public press. Resolution 72 called for dentists who advertise in a manner consistent with the Bates decision to be considered eligible for admission to membership in the ADA and its constituent and component societies.

Possessing these counterblasts from national representatives of organized dentistry, the members of this local ethics committee, who were trying to decide about Jerry Zebra, came into collision with their own prior conditioning and with the outdated ethical principles. Section 12 of the old ADA *Principles of Ethics* states:

Advertising reflects adversely on the dentist who employs it and lowers the public esteem of the dental profession. The dentist has the obligation of advancing his reputation for fidelity, judgment, and skill solely through his professional services to his patients and to society. The use of advertising in any form to solicit patients is inconsistent with this obligation.

In the end, although the committee members were loath to let him get away with what they considered unprofessionalism, they chose not to engage in a toe-to-toe legal battle with Jerry Zebra. The reason was not that he could win a large award but that he might win *any* award

—even one dollar. The government was likely to step in with an anti-trust claim as a result of this legal recognition of Zebra's complaint. There could be other civil or criminal proceedings. The committee members lacked an airtight case and would lose considerably if their dental society was made to face the real issues. They backed away from a court test and did not recommend Zebra's expulsion from the Caliope County district dental society.

The ethics committee planned a more subtle approach to disciplining Dr. Zebra. Chastisement would be achieved by preventing his practice from expanding and hoping for it to shrivel up by attrition. How could they accomplish this? By putting obstacles in the path of any new dentist he might attempt to employ.

There would be no component dental society membership allowed for any of Zebra's new professional employees. They would not receive malpractice insurance or any of the other benefits of belonging to organized dentistry. The plan: When the new dentist made his application, the chairperson in charge of such matters would say, "Dr. New Dentist, your application says you work for Dr. Zebra. He is persona non grata with this society because he is deemed to conduct an unethical practice. Membership for you is denied, since you work in an unethical office."

Theirs is a collateral attack on the advertising issue and any advertising dentist needing discipline. Dr. New Dentist will have to think again about whatever permanent arrangement he or she makes with Dr. Zebra. Without malpractice insurance, new practitioners will be vulnerable to the risk of tort law. They won't be able to obtain professional liability coverage as long as there is this disqualification from membership in a component dental society.

Dr. Zebra may bring suit, but it won't be on the same powerful issues of constitutional rights or antitrust laws. The issue will be more personal—and much weaker. As I warned in chapter 2, one's professional peers have many methods of systematic harassment to keep someone from exercising his newly won constitutional right to advertise. This simulated situation illustrates a typical conspiratorial action which might be undertaken by a professional association.

Constitutional law is also the issue for two dentists being accused of using "illegal" publicity. Michael J. Zazzaro, Jr., D.D.S., secretary of the Connecticut State Dental Commission, received an article in the mail from an anonymous source (probably from a fellow dentist), which was published in *Our Town,* a periodical sponsored by the Orange, Connecticut, Chamber of Commerce. The article focused on two dentists, Drs. Charles H. Kenney and Harvey A. Lichter, who share an office in Woodbridge, Connecticut.

Drs. Kenney and Lichter were the subjects of a news story describing their use of general anesthesia to treat retarded and hyperactive children. The publicity also detailed how the dentists used general anesthesia for routine patients undergoing nonsurgical procedures such as fillings. This anesthetic technique allowed them to treat patients who were usually difficult to handle. The information was written up, as well, in a small business-oriented newspaper, the *Bethwood News,* and circulated in Bethany, Connecticut.[3]

Dr. Zazzaro, whom a local dentist told me "is a super righteous upholder of morals," accused Kenney and Lichter of breaking a state law prohibiting dentists from advertising "professional superiority." They face the loss of their licenses.

Hearings on the charges are to be held sometime in the vague future. The two dentists retained attorney M. Mitchell Morse of New Haven, who filed a number of legal motions on September 14, 1978, and got the hearings postponed indefinitely. His motions challenged the constitutionality of the commission's charge and claimed that the advertising ban violated the dentists' rights of free speech and freedom of the press, both of which are guaranteed under the First Amendment. Morse backed his argument with the Bates ruling.

The attorney noted that the state attorney general had previously advised the Connecticut State Dental Commission to postpone further action under the statute until a U.S. district court indicated its position on a lawsuit challenging a general ban on medical advertising.

Morse also said that he questioned whether the news article fell under the statute because the two dentists didn't pay for it as they would for an ad. John Lynch, the publisher of the newspaper who wrote the story, said that neither dentist suggested the idea for the story or sought publicity. Kenney said that he and his partner simply answered questions.

Dr. Zazzaro, who brought the charges, thought differently. "It's my feeling the statements made to the reporter were very unprofessional, indicating they've been getting superior results." He stated that he is opposed to advertising by dentists. He said Kenney and Lichter "don't care if they get a suspension or a reprimand as long as they get the newspaper publicity."

If the commission upholds the accusation, it could suspend or revoke the two professionals' licenses. Then Kenney and Lichter would have to use the courts to get back their right to practice dentistry in the state of Connecticut.

## THE CONTINUING FIGHT FOR LEGAL ADVERTISING

Despite the Bates decision, the established rights and issues are factors in litigation going on right now, litigation that revolves around professional advertising in the legal profession. A suit was brought April 27, 1978, by lawyers who are fighting against rulings of their professional association. The case is likely to be tried in the next year or so.

The law partnership of Serko and Simon, formed under the laws of New York State, with principal offices in New York City, filed a complaint for declaratory and injunctive relief with the United States District Court for the Southern District of New York.

The plaintiff brought charges against the officers and directors of the Association of the Customs Bar, a professional association having the purpose of advancing and protecting the interests of lawyers specializing in customs and trade law. The association has 130 lawyer-members from 25 law firms throughout the United States. It is the only organization of lawyers specializing in this field of customs and trade law.

The defendants were accused of illegal and invalid attempts to prevent, hinder, restrain, or inhibit Serko and Simon from placing certain advertisements in trade journals and other publications, concerning the availability of the law firm's legal services. The plaintiff wanted the court to enjoin the defendants from their actions, which were alleged to be damaging the plaintiff's business and professional reputation by stating that its advertisements violated applicable standards of professional ethics.

"In attempting to so prevent, hinder, and restrain plaintiff from placing such advertisements," said the legal writ, "defendants have violated plaintiff's [constitutional] right of free speech and equal protection of the laws . . . and have unreasonably restrained trade and commerce in violation of the Sherman Antitrust Act and the Donnelly Antitrust Act."

With three law partners, four associate attorneys, five nonlawyer technical advisors, and a secretarial and support staff of approximately twenty persons, Serko and Simon, in October 1977, following the Supreme Court's Bates decision, placed a one-page ad in the *American Import Export Bulletin,* a journal that circulates among businesses engaged in international trade activities.

It was an attractive display ad showing the sun and clouds with the headline: "A New Day Has Dawned . . . For Those Seeking and Providing Specialized Legal Services. Customs and Trade Law." Then the name of the firm and addresses and telephone numbers of its two New York offices were supplied.

In December 1977, the plaintiff again advertised in the January 1978 issue of the same bulletin with a two-page insertion that contained a pen-and-ink line drawing and a long text describing the firm's services and listing its attorneys and technical advisors. It has since placed ads in *The New York Times, The Journal of Commerce, The 1978 Custom House Guide, The 1978 Transportation Telephone Tickler,* and miscellaneous yearbooks and dinner booklets.

The ethics committee of the Association of the Customs Bar met in November 1977 to review and consider the October 1977 advertisement. It determined as follows:

> An attorney may advertise his charges for performing specified services, usually uncontested, where the charge is intrinsically susceptible to advance determination. *Bates* v. *Arizona* does not authorize general display advertising by attorneys. The American Bar Association has announced its intention to publish guidelines on advertising by attorneys. In the interim, the committee's position is that, except as modified by *Bates,* no basis exists for assuming that the rules related to advertising have changed. The committee regards as improper the publication of a display advertisement, wherein the name of the law firm is displayed in an artistic setting of clouds and sunshine accompanied by a statement indicating that the firm specialized in Customs law. Committee members expressed the view that Customs law is, in fact, a specialty, and those who specialize in it should be allowed to so state. However, the American Bar Association has stated that only those in admiralty, trademark or patent law may describe themselves as specialists. The committee prefers to follow the standards of the American Bar Association, rather than to condone a challenge of such standards.

The ethics committee met again, March 10, 1978, this time to consider the plaintiff's January 1978 advertisement. It found unanimously that the ad was both "in violation of the . . . law" and "violative of standards of professional ethics."

The committee's basis for such ruling was that the textual portion of the January ad was "misleading" because it did not contain a notice that it was an advertisement. Also, it was described as "puffery" and "self-laudation," since it referred to "more than 200 years of cumulative experience" of the firm's attorneys and technical advisors, a claim that the committee stated "cannot be measured and verified." The ad was otherwise "improper" by referring to "a wide range of services" offered by Serko and Simon. It described the firm's staff and characterized the non-attorneys as technical advisors to the firm's attorneys.

Finally, the ad was alleged to have violated a "rule" of the American Bar

Association by "listing by name the courts, government agencies, and customs officers before which the law firm members appear" and by enumerating the types of service rendered by the firm.

On April 18, 1978, the board of directors of the Association of the Customs Bar, on the basis of the findings of the ethics committee, referred the January advertisement to the association's committee on discipline. On the same date, at the annual meeting of the members of the association, the president announced to the membership that these actions were taken and that disciplinary steps were being considered.

The discipline committee has threatened to take action against Serko and Simon on the basis of the January advertisement, with the intent of penalizing the firm for allowing it and the October advertisement to have been published. It is likely that the professional organization is using this penalty as an example of what will happen to other members of the association if any have in mind similar advertisements to be published in the future.

There is need for Serko and Simon to fight this inhibition, deterrence, and restraint. All of the association's members are required by the association's bylaws to be members of the bar of the United States Customs Court, the principal location of which is in New York City. For constitutional purposes, and as a matter of custom, the association functions as an agent and arm of the customs court in matters relating to the discipline of members of the bar of this court.

Therefore, not only will the prevailing threat of the association affect the plaintiff's advertising, but it will possibly constitute improper and illegal interferences with the constitutional rights of all the member firms of the association under the First and Fourteenth Amendments. For other New York law firms, the defendants' actions are alleged to constitute an improper and illegal interference with constitutional rights under Article I, Section 8 of the Constitution of the State of New York.

The plaintiff's suit seems to be on solid ground by its stated answers to the ethics committee's charges. Here are some of the points made by Serko and Simon:

- The text of the January ad contains the printed statement, "This message prepared and presented by Serko and Simon," as well as the magazine's logo specifically designating advertisements.
- While the firm states that it offers a "wide range of services," it does not state that such services are "better" than those offered by any competitor.
- Its technical advisors do in fact assist the firm's attorneys in representing clients. The way the names of the technical advisors ap-

peared was an unauthorized editorial change, made without the plaintiff's knowledge or consent, by the editors of the magazine. The advertising copy submitted for the January ad listed such persons under the separate heading "Technical Advisors," directly beneath the names of such advisors.

- As for experience, those two hundred declared years are easily added together and verified.
- Listing of the courts and other agencies before which the firm appears, and the categories of services that it renders, provides information to people seeking counsel with experience in such areas.
- Many of the law firms with whom Serko and Simon compete in the practice of customs and trade law are members of the bar of California, or of other states that permit such firms to publish advertisements in a form similar to the January advertisement. Yet, the ethics committee of the association has not threatened to apply restrictive standards and rules against those competing law firms. The sole basis for the application of standards and rules to Serko and Simon is that their principal office is in the state of New York, with its partners members of the New York bar. In this case, equal protection of the laws as guaranteed by the Fifth and Fourteenth Amendments is in violation.
- The association is in restraint of trade and commerce among the several states and the District of Columbia.

David Serko, Joel K. Simon, and the other attorneys in their firm asked for a permanent injunction against the officers and directors of the Association of the Customs Bar to enjoin them from taking any further actions to censure, discipline, or otherwise penalize the plaintiffs. They wanted no more harassment, inhibition, or interference with the efforts of the plaintiffs to place or publish the October ad, the January ad, or any similar advertisement that they may place or publish in the future.

# PART II
# Advertising

# 4

# Advertising Your Services: An Introduction

*The faults of advertising are only those common to all human institutions. If advertising speaks to a thousand in order to influence one, so does the church. And if it encourages people to live beyond their means, so does matrimony. Good times, bad times, there will always be advertising. In good times, people want to advertise; in bad times, they have to.*

—*Bruce Barton,* Town & Country, *February 1955*

As with any business, the professional person sells something. Crass as it may strike you, you're in the business of selling your expert knowledge, skill, talent, time, and various forms of specialized effort—in short, your services.

The aim of this chapter is to show you how to set objectives in advertising what you sell and acquire the final payoff you're after. It deals with basic theory in advertising—necessary before I get into the nuts and bolts of putting your message before the public.

Arthur H. Motley, president and publisher of Parade Publications, Inc., has made the short but profound statement that "nothing happens until somebody sells something." The "something" for the provider of professional services comes in two parts. You have to create one of those parts before anybody will want to buy the other—your professional services.

The first item of importance is your public image. The media, direct mail, pamphlets, newsletters, billboards, stationery, reception room furnishings, your office layout, your staff's appearance, public speaking engagements, how you conduct yourself professionally and socially, and other forms of communication are designed to sell you—your image—to the potential consumers of your services.

At once, you are both creator of that image and its best salesperson. Your talent, time, skill, and knowledge are commodities available for use by the highest bidder or by people willing and able to pay your preset fees. This is the way of free enterprise.

For the professional person, in prior years, one of business's major techniques for providing and selling services—advertising them—had been

51

banned. So-called violation of codes of professionalism or canons of ethics prevented any commercial announcement about professional services. The accomplishment of this second "something" was interfered with and made difficult.

Now that former disavowal by the professions has been rectified, you are free to present your message. You may sell your services as does anyone else in business—by advertising.

## THE TWO TYPES OF PROFESSIONAL ADVERTISING

The American Marketing Association has described advertising as *mass, paid communication* whose purpose is to "impart information, develop attitudes, and induce favorable action for the advertiser."

As far as you're concerned, professional-service advertising should function to inform, persuade, and remind clients or patients to buy your services. This is not a one-to-one proposition. Rather than to individuals, your message is directed to certain groups.

It's known that by using *mass, paid communication,* you can educate more people about your services and at lower cost in time and money than by any other means. Consumers of your professional skills are actually "manufactured" by means of the advertising of those skills. You are informing a group of people about the services you have for sale. Fortunately, they may be in the market for them. They become consumers where before they may not have known of your existence.

Advertising is many things to many people. It presents itself in a hundred forms in a hundred thousand places. Marshall McLuhan, the well-known Canadian communications scholar, says it is both the world's greatest teaching system and the greatest artistic force of the twentieth century. According to recent studies, the typical American adult is exposed to approximately eight hundred separate advertising messages every day, in one form or another. Reading one daily newspaper will give you four hundred exposures alone.

As an advertiser of professional services, your aim is to communicate to groups of prospects. Your desire will be to inform people of the services provided by you and your staff. This intent will be realized by your choosing between two types of ads. You may use either the "directional approach" or the "intrusive technique."

*The directional approach* merely points seekers of services in a direction where they can readily find those services.

The *intrusive technique* actually tells prospects what services they should have as well as where to find them.

Directional advertising has been relatively acceptable to professional associations since the advertising guidelines have been changed. Intrusive advertising has not been acceptable. Its use is still considered obnoxious and unprofessional. In time, this attitude may change as it has for the directional approach.

In directional advertising, the assumption is that a seeker of services already knows that he or she needs professional help and is on the lookout for the proper expert to provide it. The desire to buy already exists, at least in part. The only thing lacking is the consumer's knowledge of where to get this service. Perhaps consumers wish to investigate several sources; directional advertising tells them what they want to know. The classified section of your telephone directory is an example of directional advertising. Listings in dinner programs and journals of charitable organizations also are directional.

In intrusive advertising, there is a certain amount of invasion of privacy, since a message is beamed to someone who doesn't necessarily want to read, hear, or see it. Radio and television commercials intrude in this way on the attention of the listener or viewer. A set may be tuned in for news or entertainment, but the commercial breaks in with unwanted information, often about something the individual doesn't need. Direct-mail ads do this. And intrusion on highway scenery by billboards is a well-known form of esthetic pollution. Intrusive advertising will be the type most often questioned by peer-review panels and state boards of examiners.

## ALLOCATING AD MONEY FOR THE MEDIA

The success of your advertising depends in large measure on how much you're willing to spend on space and time in the media. Advertising is an investment that brings a hoped-for return, just as you would make an investment in adding another member to your staff. In buying space or time, cost will be a factor. The formula for ad expenditures is not the same for the professional provider of services as for the merchant vendor of products.

Merchants may allocate quite a bit of money for creating artistic display ads. Artistry of illustrations attracts the eye in print media. It's not likely that professionals will be buying much artwork. This is the case because most revised advertising guidelines adopted by professional associations prohibit display materials using illustrations. Your society probably will be against displays of any kind. You won't be making expenditures for creative renditions. This results in a reduced cost for ad preparation.

A rough rule of thumb for the advertising professional is that 98 percent of an ad budget will go to pay for media to carry the message. The reserve

53

of 2 percent for copy preparation may be held and used if more media money is needed. Seldom will there be a charge for copy preparation because most professional ads are straight price and service listings prepared at no cost by the media. Really, the reserve is just that—a reserve.

Each medium has characteristics of its own. Some will work for your specific benefit. Others will have you wasting dollars for things you don't want or need. The sales executives of various media have already figured into the price for time or space all of a medium's characteristics. They charge for them as a package. You'll be paying for collections of characteristics and therefore must weigh their cost-benefit ratios in advance.

The amount you have to spend should bring the biggest possible return. Repeating the same ad is one way to do this. Be aware, however, that advertisements repeated more than four times tend to lose their effectiveness.

There are four approaches to allocating ad money for the media:

1. *The "I'll spend what I can afford" approach.* Spending only what you think you can afford treats advertising as a luxury—an indulgence. This attitude reflects an underlying feeling that you really don't consider it a serious means of marketing your services. Subconsciously, you may look at commercials as wasters of dollars. In that case, you probably shouldn't be advertising at all.

2. *The "I'll match the competition" approach.* Because your colleague across the street runs a weekly six-inch, two-column ad in the local shopper, your inclination might be to do something of the same. Fight off the impulse. This is a purely defensive approach rather than an aggressive one. It's better to make a careful analysis of the audience you wish to contact and what you want to accomplish instead of blindly imitating your competitor.

3. *The "I'll invest a percentage of gross income" approach.* This more forward-looking attitude makes two constructive assumptions: (a) advertising is an investment for a larger future return, and (b) a scientific formula is necessary to figure the budget allocation.

A percentage of annual income will automatically have you taking for granted that advertising promotes the sale of services. It recognizes commercial communication as an important contributor to the expansion of a professional practice. The only danger is that your allocation based on last year's figures may be too optimistic for this year. A business cycle could dip and pull down your sale of services. Then, when advertising is necessary even more than before, you might feel the need to cut back on funds.

An engineer I know figures 5.5 percent of his firm's gross annual income for promoting new business. He makes this budget allocation no matter how the outside economy varies.

4. *The "I'll allocate so much per head" approach.* A variation of the percentage-of-gross-income method is the *unit-of-sales* approach. According to the number of new clients or patients that entered your practice last year, you designate a minimum value per head. A veterinarian in the Midwest, whom I've assisted with promotion, assigns each new anticipated patient for the forthcoming year $20 in ad budget money. He averages 1,000 office surgical operations a year that he performs on about 450 new animal patients. A $9,000 annual ad budget helped to earn him $188,000 in patient visits overall last year.

While veterinarian advertising could be simple, it should be frequent. Typical might be the small box ads inserted weekly by the Mobile Veterinary Clinic of Nassau and Queens, New York. Michael C. Posner, D.V.M., advertises minor surgery, vaccinations, laboratory services, and the like in an ambulatory-care unit brought to patients' homes by appointment. Owners of animals merely have to telephone the numbers printed in his ads, which are inserted in a pennysaver shopping paper week in and week out.

## THE FOUR R'S OF ADVERTISING

About fifteen years ago, Marshall McLuhan made a statement that has since become famous. He said, "The medium is the message!"

A few years later, in response to the hullabaloo created by what he said, McLuhan corrected himself. Over the educational station, WNDT-TV, he stated that in retrospect he had decided that the medium is the *massage.* What he meant is that some media rub people one way and some another.

Your job in picking the media that are best for your message is to find the proper ones to turn on your audience. Provide it with a therapeutic message-massage—one that makes your prospective clients or patients jump from the rubbing table prepared to engage your services for their professional needs.

The media are the mass communicative methods by which your advertising and promotion are supplied to the people. What they hear from you brings them to take an action advantageous to you, as well as to them.

Realize that your choice of the medium is part of your message. It may bring one of three possible responses: (1) optimum exposure and the volume purchase of your services; (2) no exposure and a complete waste of your investment in planning, effort, and money; (3) worse, an adverse effect that gives you poor exposure so as to drive away consumers altogether.

What approach should you take to insure against advertising failure? How are you going to optimize your investment? Is there a standard plan for communication success? Answer all three questions by aiming for the "Four R's" of advertising. Fit the "Four R's" to the talent, time, and information you have to sell. They are:

1. REACH—the determination of your market
2. READERSHIP (or listeners or viewers)—the people who are really interested in what you have to offer
3. RETENTION—the number of those who remember your message after they have seen or heard it
4. RESULTS—the selling power of what you've said and its ability to provide a return for investment

It's not unusual in advertising circles to pick the media before writing the copy or even deciding what service features to sell. The *massage* comes before the *message.*

Consequently, this chapter and the next are going to emphasize the benefits and deficiencies of the various media, and how they can be most useful for your purposes. It's a media strategy that you are after here and not necessarily the words and wisdom of your message. The message comes later, after you decide in which media you should invest your money. To the uninitiated in professional promotion, this may appear to be a topsy-turvy approach, but accomplishing the requirement of each of the "Four R's" will afford the media strategy you need.

### Reach—for Your Market

Although you may be a pediatrician, it's not likely that you'll want to voice your message to children. Their parents are the ones you wish to speak to, and primarily mothers, at that. The message will be *about* children and their problems.

If you're a gynecologist, it's quite obvious who is your market. But perhaps you specialize in the ear, nose, and throat. To whom will you be telling your story then?

Your first job before investing in advertising, therefore, is to know your market and the audience you want to reach. Next, you will need to plan how best to penetrate it—to massage it with the appropriate message. This is achieved by the art or science of *demography.*

In the advertising field, prospective customers are often identified in terms of demographic characteristics, psychological types, product usage, or brand usage. An analysis of any company's advertising problem entails, first, a working definition of the people the company is selling. In this case, *you* are the company. The people you want to reach are those most likely to respond to the message the way you want them to respond.

You are going to be purchasing time or space from the media, and each medium compiles information on its various audiences, defined in terms of demographic characteristics. The medium's information is available to you.

*Demography* is the statistical and mathematical analysis of populations based on the continuous registration of life-changes as they occur. Among media populations, the listeners, readers, or viewers are counted, and their characteristics are recorded as of one moment in time. The computation of costs per inch of space or prices per minute of time requires an accurate knowledge of the number and type of people exposed to the media.

As mentioned, the basic problem in finding a way to reach prospective clients or patients is to identify who they are in the first place. Having done that, and you're the only one who can, you then look at the audience demographics of each of the media and decide if your prospects make up most of the crowd it reaches.

Audiences usually are classified by place of residence (region of the country and size of the city) and four basic sex and age combinations: adult males, adult females, teenagers, and children. The major media also supply the audiences' income, education, and family size.

Your object is to find the media that will reach the greatest number of prospects for your services and rub them the right way with a message. This isn't a simple thing to do. For instance, if you're an accountant and want to sell your services to people with upper-middle incomes, the best medium to use for an advertising campaign may not be the one with the highest percentage of women. While it's true that women do own most of the wealth of this country at the present time, they still acquire it in the majority of instances by inheritance from their husbands. The men tend to overwork and kill themselves. At the same time, these men are looking for tax loopholes with which to accumulate the capital and keep as much as possible. Therefore, an accountant would probably prefer media exposure to male prospects between ages twenty-five and sixty-five, rather than to women in this age group.

In brief, my recommendation is to use the comparative data of the various media at your disposal. You can obtain these data from the media themselves; they use facts and figures as sales tools. Elect the few that give you exposure to the prime targets for your messages. Do this after you've gotten a handle on exactly who buys your services. In other words, define your prospects and find them demographically by their psychological or other characteristics.

### Readership—Who Sees What

It's necessary to do some matching. Match up the characteristics of the media audience with the characteristics of your consumer prospects. A way to do this is to request a readership survey from each medium to learn how many pairs of eyes per dollar per inch are being delivered. You want to know the number of purchasers of the local newspaper, for instance, in which you may buy space. And you want to learn about the people who actually read it. This way you'll get to know the true ad-exposure cost and how many in your market are exposed.

In media selection, the basic rule is to start with the medium that brings the best return and move to other media as the first becomes unavailable or loses its effectiveness.

Expect media overlapping if you use more than one. Two newspapers may reach about 20 percent of each other's audience, so that your message will probably have an impact on about 4 percent of the overlapped group. Surveys show that 10 percent of double exposures imprint themselves on people's brains, and 2 percent of each double readership take a present or future action as a result. This is a good return.

The problem of audience duplication among the media is: how much are you willing to spend on overlapping? People do tend to forget. Refreshing their memories about the services you offer is desirable but expensive. By having a knowledge of the readership (or listenership or viewership) of the media you're deciding about, you will be able to measure their ability to deliver your message with a minimum of waste.

Readership knowledge and media selection go hand in hand. Consequently, my recommendation is to study the statements put out by the media in which they disclose their basis of circulation. Such statement studies are every bit as important as studying the annual report of a publicly held corporation before investing in its stock.

Absorb the information on a print medium's circulation statement. Take note if it is audited by an outside circulation-auditing organization, as are those periodicals that are members of the American Business Press, Inc. Sometimes the medium's statement is sworn to by the publisher or owner but not audited from the outside. Other times, there is no auditing at all, and then you are buying circulation on sheer faith. Try limiting your space purchases to outside-audited periodicals.

The four organizations that do outside audits in the United States are: the Audit Bureau of Circulations (ABC), the Business Publications Audit of Circulations, Inc., (BPA), the Certified Audit of Circulations, Inc.,

(CAC), and the Verified Audit Circulation Corporation (VAC). The ABC, BPA, and CAC are nonprofit associations with boards of directors made up of people from advertising and publishing. The VAC is privately owned. All four require strict record-keeping and charge steep prices for the certification of circulation. Those may be reasons why some media are not audited by an outside organization—too much expenditure in time and money for proving the validity of circulation figures.

Viewers or listeners in the broadcast media are checked by the Broadcast Rating Council. It audits the reports of broadcast-measuring services, which take samples of households or individuals in the population as representative measurements. A survey reading will tell you the number of receiving sets in use in a particular area at a certain time and the share of that audience tuned into each station. For example, the listening and viewing audience in the usual "Nielsen A" city is splintered among an average of 4.4 television channels and numerous AM and FM radio stations. Surveys show that during an average minute in the prime 7:00 to 10:00 P.M. hours, TV sets are turned on in 49 percent of U.S. homes. While Nielson won't reveal its sampling points, a program is "A" rated when a few more than 1,000 households are tuned in. National projections come from these sample households. I will discuss the Nielsen ratings in more detail in the next chapter.

## Retention—Making Your Message Stick

Retention asks how many people remember what you said in your message after they have seen or heard it. This is determined by the significance of the advertisement's words to your audience. Does the consumer identify with your message and take it personally?

You can include sixty-five words in a thirty-second radio spot—not a lot of time—and the cost will be about $15 for broadcasting in prime "A"-class time in a medium-sized city. "A"-class time has the most listeners, perhaps those driving to work in the morning or going home in the evening. Over Radio Station WSTC in Stamford, Connecticut, where my wife and I produce a daily radio program, the cost is $17.50 for a one-minute commercial broadcast in "B"-class time. Stamford is less than a medium-sized city with a population of 125,000.

Your words have to be meaningful and must give the information quickly. Combined, the medium and the message must strike the eye or catch the ear to make an impression.

The medium guarantees to deliver your wisdom to a specified audience. You purchase so much white space on paper or so many seconds of air time.

What you do with that space or time is strictly your decision. An audience's response will depend on how well you've chosen the medium, the kind of services being offered, and how well you present the offering.

Retention of your message's meaning comes from your interpretation of the want-satisfying qualities of the services in terms of the client's or patient's preferences. The old school of advertising tends to underrate the intelligence of consumers. It thinks of the advertiser as *doing* something to the audience. The advertiser gives prospects, a stimulus that triggers the desired response. The advertiser acts and the audience reacts, says the old school. It's a form of brainwashing, hidden persuasion, or subliminal advertising. Raymond Bauer, an advertising consultant, sees a similarity between people and rats that are used in experimental psychology. He notes:

> The model of a one-way exploitative process of communication . . . is probably further reinforced by the experimental design in which the subject is seen as reacting to conditions established by the experimenter. We forget the cartoon in which one rat says to another: "Boy, have I got this guy trained! Every time I push this bar, he gives me a pellet of food." We all, it seems, believe that *we* train the rats.[1]

My advice is not to underrate modern consumers. Also, however, as an advertising professional anxious to sell services, don't *overrate* the power of your message. It has to have a certain want-satisfying quality that only consumers themselves know best.

An effective approach is to think of your advertising as a two-way exchange—an interaction between your audience and what you have to say. Avoid the tendency to pound consumers with words and *force* a response. Rather, bring knowledge of your services to them in a way that matches what you perceive to be their beliefs, values, goals, attitudes, needs, and desires. Retention of your message will result.

An expert in communication, Joseph Klapper, writes in his book, *The Effects of Mass Communication:*

> By and large, people tend to expose themselves to those mass communications which are in accord with their existing attitudes and interests. Consciously or unconsciously, they avoid communications of opposite hue. In the event of their being, nevertheless, exposed to unsympathetic material, they often seem not to perceive it, or to recast and interpret it to fit their existing views, or to forget it more readily than they forget sympathetic material. The processes involved in these self-protective exercises have become known as selective exposure (or, more classically, "self selection"), selective perception, and selective retention.[2]

## Results—from the Impact of Your Message

None of the above—REACH, READERSHIP, or RETENTION—would mean much without clients or patients coming to you to purchase services. RESULTS are the only measurements that count to justify your advertising investment.

The payoff comes from the selling power of your message. It must have certain qualities: it has to be seen or heard, understood, remembered, accepted, and cause the consumer to buy your services. Feeling satisfaction with what you've delivered, the purchaser may, in turn, make a repeat use of your services and openly refer others to do the same.

How do you achieve such results? Most important is the individual's exposure to the kinds of communications media that carry your words. As I've said, they should be the ones that rub your prospects the right way. To have them understood, remembered, and accepted, expose your words in an appealing style and consistently schedule them for appearance in appropriate media.

One of this country's most distinguished journalists, the late Walter Lippmann, once said: "For the most part, we do not first see, and then define. We define first and then see."[3] He was referring to perception of the reader, viewer, or listener when confronted by some form of communication. Advertisements are commercial communications, which draw attention to themselves when the perceivers recognize a need and develop a want. They use selective perception to fill that need or satisfy the want. Indeed, not only do consumers select what they wish to perceive, they also tend to distort the words of a message to conform to their different values, attitudes, and opinions. As Lippmann pointed out, they first define their perceptions before they see them.

The perceiver may or may not believe your advertisement. Acceptance largely depends on how well it integrates into one's existing attitudes and prejudices. Accomplish this, and you'll produce consumer *action* in favor of buying your services.

The theoretical practice that I just stated is the whole basis for success in advertising.

Yet consumer action does not take place all at once. One ad exposure usually won't be sufficient to move prospective clients or patients to respond to their wants or needs. It would be naive to expect so much from a one-time message. Each advertising placement should be an invitation to action, of course, but it should also be viewed as one of many small pushes in the direction of your office door.

The selling power of your advertisements comes into play by planting layer upon layer of messages in the mind of the consumer. Patronage of a dispenser of professional services takes place slowly. Your goals for advertising should be nothing like those of the retailer of products who is geared for quick action —an intent to influence tomorrow's buying with ads placed in the newspaper tonight. Instead, you want different effects that consist of three subtle results: (1) *awareness* by clients or patients that your services are available, (2) *knowledge* by clients or patients that there are certain advantages in making use of these services, and (3) *belief* by clients or patients that your time and attention offer the best value for the prices quoted. Achieve these goals and your advertising will eventually net a good response.

## BELIEVABILITY

Of the three above goals, bringing prospects for your services to a belief that you offer a better return for investment than any of your colleagues is the most difficult to accomplish. If you just come out and say your service is superior, the professional association is likely to have you up on charges before the state board of examiners for unethically attempting to stand out from among your fellows. More adroitness is required.

First of all, *start with the truth.* It is demanded by the covenants of professionalism and is generally more believable than lies. False statements will be recognized for what they are, resulting in undermining the consumer's confidence in your image. Only state the truth in your advertising.

Next, *appeal to the main desires* of your market. For a chiropractor's patients, it may be freedom from backaches. An accountant's clients might want lower-priced tax preparation. An attorney could feature minimum fees for title searches. In each of these professions, the appeal to prospects is identified clearly and included in the ad. People want to be well. They wish to keep the money they earn without much expenditure for government reporting. And they desire few, if any, additional costs tacked onto the price of buying property.

Then, *give some reasonable explanation* to justify the consumer's belief in what you are saying. Most people form convictions based on one of the following five reasons:

1. They have feelings and emotions about a statement.
2. They identify personally with the statement.
3. The statement forms the fabric of their own experiences.
4. They need to conform with others of their class, especially with those they consider authorities.
5. They believe what they want to believe.[4]

Finally, *use plain language* to make your statements so that prospects can picture you as their kind of person. Unfamiliar words—big ones—arouse suspicion among most people. Technical jargon may be impressive to some, but to most, it is unconvincing. This is especially true in commercial communication.

## ADVERTISING AS MARKETING

At the beginning of this chapter, I said the professional person is in business, and the service he or she dispenses is the commodity that is sold. You can sell more of your commodity if your image shines in a favorable light—made so by astute promotion. Advertising is one of the marketing methods of image building. Publicity is the other one.

Advertising has evolved from the simplest form of merely identifying a marketplace's location to a highly sophisticated means of persuasion far from the point of sale.

Under the thumb of the Federal Trade Commission, the Bates decision of the Supreme Court, and the Justice Department, professional societies have no choice but to accept the marketing of professional services by means of advertising. Speaking in 1976 before American Bar Association about its blanket prohibition against advertising by lawyers, Justice Department attorney Joe Sims said: "Since the concerted elimination of price advertising by competitors, a traditional analysis would find this flat ban a per se violation of the Sherman Antitrust Act." Another trust-buster, Bruce B. Wilson, told a meeting of lawyers: "It surely cannot be said that all price advertising is necessarily improper or harmful."[5]

The various professional organizations, unfortunately, are attempting to modify the governmental and judicial rulings and to institute the original form of no advertising among their members. It's a kind of noncommunicative advertising. They are laying down new guidelines so that current professional advertising will be practiced the way it was as early as 4000 B.C. —just listings of services and fees—routine stuff.

Advertising is a very old and honorable form of marketing activity—a means of calling attention to the availability of the goods and services provided by an entrepreneur. It reduces the personal selling costs of individuals. Isn't it less expensive in terms of time and production to place an ad in the media than to make personal contact with a large number of people? Personal contact is a frequent way of gaining new clients or patients now, but doesn't this old method squander a lot of otherwise productive time? Fairfax Cone of the Foote, Cone and Belding advertising agency, said in a 1963 interview published in the *Christian Science Monitor:* "Advertising is what you do when you can't go see somebody. That's all it is."

Advertising does serve the most useful of purposes by bringing knowledge of available professional services to those who need and want them. It is an instrument for communicating the range of skills and prices of a particular supplier. It realizes a degree of production efficiency for the professional person. And it acts as a major sales tool of our consumption-oriented economy. All of our society benefits from its existence.

The result is that many types of media in which to advertise professional services provide a forum of information for the consumer. Each has advantages and disadvantages, and those will be described in the next chapter.

# 5

# Choosing Media

*Doing business without advertising is like winking at a girl in the dark. You know what you are doing, but nobody else does.*

—*Stuart Henderson Britt*
New York Herald Tribune
*October 30, 1956*

Nothing turns on the executives along Madison Avenue, North Michigan Avenue, Wilshire Boulevard, and other advertising streets of the nation more than the attributes of various advertising media. Advertising people are exceedingly interested in the effectiveness of what they do and where they place their clients' ads. They measure media effectiveness by the number of exposures and actions of people as a result of the advertisers' messages. The ad executives make comparisons of media according to these salient points:

- Number of persons exposed to the advertising messages in each medium
- Number of persons who have their attitudes toward an advertiser changed by each medium
- Number of persons who are conditioned so that they will buy the advertised services when some reason necessitates their switch
- Number of consumers who immediately seek professional services because of advertising in each medium
- Extent to which each medium encourages present users to retain their loyalty to the advertising professional
- Extent to which each medium encourages present users to employ the services more frequently[1]

In comparing the media yourself, you'll find it valuable to be mindful that the function of a particular print ad, poster, or broadcast commercial is to communicate—to put across information and make an impression. This will induce in the reader, listener, or viewer a change in thinking or reinforcement of attitude towards the service being advertised. You want the ad to lead to an alteration in behavior that is in your favor. For this, you have to have some pertinent facts about the various forms of commercial communication available in your area.

## WHAT TO EXPECT FROM ADVERTISING

Which are the best media for you? What one or two ad facilities will influence the prospects for your services? How do you want to deliver your message? If your professional practice is a local one, from what distance can you expect to attract clients or patients? Which medium is the least offensive but the most penetrating? Can you calculate the cost-benefit ratio of each?

It's reasonable to expect advertising in any of the media to accomplish some or all of the following objectives:

- Bring in appointments by phone or mail from consumers
- Bring in requests for information from prospects
- Keep current consumers loyal and reminded of your services
- Reach key unidentified persons who influence referrals
- Uncover prospects unknown to you
- Enlighten loyal patients or clients of the full range of services you offer besides those they already use
- Call attention to your personal community activities as a good citizen simply from people being exposed to your professional ads
- Fill the need of a distracted consumer at the right place and the right time when he or she has an emergency situation

With four major decisions required relating to presenting your message: what to tell, to whom to tell it, how to tell it, and where to tell it, the balance of this chapter is devoted to helping you decide the last—that is, in which of the media to advertise.

As I indicated in the previous chapter, most ad costs are not for preparation of the ad but rather for the purchase of time or space. Preparation is an extra cost which comes out of the 2 percent reserve you set aside. Ad preparation costs will be discussed elsewhere in this book.

## NEWSPAPERS

People want local news, and newspapers are print media, daily or weekly, that provide the current-events information of a city, town, village, or local area. The written language has always been precious, and people do believe what they read. All ages, both sexes, every educational and income level, and varied cultural and recreational interests find something imperative about newspapers. Nearly everyone reads them. In fact, more people read newspapers than anything else in print.

Newspapers are timely and flexible. Your ads can be changed quickly and frequently. Regardless of the kinds of services you dispense, advertising in a newspaper will reach people who live near you and are logical prospects. The short lead time for new copy allows the placement of advertising alterations within two, three, or four days before the publication date. For an attorney, this means if a major disaster strikes your region, such as a vast multi-car accident on the nearby highway, you can quickly notify prospects through newspaper ads that you handle liability cases and practice tort law.

*The Wall Street Journal,* in a September 9, 1977, article, quoted St. Louis attorney Dennis Smith as experiencing "a tremendous increase" in his business since beginning to advertise in newspapers. Smith, a former public defender who has entered public practice, doesn't announce his availability to handle liability and tort cases, but he does advertise uncontested divorces at $125, business incorporations at $200, and adoptions at $175.

Your ad may be inserted "R.O.P." ("run of the paper"), or you can specify that it is to be put on a special-interest page that preselects your readers. An orthopedic surgeon and an osteopathic physician would probably tell of their services on the sports pages. An accountant would likely announce himself in the business section. An obstetrician might list his rates on a page of the women's-interest section. Pregnancy-termination clinics are already displayed on women's interest pages. Why not compete?

Newspaper advertising brings you quick responses and intensive coverage in a well-defined region. Both weeklies and dailies provide frequency and regularity of contact with prospects. And they offer three types of ads:

- *Display advertising*—relatively large space in the regular sections of your newspaper. It gives your message maximum visual impact.
- *Classified advertising*—a listing that reaches prospective clients or patients who are looking for services right now. Like the yellow pages, classified ads are directional.
- *Classified display advertising*—small-space "display" units included in the classified section. It combines quick information with more visual impact. The rate sometimes will be higher than the other two types.

Ad rates quoted for local display formats will be by column inches. If line rates are quoted, be aware that there are fourteen lines to an inch. (This

Advertising and Promoting the Professional Practice

measure is called an agate line.) As the amount of space you desire increases —volume rates are quoted—the cost per inch or line decreases. Volume rates may be referred to as "open," "one-time," "transient," "local," or "retail." However, such terms may vary in meaning according to the periodical using them. There may also be "frequency" and "continuity" rates, or combinations of them. If you contract for a certain amount of advertising but fall short of that, the newspaper may charge you "short" rates. However, if you advertise more than you contracted for, you will qualify for rebates on the rates.

To compare the costs of advertising in different newspapers, it is customary to use the cost per line per million circulation, called the *milline rate formula*. Using the highest rate charges by each newspaper—not the rate you are contracting for—follow this formula to make rate comparisons:

$$\text{milline rate} = \frac{\text{Line rate} \times 1,000,000}{\text{circulation}}$$

The reason for multiplying by 1,000,000 is that the larger figures are easier to compare. If the rates you are comparing are quoted in column inches, this rate can be used in the formula instead of the line rate. Just be sure to use the same rate base—the line rate or the column-inch rate—for all the newspapers you are comparing. For example, if a newspaper charges $4.90 per column inch as does *The Advocate* of Stamford, Connecticut, its line rate is 35 cents. If the newspaper's circulation is 32,000, its milline rate will be

$$\$10.93 = \frac{0.35 \times 1,000,000}{32,000}$$

Don't overlook the classified pages, especially if you want a budget way of presenting your services. Classified is the fastest-growing form of newspaper advertising. In 1974, classified billing was $2.2 billion. In 1976, it came to $2.8 billion, and by 1980, it is expected to grow to be between $3.7 and $4.7 billion. More and more people are turning to the classified sections of their newspapers to buy services—or just for the fun of seeing what's being offered.

## SUNDAY SUPPLEMENTS

In one-newspaper towns and cities, Sunday supplements reach 90 percent of all readers. I mentioned that more people read newspapers than anything else in print. Well, Sunday is, hands down, the "favorite" day of the week for newspaper reading, according to a national Roper Organization survey. Reading the Sunday paper is the number-one activity in the nation's major market areas—even outscoring watching TV.

Sunday supplements are newspaper-distributed Sunday magazines that carry fiction, nonfiction, special features, pictures, and advertising. There are two general kinds: magazines and comics, which may be national, and independent or locally edited.

Two of the more familiar national newspaper-distributed magazines are *Parade* and *Family Weekly*. There are a few others. The locally edited magazine supplements are published by individual newspapers and circulated with their Sunday editions.

Orders for advertising in a locally prepared supplement are placed with the local newspaper or its representatives. This is in contrast to the nationally distributed Sunday supplement, in which advertising is contracted for with the company that publishes the newspaper-distributed magazine. The rates for the magazine supplement of a local Sunday newspaper usually are higher priced because the advertiser may be restricted to buying not less than a quarter of a page.

### REPRESENTATIVE REGIONAL OR LOCAL SUNDAY SUPPLEMENT SPACE RATES

| Sizes Accepted[a] | | Open Rate | 6-Time Rate | 9-Time Rate | 12-Time Rate |
|---|---|---|---|---|---|
| Full page | (4″ × 14″) | $ 378.50 | $ 312.75 | $ 284.50 | $ 258.50 |
| 1/2 page | (4″ × 7″ or | 189.25 | 156.50 | 142.25 | 129.25 |
| | 2″ × 14″) | | | | |
| 1/4 page | (2″ × 7″ or | 94.50 | 78.25 | 71.00 | 64.75 |
| | 1″ × 14″) | | | | |
| 1/8 page | (1″ × 6¾″) | 47.25 | 39.00 | 35.50 | 32.25 |
| 1/12 page | (1″ × 4½″) | 31.50 | 26.00 | 23.75 | 21.50 |
| 1/16 page | (1″ × 3¼″) | 23.75 | 19.50 | 17.75 | 16.25 |

[a]Advertising may be accepted only in the sizes shown above.

## SHOPPERS

Shopping guides, or shoppers, are newspaper-like in appearance but seldom carry much news. They are almost entirely filled with advertising, which makes them even more valuable for commercial announcements of professional services for sale. When consumers open a shopper, they know very well it is going to expose them to a paper full of print ads. It's more than likely that these people are predisposed to purchasing something that catches their eyes. The eyes are gateways to the minds, which store information for immediate and future use. The shopper is a kind of mini-encyclopedia of commercial information.

Many shoppers provide readers with classified directories to services and products available locally. It is this classified section that should definitely be of interest to the learned professional. A directory involuntarily registers your availability to the consumer. Points you wish to emphasize can be brought into sharp focus when set apart by the use of headlines, bullets, boldface type, etc.

Chiropractor Dr. Fred B. Rudin of Forest Hills, New York, uses boldface type when he advertises in a local shopper—a "pennysaver." He announces that he gives full health-care services, including special treatment for spinal disorders, nutritional evaluation, and kinesiology.

(A pennysaver is a shopping guide that is hand-delivered in a controlled-circulation area of limited distance, usually to a small section of the city.)

Psychotherapist Deborah Karnbad of Queens and Manhattan, New York, finds it advantageous to tell of her services (individual, marital, and family psychotherapy on a sliding scale of fees from eight to twenty dollars) in the Queens Village, New York, pennysaver.

While pennysavers often are letter-size, shoppers vary in appearance and size. Filler material in pennysavers and shoppers is of a general nature—recipes, household hints, personal care suggestions, and a little news. Carrying advertising is their main function. Rates are charged at lower prices than newspapers—the publication will supply a rate card on request.

## DIRECTORIES

"The uniqueness of directory advertising is suggested in its name," according to Tibor Taraba, manager of the directory division of the Reuben H. Donnelley Corporation, who provided me with information about directories. The Donnelley corporation is a marketing organization that concerns itself with the effectiveness of Yellow Pages directories.

Taraba told me: "Unlike all other forms of advertising that can be used to create a desire for a product or service in customers, directory advertising speaks to consumers who are actively looking for very specific information directing them to the best source."

There are two groups of directory-advertising clients or patients, suggests the Donnelley literature. The first is divided into those who are newcomers to your area, emergency buyers who want something right away, dissatisfied people who want to change their professional service sources, infrequent purchasers who don't buy your service often, comparison shoppers, and transient or temporary visitors or residents who aren't familiar with your particular community.

The second group of consumers are those presold people who have used your skills before, have been referred to you, or have been informed about your services from having seen your advertising previously. They merely need to be reminded of your name and location, and they will call or visit you when they need your services.

In my opinion, directory advertising is the most economical means of contacting clientele. It is the only true form of directive consumer advertising whose audience is bona fide and ready to buy. There are the Yellow Pages directories that cover all industries, professions, home services, trades, and types of products in a city; and there are directories limited to single professions. Some publishing companies specialize in directories. The professional associations seem to favor directories that list services offered by their members as the primary method of living with the Supreme Court decision allowing the professional to advertise.

The directory manager of New York Telephone, Geraldine F. Ryan, told me: "Within the Bell System, there are twenty-three operating companies, each publishing Yellow Pages directories. In addition, there are many independent telephone companies and directory publishers who also produce Yellow Pages directories. The format, rules and regulations, and features often vary from company to company." In order for you to obtain more of a national profile, Ryan suggests that you contact the system coordinator for professional advertising.

Having a national profile will let you, as an individual, see what your colleagues around the country are doing in directory advertising. To acquire a profile of advertising professionals, contact William M. Cochrane, Marketing Supervisor, Directory Marketing, American Telephone and Telegraph Co., 295 North Maple Avenue, Basking Ridge, New Jersey 07920.

In the metropolitan area of New York City, Yellow Pages users refer to specialty designations of health professionals a stipulated number of times daily, as indicated by surveys conducted by the Chilton Research Services. Four out of five adults used the Yellow Pages in the twelve-month period just past. They followed up by action—phone calls, visits, or letters—84 percent of the time.

New Yorkers refer to the "Podiatrists" heading an average of 5,232 times per week, "Veterinarians" an average of 14,171 times per week, "Chiropractors" an average of 1,569 times per week, "Dentists" an average of 15,348 times per week, "Physicians and Surgeons" an average of 76,977 times per week, and "Lawyers" an average of 10,632 times per week.

## Sizes and Type Style of Directory Ads

What size should your directory advertisement be? Should you use more than a listing—make it a display-type ad instead? It's for you to reconcile your preference with the rules of your professional association. Just know that in a study conducted by Russell Marketing Research, Inc., over 200

Yellow Pages users were shown directory pages with pairs of display ads. Half of the ads had "heavy" copy—that was filled with useful information such as professional association memberships. Half the ads had "light" copy. Respondents were asked to name the supplier of services they'd call first. Here are the results:

### EFFECTIVENESS OF HEAVY COPY

| Size of Ad | Heavy Copy Outpulled Light Copy by a Ratio of |
| --- | --- |
| Large Ads (double half-column) | 3.0 to 1 |
| Medium Ads (double quarter-column) | 2.6 to 1 |
| Small Ads (quarter-column) | 1.9 to 1 |

The heavy-copy ads outpulled the light-copy ads an average of 2.4 to 1. The conclusion Russell Marketing Research came to is that the more useful information and selling copy you put into your ad, the more effective it will be in convincing prospects to call you to fill their needs.

In the same study, Yellow Pages users were also shown specific directory pages with different size display ads on them. They were asked to select a supplier in each of five different heading categories they would call first. Here are the results:

### EFFECTIVENESS OF SIZE

| Size of Ad | % Would Call First |
| --- | --- |
| Large Ads (double half-column) | 56 |
| Medium Ads (double quarter-column) | 31 |
| Small Ads (quarter-column) | 13 |

The double half-column ads outdrew the double quarter-column ads by almost 2 to 1; and the double quarter-columns outdrew the quarter-columns by close to 2 1/2 to 1. The large ads had better than four times the impact of small ads. The research firm concluded that the bigger your ad, the more you can say in it—and the better it will be able to compete for the consumers' attention and sell them on calling you first.

The benefits of directory advertising are easily measurable by building a code into your ad. In fact, you may wish to use this technique with any of the advertisements you place in the media. For instance, ads in a newspaper can say, "Ask for Mr. Montrose." "Mr. Montrose" is your code for determining which medium brought the best response.

Here are the particular benefits derived from placing your advertisements in directories:

- *Information is supplied.* Potential clients or patients are often looking for more than addresses and telephone numbers. Your ad tells much of what they wish to know.
- *Identifies you with the profession.* Prospects who need your professional services will find you under that profession's listing. (Why make it difficult for a person to find you?)
- *Display ads attract attention.* Ordinary free telephone listings are small and do not stand out sufficiently to attract patrons. Yellow Pages or other professional directories allowing for displays provide the opportunity.
- *Special services are described.* If you perform a service that no one else in the area does—say so!
- *Insures notification when the consumer wants to take a buying action.* In an emergency, or when a person finally decides to accomplish something he or she has put off until now, you are present on the directory's list of learned professionals who can put things right.
- *Advertising is economical.* The cost is comparatively small to be listed in a directory—and the listing is working for you day after day.

About 6,000 classified directories are published annually in the United States; Canada offers about 500 more. A quarter-page ad in a Yellow Pages directory for a city of 200,000 to 400,000 population costs approximately $483 per year (in May 1979). A one-column 2 1/2-inch display ad costs about $219 per year for the same medium-size city.

## NATIONAL MAGAZINES

Magazines for the consumer reach better-educated and wealthier families, who buy more services. Magazine readers seem more able to afford professional help for their problems. Even though national magazines may not appear to be within your ability and requirements to advertise, their regional editions do open certain geographical areas to you. About one hundred national magazines publish regional editions. You'll find that the market they reach comprises exactly those people who would use professional services if they knew where to find them. You can use strictly regional distribution at a lower cost and thus reach these magazine readers.

A look at *Newsweek's* regional, metropolitan, or state marketing plans will illustrate the feasibility of how you might use any national magazine that features these plans for your messages. Richard F. Bausch, associate advertising director of branch sales for *Newsweek,* supplied me with material relating to its marketing plans. Early in 1977, the magazine committed itself to a program that would "continue to refine the art of media planning and media evaluation."

*Newsweek* redesigned its metropolitan editions in the top twenty ADI markets. The ADI (area of dominant influence) is widely recognized as a standard marketing tool. It is an area in which a TV station has a commandingly large share of the viewing audience. Now applied to the circulation and audience of *Newsweek Metro* editions, it enables you to compare the efficiencies of different media and achieve more accurate market planning, media selection, and budget control in certain metropolitan areas and regions of the country. Understand, what follows about *Newsweek* is only an example of the type of marketing plans you may acquire from approximately one hundred other leading national magazines.

A one-time insertion of a black and white, half-column ad for covering just the city of Detroit and surrounding counties, for instance, with a rate base of 70,000 circulation, costs $380. This would give you exposure to 417,000 adults consisting of 243,000 men and 174,000 women. Of these people, 308,000 are age 18–49 and the other 109,000 are over the age of 49. They live in households with median incomes of $20,000+, with 202,000 of them either having attended college or graduated from one. Here, the professional/managerial class is represented by 106,000 members of the population.

This newsmagazine also offers a state marketing plan. You may buy ads to appear in any combination of states or any single state. The more circulation purchased, the lower the cost per thousand, and the higher your advertising efficiency. State marketing plan advertising is available in every fourth issue of the magazine—thirteen times a year. Five weeks preceding the issue date for black-and-white insertion is the closing date. A one-time, half-column in black and white to cover the state of Texas, as an illustration, costs $740. It would give you access to 1,091,000 adults.

Whole regions or small groups of states can be blanketed by a national magazine ad. In *Newsweek,* you could cover the southeastern region consisting of Mississippi, Alabama, Georgia, Florida, South Carolina, North Carolina, and Tennessee. You would have an estimated southeastern state circulation of 310,000 households at a cost of $1,030 for a one-time insertion of a half-column, black-and-white ad.

The editorial content of *Newsweek* is exactly the same in all its editions, including the edition distributed nationally. This is the way it is with most of the national magazines publishing regional editions.

Of the other national consumer magazines, most are edited for people's special interests. Advertising in a special-interest magazine preselects your prospects. Advertising in demographic editions lets you reach particular audiences, chosen for their professions, educational levels, spendable incomes, and other characteristics. By aiming at carefully selected audiences, you will alert the most likely prospects for your services with a minimum of waste circulation. In the end, the cost per prospect alerted to the services you make available is less expensive.

## LOCAL CONSUMER MAGAZINES

Better than any of the national magazines for your purposes, perhaps, are the local consumer publications that are independently owned and professionally edited. These may be publications connected to charitable groups, service clubs, fund-raising drives, etc. Other local publications may come out regularly, devoting themselves to aspects of living in your city or region and be profit-producing for a publisher.

Sometimes you will be inserting an ad not for its advertising value but because you feel under pressure to do so. You may not want to offend your prospective patrons who are members of the organization. In that case, the insertion should be considered a donation to build goodwill and not strictly as an ad to sell services.

The different types of local consumer magazines include the following:

- Publications of women's clubs, fraternal orders, churches, and labor organizations
- College and high-school undergraduate publications
- Seasonal sports and team programs
- Amateur entertainment programs handled by sponsoring organizations
- Theater programs of summer stock or community interest
- Society magazines that are official organs of athletic clubs, country clubs, etc.
- City and state magazines where the content is strictly local

The cost of advertising in local consumer magazines varies widely but generally runs at lower rates than regional editions of the national magazines. Rates are quoted for pages and fractions of pages. An agate-line rate is usually charged for mail-order, classified, and similar sections. If you wanted advertising space two columns wide and three inches deep, you would be charged for eighty-four agate lines.

## PROFESSIONAL JOURNALS

Advertising in journals that are read by your colleagues could be a source of referrals, especially if you are a known specialist. Professional colleagues read the journals for new information, ideas, suggestions, and case reports. Your ad can be among the various informational resources.

Professional journals are thought of as business papers by the advertising industry. Some are called industrial papers and are edited for professionals such as architects, who buy little themselves but often exert strong influences on what others buy through their specifications and recommendations. More than half of all the business papers published are industrial papers. Many business papers (in magazine format) are the official organs of the professional associations—their journals—and subscription to them is included in the membership dues.

Information about the various business papers and other periodicals can be found in a publication put out by the Standard Rate and Data Services, Inc., available at your local community library. You can also buy the data for one year (12 monthly issues) for $76, which includes postage. Market information, circulation breakdowns, analysis of editorial policy and content, advertising revenue comparisons, success stories, and many other types of complete, useful information go into the *Standard Rate and Data* listings. Contact the Standard Rate and Data Services, Inc., 5201 Old Orchard Road, Skokie, Illinois 60076, to subscribe to the publication of rates and data for periodicals, to be received monthly. Geographic and demographic editions are included as well.

## TRANSIT ADVERTISING

Over 40 million Americans travel in and around their cities by bus. Almost every major artery in every major city is covered by a bus route. That's mass transit! And transit advertising has a place in the media mix to carry your professional-service message.

Transit advertising takes a natural resource—the existing bus routes— and harnesses it to fit your need to communicate. Joseph Palastak, executive director of the Transit Advertising Association, Inc., located in Washington, D.C., points out that there are two types of transit media—two audiences for transit advertising: transit outdoor advertising, and transit in-bus advertising. In both cases, the transit rider is helping to pay the bill for transporting your message at low cost.

The Batchelder Company, a member of the Transit Advertising Association, which sells and services transit ad space in twenty midwestern cities, had a recent survey of in-bus ads performed by the media research firm of R. H. Bruskin Associates. The Batchelder Company's vice-president and national sales manager, Ben Joseph, supplied me with the survey results. Five different interior bus advertisements presented to the residents of New York City's five boroughs were remembered by 39.1 percent of those who viewed them on a bus. Seven out of ten (68 percent) of all New York City adults ride the metropolitan area buses every two weeks. The average ride lasts twenty-three minutes. This indicates a longer exposure time to your message than any other form of advertising.

Your office may be located on one or more regular bus routes—and this can be an additional stimulus to consumer response.

Rates are moderate but variable for transit ads. Prices are dependent on the average monthly ridership of buses in a given city, and on the number of vehicles in which your ad is posted. A city like Milwaukee, Wisconsin, with a population of 1.5 million could give you as many as 523 vehicles in which—or on which—to advertise to 6,198,261 average-monthly riders. You could have outside ads or in-bus ones. The outside ads might be posted on the side of the bus, the rear of the bus, or at the roof line. The interior ads could be in a full run of buses with one card in every bus in the fleet, or a half-run with one card in every other bus.

The in-bus transit ads are like magazine advertising. Almost any magazine ad can be adapted easily to the "in-bus magazine." Ads aren't buried in editorial material. Such inside space in an 11- by 28-inch card size costs $2 per unit. A card 22 by 21 inches costs $4.75 per unit.

In New Jersey, the Passaic County Bar Association advertises in buses in English and Spanish. On a 42- by 21-inch card displayed in multiple vehicles, it states: "Private lawyers referred. If you need the services of an attorney and do not know one but can afford to pay one, call the lawyer referral service of the Passaic County Bar Association (201) 525-8011."

The outdoor transit ads are like billboard-bulletin techniques. They reach virtually everyone more times in more places, and at less cost than almost any other medium. Such exterior space costs $75 per unit at the roof line, $45–$60 per unit at the side of the bus, and $30–$35 per unit at the rear of the bus. Write to the transit company in your area for a rate card.

Subway ads are transit advertising, too. In the New York metropolitan area, nearly three out of four workers use the subways for all or part of their journey to and from work in Manhattan. Subways are ridden 2.3 times more than buses, 5.5 times more than autos, and 7.3 times more than railroads. These statistics include 392,508 suburbanites from 18 suburban counties surrounding the city.

Subways supply a captive audience with darkened windows and few distractions, an average 53 percent copy recognition, full color at no extra space cost, and impressions delivered just minutes and steps away from your office. A New York subway ad costs $4,522 per month for a 1–2-month run in 1,500 cars of an 11- by 14-inch card on the combined IRT-IND-BMT divisions, says the New York Subways Advertising Co., Inc. This includes typesetting but not special artwork you might want for eye-catching appeal.

Like outdoor posters, the transit indoor and outdoor ads give viewers close, clear, detailed messages with minimal layout restrictions. There are no service area restrictions either as are levied on other visual out-of-home advertising such as billboards and posters.

## BILLBOARDS AND POSTERS

Some 250,000 signs have been erected around the United States by the billboard industry. Sales have climbed by 20 percent in the preceding three years to $462 million in 1977. Outdoor advertising, says the Outdoor Advertising Association, is benefiting from the new interest taken in "commercial speech" by the learned professionals. A report, prepared at the time of the Bates case by the Axiom Market Research Bureau, Inc., a subsidiary of the J. Walter Thompson Co. of New York City, tells buyers how many people of certain categories they will reach with their messages. The billboard industry anticipates figures to be reported in the spring of 1979 will show a 12 percent growth in outdoor advertising use in 1978.

Billboard advertising reaches the people on the street, in cars, and on mass transit. It doesn't ask for a moment of their time. They read your message without expending effort and are subjected to a subliminal effect. Billboards give repetition, reach everyone who steps outside, and create a memorable impression 85 percent of the time. They penetrate quickly, and the cost is small in relative terms.

Poster advertising functions only in retail shopping areas as panels placed at eye level, on prominent wall locations so that the advertising professional's message will be exposed to the greatest number of shoppers as they move in and out of a given shopping area.

Billboards and posters are usually erected after careful studies of traffic and pedestrian flow. Space is sold based on the promise that they can provide the same type of saturation advertising that is possible in magazines, newspapers, and the broadcast media.

They are about as effective as the ten-second television spot message, since they are viewed by passersby for an exceedingly short time. A number of billboards or posters are required in various locations to get your messages impressed on the minds of prospects.

Mainly, there are just two points to be conveyed by such outdoor advertisements—your name and the services you dispense. Since people only view signs for a few seconds, the messages must be simple and swift. There is no place for long, subtle copy here.

Usually, two sizes of billboards are available for rent. One is the painted bulletin that generally is 14 feet high and 48 feet wide. The other is the poster panel that runs 12 by 25 feet. Prices vary sharply from location to location. Discounts are offered for package contracts. In the Northeast, posting your message on a large-size billboard for thirty days (called "thirty sheets") costs in the vicinity of $250 for one billboard. If you buy thirty sheets in a six-sign package, the price is discounted at $1,110 for the whole package (six billboards for thirty days). This does not include artwork for the ads, which is extra.

For $123,000 a month, Foster & Kleiser, a division of Metromedia, Inc., the industry leader with 35,000 structures, will provide a package of 580 poster panels in Los Angeles, the fullest coverage offered. The same comprehensive coverage in Dallas requires 128 posters and costs $18,000. A giant Foster & Kleiser billboard outside Chicago's O'Hare Airport (which I am by no means recommending here)—seen by 200,000 a day—sells for $12,000 a month.[2]

## THEATER SCREEN ADVERTISING

Film advertising on the neighborhood theater screen is another form of poster advertising. Movie watchers are a captive audience, but they have come to accept screen advertising along with previews of coming attractions. Your ad, from forty to sixty seconds long, may appear on a slide or film, in black and white or in color.

Rates are based on theater attendance and what the advertising traffic will bear. It ranges from $500 to $1500 for daily showings over thirteen weeks, which is the usual life of the contract.

## SPECIALTIES IN ADVERTISING

A form of outdoor advertising is advertising specialties given away—such as book matches, pens, pencils, combs, memo books, paperweights, clips, and gadgets of various kinds. A small space for your message is provided. It may tell the consumer who you are, what you do, and where you're located. Its worth as an advertising medium is questionable unless you are assisted with a plan provided by the company that supplies the specialty items. Such a plan would analyze your client distribution potential to avoid a waste of the specialty items.

79

It's better to distribute specialities that are tied in some way to your profession. Engineers could give away a handy measuring device. Accountants could supply an inexpensive pocket calculator. These gadgets are more an expression of appreciation for patronage and an invitation to continue to utilize your services. Their costs are variable, depending on the value and quantity of the specialty-advertising items ordered. The National Pen Corporation of Hollywood, Florida, for example, sells "Memory Helper" wall calendars at 75 cents each for quantities of 150, or 66 cents each for quantities of 1,000 or more.

## DIRECT MAIL AND DIRECT ADVERTISING

Karen Burns, assistant director of Informational Services for the Direct Mail/Marketing Association, Inc., of New York City, provided me with information about direct-mail and direct advertising. The difference between the two is only in the method of delivery. Direct-mail advertising is sent through the U.S. Postal Service. Direct advertising is handed out by deliverers who distribute house-to-house.

Direct mail is the third largest advertising method. (Television is first, newspapers second.) In 1976, more than 60 billion dollars worth of goods and services were sold to American consumers through direct-mail marketing. This amount of selling occurred because advertisers were able to preselect those who should receive their messages. They advertised only to people who could use what they sold.

As a direct-mail advertiser, you can alert as few or as many people as you wish. You can limit your mailing area to a few city blocks, or distribute regionally or nationally. What you say and how you present it may be simple or elaborate. There are no page limitations or lead times, no deadlines or broadcast schedules. In direct-mail advertising, the control is entirely in your hands.

It's not uncommon to refer to direct mail as "junk mail." Admittedly there is too much "junk" received by too many people. That's because of abuse of mailing lists of names improperly selected by lazy advertisers. They blanket an area or class of people without any consideration of whether these recipients are actually prospects for what is being advertised. The following are some sources you can use to build your own mailing list of true prospects for your professional services:

- The names and addresses of present clients or patients or those who had visited you for services in the past.
- Reverse telephone directories (in local library) where names are

listed by streets. Send to those in your neighborhood.
- The classified section of the telephone directory of your town. Send to those businesses regularly in need of your kind of professional services.
- City directories.
- Professional, trade, and industrial directories.
- Rating books of local and national credit bureaus and reporting companies. Send to a class of people that buys your services.
- Inquiries received from your advertising in other media.
- Newspaper announcements of births, engagements, marriages, wedding anniversaries, business promotions, deaths, accidents, disasters, mergers, new business openings, etc.
- Permits for new buildings, additions, remodeling, repairs, and other changes.
- Municipal and county records.
- Companies that compile lists for sale. Lists are compiled by area, title, business, profession, census track information, age, sex, median income, and any other information of record that compilers have put into their computer banks.
- Membership lists of service clubs, parent-teacher associations, women's clubs, fraternal orders, professional societies, churches, and similar groups.
- Business, trade, and professional periodicals.

The list you build should be kept up to date, since it is not unusual for 25 percent of list entries to change in a single year. Compiled lists sold by a broker run $20.00 and up. Hand addressing is expensive except in small quantities. Computer addressing in quantities of 10,000 and up costs $1.20+ a line. Computer letters must be bought as a computer form and trimmed into letters after imprinting. This service costs about $10.00 per thousand. Folding, inserting, tying, bagging, and mailing the outside envelope, your letter, and one other piece costs about $10.00 per thousand. The preparation of 100,000 pieces averages $150, not including postage.

## The Best Days and Months for Direct-Mail Ads

Which month is the best to mail? A recent study of seasonality of mailing undertaken by the Kleid Company of New York City, a leading list broker and consultant firm, revealed data on the best days and months for mailings. The Kleid Company says: "If the time of delivery could be controlled, it would be desirable to reach the consumer on Tuesday, Wednesday, or

Thursday. Avoid Friday, Saturday, and Monday, and several days before and the day immediately following a holiday."

There are four top months for providers to make mailings in different categories of services advertised. Following are the categories of mailings and (in order of effectiveness) the best four months to mail:

- *Business/financial services*—January, September, December, July
- *Cultural services*—January, September, July, December
- *Entertainment services*—January, December, July, September
- *Educational/technical/professional services*—September, January, July, May
- *Fund raising (non-political) services*—November, October, February, April
- *Home interest services*—December, January, July, August
- *Hobby-related services*—January, July, February, October
- *General services*—July, December, January, September
- *Self-improvement services*—December, February, January, August

The post office will return undelivered third-class mail if you print on the envelope, "Address Correction Requested." There is no charge for a lightweight piece returned with the new address. You pay a small fee for each undelivered piece returned with the addressee's new address if your piece weighs more than six ounces and you have stamped "Return Postage Guaranteed" on the envelope.

## NETWORK TELEVISION

Network television is expensive because it reaches more people daily than any other medium—about 37 percent of all Americans. The Television Bureau of Advertising, Inc., of New York City, through its representative, Barbara Zeiger, revealed the ad budgets of the top one hundred advertisers in the country. National advertisers spent $5,772,021,500 in 1977 and of this, national television received $4,343,914,500, exactly 75.3 percent. (Incidentally, in 1977, magazines received $918,065,000, or 15.9 percent of advertising revenues; radio was paid $249,609,700, or 4.3 percent; outdoor advertising got $155,997,900, which was 2.7 percent; newspaper supplements grossed $104,434,400, amounting to 1.8 percent.)

National television enjoys top popularity for three simple reasons: (1) customers and potential customers use it—viewing almost daily for long periods of time; (2) TV's sight, sound, and motion let advertisers communicate their messages to these people; (3) somehow it works in dollars returned. Some critics may consider network television mind pollution, but it does produce product and service sales. And sales are what count to the commercial thinker. For twenty-three years, as I have indicated, TV has been the major medium for the largest U.S. national advertisers. They are the research-based companies carefully checking to see what their advertising dollars buy and return.

The three television networks—CBS, NBC, and ABC—all are thriving. They furnish programs to radio and television stations and help solve local stations' problems with entertainment that brings sufficient listenership or viewership. Each local station is provided with a varied program schedule, and local advertisers are encouraged to tag on their advertising messages.

There are no local networks, but there are regional ones. Regional networks are miniature national networks. They cover one concentrated area and cater to regional tastes and preferences in such areas as news and weather. Sports programs often are regional. They are broadcast on "tailor-made" networks. These regional networks might be the best programs for inserting your own messages.

National television networks receive about 70 percent of advertisers' payments for programming. A local television station keeps only about 30 percent. The percentage may seem disproportionately small for the local stations. They actually make most of their money selling you time "spots" *between* network shows. You're charged a premium price for a spot that is next to a highly rated national program.

According to television and radio advertising experts Gene F. Seehafer and Jack W. Laemmar, there are five basic advantages in network broadcasting:

1. Excellent physical control over program and commercial production
2. Simultaneous coverage with good broadcast hours on local affiliated stations
3. Prorating of costs among stations at a low net cost per station
4. Single billing for time and talent costs
5. Last-day change privileges both in live program content and in live commercial content[3]

The A. C. Nielsen Company uses the audimeter, an electronic device attached to each receiver in a home, to measure national network television program popularity. The audimeter automatically produces a minute-by-minute record identifying the times home sets are turned on and off and the stations tuned in. Broadcast audience ratings give the sponsor some guide upon which to base future advertising decisions. Continued sponsorship of a declining program is not only a poor investment, but it may also adversely affect the prestige of the sponsor.

By selecting the station, the program, and the time of the broadcast, you can reach almost any group of buyers you want.

## LOCAL TELEVISION

Local television is transmitted by 569 TV stations in this country that are privately owned and operated under license by the Federal Communications Commission (FCC). This federal agency, which acts in the public interest to protect against the misuse of the airwaves, is concerned with the problem of crowded airwaves. Every three years, each broadcasting station is reviewed by the FCC to determine whether its license is to be renewed. One of the conditions of the broadcasting license is that the station must air a certain amount of public-interest or educational programming. By enforcing this requirement, a professional association can assist its members with good public relations. It can promote the use of its members' services by broadcasting public-service messages about the benefits of receiving regular professional attention.

You can benefit individually, even more. Whether you need to talk with the woman of a household or her husband—with the working woman or the high-income man, the city-center-apartment family or the suburban-ranch-home family or the farm family—the same TV is reaching them all. It's in 97 percent of all local homes at least part of the week.

Repetition is an important advertising technique. You can reach TV's many audiences often because they spend so much time viewing. Would you believe the average home spends over six hours a day watching TV—all year long? It's an astounding figure that keeps growing year after year.

Information regarding when each type of person watches television is available. Your local TV station will assist you in scheduling commercials for programs selected for your particular audience. This information is in the media data mentioned in chapter 4. Local TV will help you create involvement with the television viewer, help the viewer hear your message, feel what you feel, appreciate what you appreciate, accept what you say—and buy the services you sell.

People seem ready to accept what they see for themselves on television. TV has long been most people's chief source of news. The Television Bureau of Advertising, Inc., assures us that people believe TV is also the most believable source of news. This environment of acceptance helps you to earn acceptance for your message, too. One way to accomplish this believability even more is to try to have your message present information that is news. How you do that will be discussed in Part III of this book.

Television has become so important to people that they spend almost as much money buying new sets as all the advertisers combined spend in trying to reach them on TV. Many of these viewer dollars are going for color sets —now in over 90 percent of all higher-income homes.

The public's attention to television saves you money. You don't need to fight for viewers' attention in your commercials. Also, you save money by the trend toward shorter commercials. You save in commercial production and in the amount of TV time you need to buy. This lets you run more messages more often—and so reach more people more often.

A thirty-second TV spot announcement costs about four hundred dollars. It creates an immediate response to your message because so many people see it in your area. You will also know the age, sex, income, and education of your market by the local station's surveys. Spot announcements offer more flexibility than sponsored programs or features. You can vary the number of spots for different degrees of intensity and impact.

There are three kinds of spot announcements. A *fixed spot* is guaranteed to be broadcast at a time you choose and contract for. A *preemptible spot* is "semi-fixed": you pay a reduced rate for the time you choose, but risk being bumped by an advertiser willing to pay the higher fixed rate. A *floating spot* gives you little or no control over when it is to be broadcast. It is the lowest-price spot, and the station decides the broadcast time of the floater. *Run-of-station* spots (ROS), like floaters, are broadcast whenever time is available, as decided by the station.

## LOCAL RADIO

Local radio gives immediacy and "personality." It can reach a large portion of your market no matter where it is or what it is doing, almost instantly and at any given time. Depending on the program you choose to sponsor, you can select your market with care and get maximum client/patient exposure. Stations will provide you with a list of rates.

Radio has long been a workhorse for the local advertiser. For most radio stations, programming is designed to segment audiences, to appeal to particular groups of people. They are selected by age, income, buying habits, or other demographic factors. In theory, this permits the station to deliver a specific group of highly desired, identifiable prospects to advertisers, to help them get the maximum effect for their money by advertising only to an audience segment that can (and desires to) use their types of services.

I mentioned in the previous chapter that with my wife, Joan, I have for almost ten years produced a daily radio show over WSTC in Stamford,

Connecticut. Sponsors flock to advertising on "Keeping Slender" because they are certain of beaming their messages to homemakers at 10:55 A.M. (six days a week).

For five years prior to this current show, when I was a practicing podiatrist, I broadcast my own daily sponsored radio program on foot health, also over radio station WSTC. It educated listeners about care of the feet and created public awareness of the podiatry profession. In chapter 15 I will explain how you can get your own show on radio or television.

The characteristics of radio are more varied and may provide greater advertising benefits than any other medium. The following are twenty features of radio that make it deserving of your advertising dollars:

1. Radio transmits the persuasive voice of the salesperson directly to the consumer.
2. Radio can be presented at selected times.
3. Radio is flexible in that it can be used nationally, regionally, and locally.
4. Radio is given credit for providing entertainment.
5. Radio is able to give news happenings immediately.
6. Radio is the only medium appealing to the ear alone.
7. Radio permits the listener to do other things while listening, hence can be the "constant companion."
8. Radio has a low cost, whether network or local.
9. Radio copy can be changed on short notice.
10. Radio gives the advertiser the opportunity to blend his commercial with program content.
11. Radio can build a faithful following.
12. Radio does not demonstrate as television does, but it suggests, and appeals to the imagination of the audience.
13. Radio reaches persons in a wide number of places, engaged in a wide range of activities.
14. Radio can be selective in the audience to which it appeals.
15. Radio provides the advertiser a "last word" with prospects before they leave their houses or automobiles.
16. Radio is a good complementary medium, as its economy makes it useful in evoking the messages implanted by other media.
17. Radio has changed from a group medium to a personal one.
18. Radio has primarily an adult audience, one that buys professional services. Children have switched to television.
19. The great number of stations and time periods of radio make it possible to saturate markets.
20. Radio has tremendous reach into people's lives.[4]

# 6

# How to Develop Ads

*The reader has bought the publication for news, entertainment, or instruction which is of helpful personal value. So that is what your advertisement also has to provide—if you are to stand any chance of competing with the publication's editorial matter for the interest of the reader. And then, to make him pay you for your product [service] you must make it pay him to read about it.*

—*Victor O. Schwab,* How to Write a Good Advertisement, *1962*

Convincing and action-provoking advertising not only circulates information; it permeates public thought with desires and beliefs. It penetrates any wall of ignorance that blocks the use of professional expertise. In a subtle way, you want to have a share of the minds among those who would buy your services. Professional-service ads will locate those minds and bring them to you.

In developing your ads, there are five basic points for getting the results you desire. Perhaps you'll have to hammer away at achieving these points by yourself, using brain power and suffering in the process. Charles Brower, former president of Batten, Barton, Durstine, and Osborn, a renowned Madison Avenue advertising agency, said: "When you try to formalize creative activity, the only sure result is commercial constipation. . . . The good ideas are all hammered out in agony by individuals, not spewed out by groups."[1] Whether the effort is painful or not, memorable advertising reflects your own creative effort, for you know best what it is you have to offer.

## THE FIVE BASIC POINTS FOR DEVELOPING ADS

When considering an advertising campaign for the sale of your talents, keep in mind the silent words of anyone in the market for your services: "I am the potential client or patient. I don't know who you are. I don't know your office policy or attitude. I don't know what skill or knowledge you have to satisfy my need. Now, what professional services do you want to sell me?"

Advertising and Promoting the Professional Practice

Your ads are your mass communicative sales aids. They are the mirrors of your own thinking. As such, they must establish a positive buyer response —building consumers out of people who are prospects. In developing your advertising, there are five particular points to have at the forefront of your creative effort:

1. Your advertising must be *consistent* if it is to attract the attention of present clients or patients, and reach new ones.
2. It must *create and stimulate a desire* for people to purchase your special kind of service.
3. It must offer the consumer a *real dollar value*—exceedingly important for adding new buyers to build volume.
4. The advertising must *convince* readers, listeners, or viewers beyond the shadow of a doubt that they can obtain *quality services* and that their *satisfaction* is the most important object for you.
5. Every professional service ad you run must project such *a favorable image* to the client or patient that he or she will make a special effort to have only *you* be the purveyor of those services.

## Point One: Be Consistent

Any advertising effort always has an overall aim—an underlying goal— that keeps you from drifting tangentially. This is important for you, especially since you don't have the financial resources of a large corporation to squander on experimental advertisements.

Your advertising ought to be a *campaign* dedicated to systematically persuade people to buy your professional services. Derived from the medieval Latin word *campania,* or "level country," a "campaign" described battle maneuvers executed on the plains. Your advertising maneuvers, like well-executed battle plans, should win the confidence of prospects and turn them into consumers.

A single advertisement can be memorable and persuasive. But it takes a campaign—a series of different advertisements with just one underlying goal—to win the battle for a place in the consumer's memory.

The first rule for an advertising campaign is that it be consistent—that it stay on target—with the same continuous theme. What is that theme? You alone are the one to select the sort of image you wish to project and consistently but indirectly present it in your ads. Later in this chapter, I shall provide the model for a consumer questionnaire to uncover the professional-practice image you are now projecting.

Joseph Serian, an optometrist of Columbus, Ohio, follows a consistent theme in advertising his 20/20 Contact Lens Service. Serian's service employs opticians who are technicians using their skills to make eyeglasses to prescription. An optometrist is a nonmedical specialist licensed to examine the eyes and prescribe corrective lenses or eye exercises. If the optometrist finds evidence of eye disease, he refers the patient to an ophthalmologist, who is a medical doctor specializing in the eyes.

Dr. Serian has been heavily involved in price advertising since the spring of 1976. 20/20 Contact Lens Service, the first such operation in the nation, sells products at considerably lower prices than those of most optometrists. It serves the consumer in his best interest and serves Dr. Serian by stimulating volume sales. He follows a line of reasoning that provides him with a theme for his ads and helps create his professional image.

"For all too long, the optometrist has been groping somewhere between the jewelry store and the eyeglasses shop," says Serian. "It's time to break away from the nondescript image with which we're associated. We are professionals, practicing in a specialized area of health care, which is of tremendous value to the American public. Here, at last, is the opportunity for the optometrist to build the identity he deserves."

Serian does it by consistently separating sales and services into two distinct categories in the eye-care field. He likens optometric services with those offered by the physician. Today's M.D.'s don't examine and prescribe medication for patients, then turn around and sell those patients the prescriptions they've just written. It's true that this is how medicine once was practiced, but professionalism won out over commercialism in the latter part of the last century. The separation of professional services and pharmaceutical sales didn't put the medical doctor out of business. Serian says that neither would the separation of ophthalmic services from eyewear sales.

"Division of sales and services is crucial to the image-building task we must tackle," he says. "We must recognize and respect the position and role of opticians. Such action on our part, combined with greater public awareness of who and what an optician is as revealed through advertising, will provide the sorely needed definition of the difference between us and them. Quite automatically, the position of the optometrist will be elevated. His importance in the vision-care field will become clear. The consumer, faced with increasing amounts of eyewear advertising, will quickly learn. He will readily see the difference and know which is the 'real doctor.' And we, as 'real doctors,' will benefit tremendously from the alleviation of confusion that has plagued the public."

The theme in Dr. Serian's advertising is that he, the optometrist, services patients. An optician, who is a technician, is on duty in his office to service and sell optical products. Serian's theme is consistent in thirty-second television spots, on radio, in newspapers, on billboards, on taxicab and bus signs, and elsewhere.

Thus, the 20/20 Contact Lens Service runs an advertising campaign that divides service and sales into two parts. Its ads indicate that an optometrist-doctor does the servicing of the patient's need, and an optician-technician services the optical products. There is a fee for service and a separate smaller one for products. Both fees are advertised.

Before leaving the subject of Dr. Serian's type of advertising, one danger should be acknowledged in separating the price of service from the price of product, especially in optometry. Be warned, for example, by the following:

A pair of hard contact lenses doesn't cost an optometrist more than $10 to $20. It is not uncommon, however, for a pair of hard contacts to cost the consumer $200. Soft contacts sell for $300. The "price" has little, if anything, to do with "quality" in contact lenses. Quality care comes from the time, attention, and skill offered by the doctor himself. The markup is made for the service of the optometrist and not for the contact lens product.

The danger in separating price into service charges and product charges comes from a sudden disillusionment by consumers with the way doctors have scheduled prices until now. Serian admits that with increasing amounts of price advertising such as the theme repeated in his campaign, optometrists could wind up looking quite the fools. The American public will then learn the true cost of glasses and contact lenses. "With a knowledgeable consumer 'shopping around' for his ophthalmic products and finding we've misrepresented the facts, it will only widen the crack which already exists in our image as professionals," he says.[2]

The Federal Trade Commission, as I've indicated in previous chapters, is working steadily to widen the crack. On May 24, 1978, the FTC formally adopted a proposal that would lift restrictions on advertising the cost of eye examinations, eyeglasses, and contact lenses. More than forty states had laws that prohibited the eyewear industry from listing its prices. In other states, professional groups representing the industry barred their members from advertising prices. Now, however, the agency's action has changed all that.

More than forty thousand ophthalmologists, optometrists, and opticians are affected. The FTC had found that prices for the same pair of glasses could vary as much as 300 percent within the same city. The agency said that prices for eyewear were generally 25 percent higher in states with advertising bans than in those states that permitted some advertising.

The new FTC order also requires ophthalmologists and optometrists to give their patients copies of prescriptions so that patients can shop for the lowest price to fill them. The Opticians Association of America endorsed the commission's action because opticians can then fill prescriptions at lower prices than optometrists, who also sell eyeglasses. Of course, the American Optometric Association condemned the May 24 advertising rule and accused the FTC of "overstepping its power as a federal regulatory agency." The AOA remains miffed with optometrists who advertise.

Pioneering optometrist Joseph Serian persists with his campaign, even in the face of criticism by his professional colleagues. He also follows the first basic point for developing ads: advertising that is consistent. He doesn't fly off in all directions but sticks to a central theme of separating service from sales.

A consistent campaign allows you to concentrate on better ways to communicate the same theme rather than to keep testing new ideas. When consumers become familiar with your theme, they do some of the communicative work for you. They will read the extra thoughts from a sixty-second commercial into a thirty-second one. Even though you don't include part of your message, the prospect who has seen your ads previously will subconsciously supply what's missing.

Your familiar ad will stand out on a crowded newspaper page.

The smaller your investment in advertising, the more important it is to have a consistent campaign.

## Point Two: Stimulate Desire

Advertising is a particular type of persuasive communication—identified as to source, controlled as to content, and delivered to receivers by mass communicative methods. It is not a force that manipulates passive masses at the whim of the advertiser, but it does create desires in people who previously did not recognize them, and it stimulates consumers to satisfy those desires.

All of us have different desires—determined by how old we are, how much money we have, what vocation we follow, the tastes we acquire, our age and sex, and other things. An old marketing axiom is that no service is bought by every person. "The market" for any service is really a restricted group of people—or market segment—who tend to have certain basic characteristics in common. As emphasized in the two previous chapters, one of your main jobs in advertising is to know your market before turning out ads. Then you'll be able to create and stimulate desire in that market.

Three characteristics of the market may sway your thinking about how you will reach it and what you should say.

*First,* can the market pay for your services? The ability to pay does not depend solely on total or disposable income. Some service vendors are quite concerned with the client's financial competence. Others are not. If you're a health-care provider, your patients' enrollment in surgical-medical insurance plans may be more important than their being in the upper- or middle-income brackets.

*Second,* does your market have the power to make buying decisions? This does not mean that the buyers themselves actually make the decision. Potential clients, if you are in the law profession, may come around seeking your help. But the real decision in favor of their wanting your services may have been made by whoever brought suit against these clients. You could be the attorney specializing in the rules of law in question.

*Third,* will the people in your market receive true satisfaction from having received your services? The satisfaction might not come from the acts you actually perform, but rather from the end result of those acts. Patients with broken legs may be unfavorably impressed with the personalities of their orthopedic surgeons, but the limbs end up being as strong and useful as before the injury. That's satisfaction!

The stimulation of desire by advertising in prospective clients or patients is both a sociopsychological art and a behavioral science. This was recognized by the advertising field as early as 1895, when the editor of *Printer's Ink* wrote:

> Probably when we are a little more enlightened, the advertisement writer, like the teacher, will study psychology. For however diverse their occupations may at first sight appear, the advertising writer and the teacher have one great objective in common—to influence the human mind.[23]

To influence minds in your market, you must spark motives that channel purposive, or goal-directed, behavior. You have to provide the stimulus that brings on a response. The stimulus will create a state of tension or disequilibrium within prospects that activates or moves their behavior toward the objective or goal you have set. Your professional expertise will then come into play to supply a satisfaction of those inner striving conditions described as needs, drives, wants, urges, and motives.

How can you motivate the market so as to satisfy its disequilibrium? You might start by making a list of motives that move the people you want to service.

There are two kinds of motives: "primary," or biologically based needs that are physical; and "secondary," or social desires that are acquired from the environment and experience. The acquired motives are sometimes labeled "psychogenic." While biological needs, such as hunger and thirst, are present in all of us, psychogenic motives are variable and individualistic. The following is a list of psychogenic or socially acquired motives or desires:

- To obtain group approval and conform to its standards
- To feel superiority over others, for extra achievement
- To control material objects
- To master and control the environment
- To be liked, admired, respected, and wanted
- To have economic security and avoid want and deprivation
- To play, for diversion and amusement
- To care for loved ones and fulfill the parental need
- To have good health and maintain one's physical body in good repair
- To acquire information, to learn
- To own material objects for the feeling of possession
- To investigate and experiment in order to satisfy curiosity
- To achieve comfort and enjoy convenience
- To sustain and maintain economic, political, religious, and social structures for purposes of group preservation
- To feel personal accomplishment for the sake of self-realization
- To have a sense of dependability and feel reliability[4]

The national Blue Shield organization creates and stimulates desire among its members by marketing one of these messages. An advertisement that has received widespread publication shows the expanded abdomen of an obese man. The appeal to the desire for health, or to maintain one's physical self in good condition is played up by the headline:

WHEN GOD CREATED MAN, IS THIS WHAT HE HAD IN MIND?

The text goes on to say that Blue Shield doubts it and that people aren't born with those extra rolls around the middle. Blue Shield's final pitch is:

Our prepayment programs and our working relationship with the medical profession allow us to make better health possible for everyone by removing financial barriers.
We don't like to see people eating their hearts out.
Your good health is our greatest concern.

In a related advertising program, a regional insurer, Blue Cross and Blue Shield of Greater New York, with the help of the J. Walter Thompson Company, is offering a $5.95 book entitled, *Take Care of Yourself: A Consumer Guide to Medical Care* by Donald M. Vickery, M.D., and James F. Fries, M.D., for $2.00. Concerned about soaring costs of medical care, the citywide health insurance company is endeavoring to encourage preventive medicine and self-care.

The first ad, 800 lines under the headline, "The Hospital Is No Place to Rest," ran on April 13, 1978, in general circulation newspapers in seventeen New York State counties and in *The Amsterdam News.* Two other ads ran periodically from April to October 1978; they were headed, "50% of All Visits to the Doctor May Be Unnecessary," and "What's Preventive Medicine?"[5]

### Point Three: Offer Real Dollar Value

Where consumer ignorance exists regarding the relative merits of services supplied by you or your professional colleagues, advertising will have a major influence on decisions. This is not because prospects accept advertising as a source of information more readily than others, but rather because advertising makes an important distinction among service vendors. Ads serve as guides to decision making. When in doubt between advertised and unadvertised services, an individual is most likely to go along with the familiar. Don't you?

In choosing a known, highly advertised provider of professional services over a colleague across the street who doesn't advertise, consumers are simply doing their best to cope with the lack of objective information concerning service quality and price. This is a reasonable method of minimizing risk. Consumers regard the ad as an implied warranty of performance. Their inference is that they are getting full value for what they are paying.

Your advertising can have a major impact on consumer purchasing decisions even when your service is of average quality and consumers behave in a neutral fashion toward everyone in your field. A price discount will be the magnetic attraction. Risk of purchase is reduced for a client or patient. Discount information will allow the consumer to predict some characteristics of unknown services. In other words, even if he or she doesn't know much about your profession in general, and the quality of your services in particular, offering a lower fee (in fact, merely stating the fee) openly in ads will persuade the consumer that you give real dollar value.

Consumer decision making prior to the purchase of professional services comes about from various important sources of information: the consumer's own experience with your services; word-of-mouth referrals from others who have observed or used your services; national and regional directories that aim to provide "objective" information regarding the providers in the field; and advertising. Of these, only the last one is absolutely under your control. It is the sole place you can establish your fees in no uncertain terms —in the public's eye and ear—to stand out from the others in the profession. You cannot praise your own quality of service delivery, but there is no question that you may publish its price.

For example, Jerrold Heller, D.D.S., and Paul Rosen, D.M.D., in partnership in Jamaica, Queens, New York, advertise "Quality Dental Care at Prices You Can Afford!" Their fee schedule is exceedingly low—including an examination for $5, a full set of X rays for $10, silver fillings for $6 and plastic fillings for $8, extractions for $15, root canals for $50, fixed crowns for $115, and full denture plates for $150.

Drs. Heller and Rosen announce that they accept all union plans and Medicaid. All repairs on plates are done in one day. All phases of the dental work are done on the premises and performed under nitrous oxide (laughing gas) if desired. They speak Spanish and English and are patient when working on children.

Their advertisements offer real dollar value in dental care. Prospective patients are made to feel confident in the two doctors even before meeting them.

### Point Four: Convince Readers They'll Get Quality Service

People don't just buy your attention and time processed to certain specifications. They want and buy your image, which includes not only the picture they have of your intrinsic qualities but also the ideas they have about you —the sort of clients or patients you take care of, your honesty, humaneness, cleanliness, and other virtues. This bundle of service attributes is referred to as the professional image. It is measured in values resulting from the interaction of perception, learning, and motivation.

The concept of professional image helps explain why two architects who are technically identical are patronized by different types of people for different reasons. One architectural firm, let us say, is preferred by young, college-educated couples, and a neighboring firm is preferred by well-established couples over fifty. Economist John Kenneth Galbraith says that there is no such phenomenon as identical services, or the "undifferentiated market," in the modern economy of monopolistic competition:

95

> If the number of sellers is small, they will always be identified as distinct personalities to the buyer. And although their products [and services] may be identical, their personalities will not and cannot be. There is always, accordingly, a degree of product [service] differentiation.[6]

Since advertising is one-way communication with no opportunity for the prospect to ask questions or even indicate whether your message has been received, it's not easy to let people know that you give quality service unless you actually say so. A lesson on how to do this in a subtle and acceptable way may be gained from looking at the message text of the Denture Center in New York City, which I described in chapter 2. The Denture Center ad reads:

> Last year, when the Denture Center office opened on East 29th Street, it opened up a new way for New Yorkers to get custom dentures as well as other dental services. Now we've opened a new office on West 72nd Street, east of Broadway. You'll get the same professional service and reasonable prices that have helped make all our locations so successful.
> FAST, BUT THOROUGH SERVICE
> Whether you need a full denture or a simple filling, our doctors will take the time to explain to you the techniques they will use. You will also be advised of the costs prior to incurring them. We will perform our services as quickly as possible with a minimum of inconvenience to you.

Notice the implication here that the patient's satisfaction is the most important object of the doctors of the Denture Center.

## Point Five: Project Your Most Favorable Image

Related to point four, this basic point for developing ads—projecting your most favorable image—comes from knowing the appeal you have for clients or patients.

A superbly written and displayed ad about coffee published in the Salt Lake City *Deseret News* or an even better one for pork sausage printed in the New York *Jewish Daily Forward* would fail to build the image of these products. Why? Because Mormons living in Salt Lake City disapprove of drinking coffee and Jewish dietary laws forbid the eating of pork in any form. There is nothing favorable that could be said in these ads that could enhance these products in the eyes of the two audiences.

It is not enough for you to know the character of your clientele. You also must know what it is in the personality of your practice that appeals to the composite or group personality of those who come to you for services. Such knowledge is difficult to come by. Oftentimes, patrons themselves do not understand the forces that have brought their fingers to dial your phone number. When asked to explain their behavior, they cannot or will not explain it in a valid way. If they dig into themselves and truly attempt to describe their behavior, they are likely to give you information that is expected, even though it may be less than accurate.

Ask a junior executive, "What magazines do you read?" and he will probably name those he thinks he *should* read, such as *Forbes, Business Week,* or *Newsweek. Playboy* or *Runner's World* may be the magazines he spends the most time reading, but they don't conform to his concept of being an important junior executive on the way up.

The same is true of the people who come to you for expert advice. They won't be able to tell you what there is in the appeal of your image that actually attracts them. They will give conventional answers—or rationalizations. To get the truth, you have to do market research.

In the precise sense, the term "research" refers to formalized procedures using scientific method, especially statistical techniques, to gather and evaluate information. However, as an advertiser of professional services, you don't have to go that far. A simple questionnaire, as part of your patient or client history, filled in by the consumer or one of your assistants, will be sufficient to reveal the most favorable aspects of your projected image.

Make it an in-depth questionnaire by focusing on feelings. Avoid questions that ask for answers using evaluative intelligence; do not ask for judgments—just feelings. Try to get responses from the emotions such as the direct restatement of implied feeling.

This form of interviewing in questionnaires has been developed by the Bureau of Applied Social Research at Columbia University. The focused interview aims to particularize the effective stimulus in the objective situation, and to characterize the subject's response to it.[6]

The twenty or more questions I supply here may be pure lead-ins as a result of the individual's prior responses, or they may be quite specific and undeviating. You don't have to use all the questions. They are only guideposts for your own inquiries. The technique employed will vary with the skill of the interviewer. Remember, the object of the interview or of filling out the questionnaire is to learn just what it is in the personality of your practice that appeals to those who come to you for professional services. You want to learn what is your most favorable image projected to the public. You are conducting marketing or advertising research.

The following is a sample questionnaire you can give to your clientele to fill out or to your assistant to use as a guide in interviewing:

## Consumer Questionnaire for Uncovering
## Your Professional-Practice Image

1. Do you remember at what time of day you first heard or read of the services offered by this office?

2. How did you happen to learn of this office that first time?

3. How did you feel about employing our professional services when you first heard of them?

4. Do you remember what was said when you made up your mind to inquire about these services—anything in particular that appealed to you?

5. Did what you heard then impress you more than other things you were told or had read about this practice? Why?

6. Did you think of any reasons why you shouldn't make use of these professional services just then—that is, did you argue with yourself about it before you made up your mind definitely to seek help for your problem?

7. What made you go ahead and schedule an appointment with us?

8. How would you have felt if you hadn't taken an action just then and made your appointment?

9. How did you feel *after* you made your appointment?

10. Did you have any doubts after you had made your appointment to visit us? Why?

11. With the appointment set, what were you mainly concerned about?

12. Were your feelings about this office after you had become one of its clientele any different from your opinion previously? In what way?

13. Why did your opinion change?

14. Did you discuss seeking services from this office with anyone prior to your scheduling an appointment? What did they say?

15. Did you speak with anyone receiving professional help from this office after you scheduled an appointment? What did they say?

16. Are there any reasons besides the particular problem that you've mentioned has brought you here for wanting to make contact with this office? What are they?

17. Do you feel you acted on impulse to seek professional assistance? Are you glad you did anyway?

18. Given a chance to reconsider, would you make the appointment again? Why?

19. What do you hope to achieve by this visit?

20. Do you anticipate that this office has the ability to satisfy your needs? Why?

## MARKETING RESEARCH

A distinction exists between marketing research and advertising research. The first is concerned with the description and measurement of a particular market—the groups you attract—while the second evaluates the impact of your message on the market. But advertising research is a form of market research.

You can sell more of your services more effectively by doing marketing research. It can help you vary your approach to service delivery for building the best image; determine who wants your services and why they want them; pinpoint the exact population for your messages; select the media giving greatest return on investment; determine channels for putting out your effort; report on competitive trends in the profession; suggest advertising approaches and appeals; pretest ads before publication, and check on advertising results after publication.

Marketing research will give you solutions to problems in communication with clients or patients. It provides precise answers to specific questions. It is an aid to the decision-making process rather than a search for certain unconditional truths. Marketing research uses scientific methods in exploring the marketplace for your professional skills.

The scientific method is not a system of formal procedure, remember, but rather an attitude and a philosophy that approaches a problem in an objective, systematic manner, as opposed to an approach guided by opinion or intuition. Research before marketing and advertising your services will reduce your areas of uncertainty in which judgment and experience must operate.

*Advertising Age* magazine publishes an annual descriptive list of available market data issued by media and trade associations. There may come a time when the magazine also publishes marketing material for the dispensing of professional services. Another useful bibliography of available data is the monthly *Marketing Information Guide* published by the U.S. Department of Commerce. Both data guides are adaptable for professional people to use in doing market research.

Better still, for getting market research, is a regular research firm that will take your requirements, find facts, and collate answers to your many marketing questions. Such firms may be found in an international directory of marketing research companies. The "Green Book" is published by the New York chapter of the American Marketing Association, 60 East 42nd St., New York, NY 10017. It has 134 pages and costs $15.

Listed here are some syndicated media research services that conduct regular surveys for information such as what publications people read, which stations they listen to, which advertisements they read, which programs they listen to or watch, what their reaction is to programs and commercials, what types of products and services they use, and other information. Among the most important services for you is the demographic information about people and their relationship to your profession —in your locale in particular. For the latest such marketing information as it relates to your requirements, contact the following syndicated research services directly:

American Research Bureau
4320 Ammendale Road
Beltsville, MD 20705

Brand Rating Research Corp.
745 Fifth Avenue
New York, NY 10022

Gallup & Robinson, Inc.
44 Nassau Street
Princeton, NY 08541

N. C. Rorabaugh Co., Inc.
347 Madison Avenue
New York, NY 10017

W. R. Simmons & Associates
Research, Incorporated
235 East 42nd Street
New York, NY 10017

Sindlinger & Co., Inc.
Winona & Mohawk Avenues
Norwood, PA 19074

SRDS Data, Inc.
235 East 42nd Street
New York, NY 10017

C. E. Hooper, Inc.
750 Third Avenue
New York, NY 10017

A. C. Nielsen Company
1290 Avenue of the Americas
New York, NY 10019

Alfred Politz Research, Inc.
527 Madison Avenue
New York, NY 10022

Daniel Starch and Staff
Mamaroneck, NY 10544

The Pulse, Inc.
730 Fifth Avenue
New York, NY 10019

Trendex, Inc.
200 Park Avenue
New York, NY 10017

Yankelovich, Skelly and White, Inc.
969 High Ridge Road
Stamford, CT 06905

There is no way to judge the costs of market research supplied by one of these syndicated research firms versus what you do on your own. Your requirements, the information you want and need, the area of your field of interest, the distance from your office for the consumer sample, the sampling patterns employed, and the methodology in general will determine the costs. Of course, everyone's requirements are different.

John Gilfeather, an executive with Yankelovich, Skelly and White, Inc., told me the big eight accounting firms, for whom his firm does some market research, are facing this problem now of determining how and where to advertise, the proper means of marketing, and their audience for such marketing efforts. This is where market research comes in.

Major law firms or giant accounting firms are spending an absolute minimum of $15,000 and up for market research. Their constituency is fairly wide. The local professional person would probably do something rather informal.

Suppose a podiatrist wants to learn who his patients are. A market research firm would define how many pairs of feet there are in a community, which of these have problems, what age groups are affected the most, segment the market, the scope, and other items. If you have only five people within a hundred miles and the incidence of foot problems is 20 percent, you would have only one patient. If your city population is 100,000, your prospects might be 20,000. Since this is enough of a draw, you wouldn't waste your money advertising in the outlying areas.

If foot problems occur more among older people than younger people, you should choose your media accordingly. You may prefer to advertise in the senior citizen news. With two papers, one more downscale than the other, you would want to use the more upscale one that older people read. This is all market research: defining the parameters of the market.

Marketing research determines what your message should say—what turns people on.

President Jimmy Carter, during the 1976 election, had a market of fifty states, all of which he visited. But his marketing approach was based upon what the country wanted—trust and honesty. The people did not want positions on issues, so Carter did not take clear positions, but he spoke about integrity, and it won him the election.

It is costly to find your market if you use a market research firm. However, you can use a part-time or full-time consultant ranging in fee from $100 to $500 per diem. You can find such consultants at a local business school, where professors are eager to pick up consultation fees doing market research. You might, in fact, get it free if the challenge is picked up as a class project.

# 7

# Writing an Excellent Advertisement

*After all the meetings are over, the phones have stopped ringing and the vocalizing has died down, somebody finally has to get out an ad, often after hours. Somebody has to stare at a blank piece of paper. This is probably the very height of lonesomeness. Out of the recesses of his mind must come words which interest, words which persuade, words which inspire, words which sell. Magic words. I regard him as the man of the hour in our business today.*

*—Leo Burnett, address to American Association of Advertising Agencies, October 19, 1955*

Each segment in an advertising campaign ought to be planned in advance. Like building a house from a blueprint, planning prevents weaknesses from developing in the structure of separate ads.

The creative task of actually writing the ad needs more planning than any other campaign aspects. The words are important, and anyone who would presume to own a formula for writing successful advertising is not dealing in reality.

## FIRST STEPS

In planning the words to be used, you first have to recognize and admit to the quality of your own professional services. Are they excellent, mediocre, or poor?

Charles F. Adams, executive vice-president of the advertising firm of MacManus, John & Adams, Inc., writing in *Common Sense in Advertising,* says: "If a product [service] is unworthy or its market inadequate, advertising performs a true service in bringing the shortcomings more quickly to light. In fact, advertising may on the whole be more valuable in hastening failure than it is in speeding success."[1]

Writing the words for your professional service ads thus relates to quality in several ways:

First, advertising can't sell your poorly delivered service more than once. Indeed, such advertising will make it harder for you to regain a lost reputation than to build a new one from scratch.

Second, ads can give you a reputation for poor quality simply by promising more than you are able to deliver. The effect could be the same as if you were totally incompetent.

Third, extensive advertising will accelerate the failure of your lack of talent, just as it can accelerate the success of your excellent one.

Adams also offers several other basic thoughts on advertising writing:

- Before you pick up the pencil, pick up the facts. Detachment is fine, but ignorance is inexcusable.
- First make sure you have something to say that is worth saying. Then communicate it in a way that people can understand. Remember that too much creativity can often obscure a good message.
- Make certain that you are neither insulting your prospect's intelligence nor offending his judgment. Remember that it's better to impress a small audience than to offend a large one.
- Following the new leaders is just as dangerous as following the old leaders. Imitation may be the sincerest form of flattery, but in advertising, it can also be the shortest route to disaster.
- Make sure that the principal thought in your advertising appeals to a human emotion. . . . Then use your talent and ingenuity to present that thought in the most intriguing and provocative way. Try to be different, but first try to be good!
- You must train yourself to communicate with people on their level, not yours. When a reader decides to look at your ad, he gives you a slice out of his life. You had better reward him by talking to him in his own language. One nod from a customer is worth two awards on the wall.[2]

## FIVE FUNDAMENTALS IN WRITING AN EXCELLENT AD

Any guidelines for excellent ad writing operate in a climate of constant change. There's always something new. An idea that was worth a million in income last year may turn out to be an aid and comfort to the competition this year. It could be an interesting idea to the wrong people. Your prospective clients or patients may not have the same interests in things in which you are interested.

Consequently, after insuring that you deliver quality service, write your advertisement following five fundamentals:[2]

1. *Get Attention*—Nobody is waiting for your ad to appear except you. Don't underestimate the fierce competition you face in getting people to focus on your message. The reader or listener has bought or tuned into the media for news, entertainment, or instruction, which is helpful and of personal value. So this value is what your ad has to provide, as well. To

103

make the client or patient pay you for your services, you must make it pay for him or her to read about them. Among other things to do, use a headline to get attention.

2. *Show an Advantage*—The thing people want to know above everything else is: What will your professional services do for me? Tell how it will increase their mental, physical, financial, social, emotional, or spiritual stimulation, satisfaction, self-respect, well-being, or security. Or show how it will decrease their fear of poverty, illness or accident, discomfort, boredom, offense to others, and the loss of business, personal, or social prestige or advancement. Use body copy to accomplish this, but keep the copy short.

3. *Prove the Advantage*—Proof material may be introduced into any part of the ad, from headline to close, but facts are necessary. As a professional, the facts you can offer are your degrees, services performed, fees charged, time involved, and other items. Use understatement because it carries more conviction than overstatement. Use the consumers' viewpoint, and see the services through their eyes.

4. *Persuade People to Take Advantage*—It's necessary to paint a quick and summarized mind's-eye portrait of what the service will do for your potential client or patient, and how easy it is for him or her to get it. Tell your location, your access to transit lines, ease of parking, number of professionals on the job, charge cards you accept, insurance plans honored, and so forth. It is wisest to plan your ad to persuade the most difficult target in your audience.

5. *Call for Action*—When Cicero completed an oration, people used to say: "What a marvelous orator! What an excellent speech!" But when Demosthenes thundered his denunciation of Philip of Macedon, people leaped to their feet. Roaring with rage, they shouted: "LET US MARCH AGAINST PHILIP!"

The same is true of your professional advertising. It can make consumers leap into action, but you've got to ask for that action. There has to be a concluding "do-something" statement that makes it simple, easy, and specific. Use several approaches that are included later in this chapter.

### Getting Attention

The written part of an advertisement is called copy. This includes the headline, the body copy with its own structure, the important closing that asks for action, your characteristic signature (logo) or a logotype that always appears in your ads, and basic office information such as hours, address, and phone number.

As you begin to write, you're aware of the need to get attention for your

# QUALITY DENTAL CARE AT PRICES YOU CAN AFFORD

Children Full Series of
● X-Rays ● Oral Examination
● Treatment Plan ● Cleaning
● Florida Treatment and
● Completion of School Note

$25⁰⁰

1) All phases of dental work done on premises (extractions fillings, partial & full plates, crowns, bridges, root canals)

2) All work done with $N_2O$ (nitrous oxide, laughing gas) if desired

3) Spanish and English spoken

4) All repairs on plates done in one day

5) Extra patience given when working on children

## FEE SCHEDULE

| | |
|---|---:|
| Examination | $5⁰⁰ |
| X-Rays (full set) | $10⁰⁰ |
| Cleanings | $10⁰⁰ |
| Fillings (silver) | $6⁰⁰ |
| (plastic) | $8⁰⁰ |
| Extractions | $15⁰⁰ |
| Full Denture Plates | $150⁰⁰ |
| Partial Denture | $150⁰⁰ |
| Fixed Crowns (caps)Acrylic Veneer | $115⁰⁰ |
| Fixed Crowns (caps) Porcelain Veneer | $140⁰⁰ |
| Root Canals (Front Teeth) | $50⁰⁰ |

Casey Fritz Archibald, D.D.S.
and
Hiram H. Schesingine, D.M.D.

187-88 Main Boulevard, @ 32 St.
Someplace, Arizona, U.S.A.
(602) 506-7641

105

advertisement among the thousands printed in the newspaper or other media viewed by the public. To arouse the reader's interest, you must think of your practice, the services you have to write about, the kind of advertisement your copy will go into, the medium it will run in, and the potential consumer who reacts to all of these elements.

One more factor bears a reminder: Your ad should be part of a campaign concept repeating a *unifying theme* that runs through all of the messages.

The ad writer's job divides itself into two co-equal and commingling parts, according to author John W. Crawford. He writes that copywriting is:

> 1. A never-ending search for ideas—the "what to say" in an advertisement that provides the brilliant solution to an advertising problem, and
> 2. A never-ending search for new and different ways to express those ideas—the "how to show it" techniques of preparing an advertisement that provide the brilliant execution of the ideas the copywriter wants to convey.[3]

To express an idea in the least number of words and simultaneously get the reader's attention, one uses the *headline.* A headline stops the eye and pinpoints mental concentration for at least a split second. Just because it comes first, however, doesn't mean that you write the headline first. Just as the title of a book reflects the contents of that book, the headline is determined by what's in the ad.

A headline has an eye-stopping function, of course, but equally important is its effect in selecting the potentially interested audience—your prospects. Something in the headline's words tells the audience, "Read More! This ad is of interest to you!" The headline doesn't tell the whole story but centers around the major selling point of the ad.

Any really good headline informs the reader, selects the audience, provides a hint of benefit, and arouses curiosity.

For an architect, a good headline would be: FUNCTIONAL AND BEAUTIFUL ARCHITECTURE AT A FAIR FEE.

For a veterinarian, it might be: COMPLETE HEALTH CARE FOR YOUR PET AT LOW COST.

For an accountant, it could be: A CLIENT-CONCERNED ACCOUNTANT SPECIALIZES IN SMALL BUSINESSES—FREE CONSULTATION.

One board-certified psychologist, Jeffrey J. Felixbrod, Ph.D., of Forest Hills and Manhattan, New York, uses a variety of headlines in his ads. All of them have emotional appeal. They include:

PROBLEMS OF CHILDREN AND ADOLESCENTS
MARRIAGE PROBLEMS
FEARS AND PHOBIAS
WEIGHT CONTROL
RELAXATION TRAINING
PSYCHOLOGICAL TESTING
SOCIAL AND INTERPERSONAL SKILLS TRAINING

In the advertising of professional services, an illustration, which ordinarily shares the chore of grabbing the prospects' attention, may be absent. As I've discussed, this absence occurs out of fear on the part of the advertising professional of violating the new guidelines drawn up by his or her professional association. Any advertising expert knows that usually the attention-getters in a print ad are the headline and illustration together. They share the attention-getting effect. Without an illustration, the full burden of attracting your prospects' notice and getting them to read the body copy rests solely on the headline. It's like running a marathon with your shoelaces untied. You have to be mighty careful where you put your feet down—or what you use for a headline.

The same advice about print headlines is valid for the opening words of a broadcast commercial. The first few thoughts stated in the commercial make up your broadcast headline.

A potential client or patient is mainly interested in what he or she will get out of your service, not what you put into it. Therefore, reader self-interest is the key to successful headline writing. It must promise a personal benefit or satisfaction to the prospect.

John Caples, a veteran ad person who wrote the famous headline, "They Laughed When I Sat Down At The Piano," supplies us with the following rules for writing a good headline:

- Try to get self-interest into every headline. Make it suggest that here is something the prospect wants.
- If you have useful news, such as a new service or technique, or a new use for an old service, be sure to get that news into your headline.
- Don't use merely curiosity headlines, but combine curiosity with self-interest.
- Avoid painting the gloomy or negative side of the picture. Take the cheerful, positive angle.
- Suggest in your headline that here is a quick and easy way for the individual to get something he wants.[4]

## Showing an Advantage of Your Service

The self-interest attraction of the headline is continued in the body copy and sub-headlines. Show the want-satisfying qualities of your service and include price information. Not publishing prices will have many prospects implying a price quite different from reality. If their guesses are much higher than your charges, then those people might never seek additional information. Supplying less information is a way to discourage inquiries about buying your services.

Readership studies, surveys, and other techniques conducted by the advertising industry to measure consumer interest in ads support the principle of including specific and full copy information. As the advertiser, you may have longer copy and require more magazine space or broadcast time to deliver it, but it has been proven over and over that a good headline alerts consumers and leads them into reading longer copy. Just supply the full information they seek.

When a person suddenly needs legal assistance, medical care, or some other professional help, any advertisement for this sort of service will almost surely be noticed. All copy will be read. Don't turn the prospect away by not supplying sufficient information. Make it compelling and usable copy for a prospect's full consumption. Get people involved.

An example of reader involvement is a national ad published by the American Cancer Society that discourages smoking. The ad shows an ordinary man in a trench coat puffing on a cigarette with just one word as the headline describing him:

DAREDEVIL

The body copy goes on to explain:

> No, he's not a free-fall parachutist. Or an X-15 test pilot. Or a stock car racer. With a wife and kids to think about, he can't afford to take chances.
> But he goes on taking the *big* risk . . . clinging to a habit which *every day* causes 100 deaths from lung cancer and contributes to many more from coronary artery and respiratory diseases. Studies show that the death rate from lung cancer alone for cigarette smokers (one pack a day or more) is 10 times higher than for nonsmokers.
> Nobody says it's easy to stop. But living *that* dangerously often winds up in not living at all.

In this case, the male reader is looking at an illustration picturing a person just like himself in a situation just like his own. The body copy speaks his kind of language. While many advertising professionals may not be using illustrations of this type, they can build a mental picture in the prospect's imagination with words. They can make it vividly clear so that the reader can easily project himself into the picture. Do it by using second person singular and active verbs.

Employ body copy in some respects similar to the following proposed ad text:

> Make yourself this promise: I will provide myself with the most competent professional services I can find. I will permit myself the payment of a fair fee for services rendered by a humane, warm, friendly, and interested professional person. I want only the best help available but at the most reasonable price possible. I will immediately contact . . .

Show the prospect the advantage of buying your assistance by speaking with sincerity in your message copy. Find the drama in your services and present it frankly, simply, and straightforwardly. Believe in yourself. One way to reflect honesty in your body copy is to write for an individual person instead of writing to a mass of anonymous prospects. Write in the same way you would send a personal letter or an invitation to have a friendly chat. Your advertisement is, after all, an invitation to people to avail themselves of your professional services.

### Proving the Advantage of Your Service

Sincerity of presentation and an invitation to use his professional services are projected by Joel Hyatt, a new, young lawyer who is owner and director of at least four legal clinics. He opened them all in Cleveland, Ohio, within a six-month period. He keeps the ten attorneys who work for him busy by advertising on television extensively.

Using a variety of thirty-second TV spots between segments of a soap opera, Attorney Hyatt sits before the camera in tie and shirtsleeves at a desk in front of a shelf full of law books. To the TV viewer he says: "My name is Joel Hyatt. And I'm an attorney with the Hyatt Legal Clinics. We're a new law firm specializing in legal services for *people,* not businesses or corporations. And we offer these services at very reasonable fees."

Appearing as his own pitchman, the twenty-eight-year-old lawyer is handsome, athletic looking, friendly, and personable. He projects competence and engenders confidence. He is a Yale law graduate.

Using borrowed capital from friends, young Hyatt is spreading word of

# So You're Being Sued...

Personal injury suits can be complicated, and few citizens can be as effective as a trained professional in protecting their own rights and interests.

As specialists in this area, we offer each of our clients experienced and highly individualized service so their rights and interests receive full consideration under the law.

No fee is charged for the initial in-office consultation and all fees and associated costs are fully explained before any work is undertaken on your behalf.

Call 334-6000 for a private and totally confidential appointment.

## HANSEN & HANSEN

7750 Bonnie Boulevard

his exceedingly low-priced legal services throughout the metropolitan Cleveland area. He spends $1,500 a week for the TV ads. By 1980, within three years of opening his first office, Hyatt anticipates that he will be the H & R Block in the practice of law for the State of Ohio. He will owe much of his success, he acknowledges, to television advertising.[5]

The candor and proof of performance he projects over the air is unquestioning. "You can discuss your problem with an attorney for only fifteen dollars," he says in his ads. "And if it's a routine problem—such as an uncontested divorce, personal bankruptcy, or simple will—we have a standard fee. Now there's no reason to be your own lawyer."

He really does perform well both as a pitchman and as a lawyer. The one thousand clients who sought his help in the first six months of his opening came because of the TV commercials. Four hundred fifty of them each paid the fifteen dollar consultation fee to have their problems outlined, the solution explained, and the cost quoted to have it taken further, if necessary. Either they were told that they had no legal recourse, or they chose not to make a further investment in legal services.

The other 550 clients did pursue their legal needs to a conclusion. They sought no-fault divorces at a standard charge of $200, had simple wills drawn for $35 each (wills for husbands and wives together cost $50—even the $15 consultation fee is a credit toward drawing the wills), took legal actions in personal injury cases for a 25 percent contingency fee (30 percent if the case went to trial), or pursued other legal matters that did not fit into any standard category at a relatively modest $40-an-hour charge.

## Persuading People to Take Advantage

There are at least twenty ways to persuade people through advertising to take advantage of what you offer in professional services. Victor O. Schwab, former president of Schwab, Beatty and Porter, a leading advertising agency, says that everything depends on your readable copy: the headline, sub-headlines, and body copy. To sway consumers in your direction, I suggest that you use any number of the following techniques which I've put together from Schwab's advice:

1. Ask questions in the ad that stimulate a response in favor of your kind of service.
2. Have the headline present your strongest consumer benefit.
3. Put newsworthy information in the sub-headline.
4. Be concrete and specific. Focus on just one item and not on generalities.
5. Identify what is said with the reader's needs and desires.

6. Concentrate on appealing angles and nothing that is of minor value.

7. Use emotional appeals that deal with vital decisions.

8. Touch people with familiar situations to make them put themselves in the picture.

9. Humanize facts and don't make flat claims.

10. Be natural and personable in your copy.

11. Make it entertaining to read, watch, or listen to your ad.

12. Don't distract with irrelevant information.

13. Use short, simple sentence construction similar to the way this list is written.

14. Use the present tense, singular instead of plural. Direct your message to one person—the second person "you."

15. Use pictorial nouns and active verbs.

16. Where possible, avoid adjectives, adverbs, pronouns, demonstrative articles, dependent clauses, and the subjective mood. Take Mark Twain's advice: "As to the adjective: when in doubt, strike it out."

17. Punctuate for clarity and vigor. Good punctuation makes your copy march forward.

18. Longer copy is OK, but don't let it be loose. Keep copy compact and say just what you mean.

19. Follow Ernest Hemingway's advice: "I use the oldest words in the English language. People think I'm an ignorant bastard who doesn't know the ten-dollar words. I know the ten-dollar words. There are older and better words which, if you arrange them in the proper combination, you make it stick."[6]

20. Employ the correct grammar to lead from one interesting point to the next. Good grammar makes for clarity.

### Call for Action

Today the professions are generally testing mass advertising to drum up patients and clients. They are seeking action from potential patrons by offering action in their ads. The low fees are but one appeal technique. Also calling for response from readers, viewers, and listeners are offers of "freebies" such as free consultations, free portfolio evaluations, free examinations, free informative booklets, free parking, and other things. The learned professionals don't advertise superior quality of service, since this is against every published professional guideline, old or new.

Murray R. Davidson, D.P.M., chairman of the Podiatry Department at the Community Hospital of Phoenix, Arizona, uses billboard advertising. He calls for action from prospective patients by offering free foot examinations.

Donald S. Pritt, D.P.M., of Parkersburg, West Virginia, uses small boxed newspaper ads. He gives away free booklets that he has written on foot health.

The Dental Associates of New York, including the Queens Orthodontic Associates, the Queens Hillside Dental Group, and the Manhattan-Chelsea Dental Group, all offer free two-hour parking in their pennysaver advertisements.

Zuflacht and Gonzalez, attorneys-at-law on Long Island in New York State, offer free consultations in their shopper ads.

The Forest Hills Transplant Center of Forest Hills, New York, advertises a free evaluation by plastic surgeons to determine whether your own hair may be transplanted to areas of your hair loss.

Giving something "free" is a direct request for action from potential patrons. It calls for a response. Prospects often take what's free, and may avail themselves of other purchasable services if you inform them of those you render.

## THE DESIGN AND LAYOUT OF YOUR AD

I don't recommend that you design and lay out your own print ad. You might suggest a concept, even make some sketches, but the actual ad construction with its copy should be placed in the hands of a commercial artist. These professionals have the science of advertising as part of their art training.

Lewis Mumford, the noted author and critic, once said that the artist does not illustrate science, but he frequently responds to the same interests that a scientist does.

You find a commercial artist by looking in the Yellow Pages under "artists—commercial." There shouldn't be any difficulty in locating a free-lancer or a full-service commercial art studio to do your artwork. Another phone book classification might be "designers," and as a last resort check out a small advertising agency.

Rates vary throughout the country depending on individual cost and standard of living in the region, the prominence of the artist, the kind and quantity of services desired, and whether charges are on an hourly basis or a whole job basis. Gerry Salomon, creative director of the Romax Studio in Stamford, Connecticut, a complete art service enterprise including advertising, told me how to approach an artist. He said, "Ask for a quotation. Show the art director your job and ask for the price on an open basis or on the total assignment. Some artists work on an hourly basis. An average freelancer may charge anywhere from $15 to $60 per hour. Paste-up alone is charged at a lower rate than design services. Something conceptual costs more. My quote for a total project is for design, typesetting, paste-up, all camera-ready that the newspaper uses as is."

Logo designs would cost more. Incidentally, logos are frowned upon by professional associations. They seem to make your advertisement stand out too much from the rest of professional service listings. Harry Choron, a dentist in Teaneck, New Jersey, used a simple five-line stick figure in his newspaper ad and quickly received a letter of protest from the state dental association. He eliminated the stick figure logo.

Many newspapers offer their own newspaper advertising services, including some artwork. Typically, these newspaper ad people have some reasonable expertise in what you're trying to accomplish. You have to discuss what you have in mind. The selling of services is more difficult than the selling of products. Consequently, the newspaper art designers may be insufficiently skilled—they are more interested in dealing with mechanicals than in creating images.

A mechanical is an assembly of pictures and proofs of type, pasted in a desired arrangement (usually on pieces of cardboard), to be photographed for making into a printing plate. They are also called mechanical layouts.

You have to supply the photo-ready mechanical in the form of photostats in various sizes. Or, you might hand over a typeset format for the newspaper advertising department to have them run off photostats. Photographs that might be inserted have to be scaled to the proper size.

Maybe it's needless for me to warn you once again that your professional association is not likely to look kindly on your using photographs, logos, or other illustrations. Look at the trouble Serko and Simon, a New York City law firm, is having with the ethics committee of the Association of the Customs Bar. Serko and Simon used some fine illustrations in its ads: I described the ongoing litigation of the firm and its professional association in chapter 3.

If you don't want to engage the services of a commercial artist because of cost or if you have confidence in the newspaper's art department, you have an alternative. You can go to a professional writer. Take the writer's copy to the newspaper or a printer and have the craftsman lay out the message in a number of different type styles. Make your selection and have the craftsman run a proof to make sure you like what's been done. Then present the final copy as camera ready.

If you use the services of a commercial artist, there is a lead time to take into consideration. Gerry Salomon says, "I think one week's time is a reasonable lead time in any kind of assignment, unless it's an exceedingly large assignment. There is even a possibility that sketches could be accom-

117

*Newly Approved*

# Physicians & Surgeons

now have the opportunity to place expanded information in telephone directories—an <u>assist</u> to <u>your</u> <u>office</u> <u>personnel</u> and <u>patients</u>

- Identify your specialty
- List your office hours
- Direct people to your office location
- List alternate or emergency phone information
- Avoid nuisance or unnecessary phone calls
- Identify additional facilities and services

---

Yellow Pages users in the metropolitan area refer to the Physicians and Surgeons heading an average of 76,977* times per week

---

Yellow Pages users are categorized as being either **KNOWN** or **UNKNOWN** to your practice

**KNOWN**
Recommended
Former or
Current

**UNKNOWN**
New
Transients

**4** out of **5** adults used the Yellow Pages in a 12 month period. **84%** followed-up by action — a phone call, visit or letter**.

*Estimated—representing the average number of times per week this category was consulted by residence telephone subscribers in the Metropolitan New York area.
SOURCES: *AHF Marketing Research
**Chilton Research Services

Here are samples of Yellow Pages units that are available and suggested copy to clarify the services you offer to your patients

This "Display Ad" offers an opportunity to inform directory users, by listing in detail, the various services you offer.

> ## Dr. John A. Smith
> ### FAMILY PRACTICE & SURGERY
> Office Hours: Mon, Wed, Fri & Sat 10 AM to 4 PM
> Wed Evening 7 to 9 PM     Free
> 1001 Broadway (Doctor's Building)   Parking
> ### Medicare • Medicaid • Most Medical Plans
> • Pre-School Examinations • Annual Physicals
> • Pre-Marriage Examinations • General Surgery
> • Workmen's Compensation Physicals • X-Ray Facilities
> • Weight Loss Programs • Laboratory on Premises
> —Member: ABC Medical Association—
> ## 999-1212

This "Space Listing" offers an opportunity to mention the most important services you offer.

**SMITH JOHN A**

| GENERAL SURGERY | **FAMILY PRACTICE** |

**MON-WED-FRI-SAT 10 AM-4 PM**
**WED EVENING 7-9 PM**
- Pre-School, Pre-Marriage Exams
- Annual Physicals, Weight Loss Plans
- Workmen's Compensation
- X-Ray Facilities
- Laboratory on Premises

**1001 Broadway**
**Dr.'s Building** | **999-1212**

This "Bold Listing with Extra Line" offers an opportunity to highlight your services and feature your name, phone number and address.

**SMITH JOHN A**
*Office Hours Mon-Wed-Fri*
*Sat 10 A.M.-4 P.M. Wed Eve 7-9 P.M.*
*Family Practice-Surgery*
1001 Broadway ............**999-1212**

A "Specialty Guide" is also available for listing your name, address and phone number plus limited information under the field of medicine you may limit your practice to. Shown is the attractive masthead for the guide.

 **PHYSICIANS & SURGEONS**
**Grouped By Practice**

*The following doctors have arranged to list themselves by the field of medicine to which they limit their practice.*

**Guide**

---

Prepared for New York Telephone, Publishers,  by The Reuben H. Donnelley Corporation, Publisher's Representative

Your local telephone company office will send you, upon request, flyers describing their classified services for your specific profession.

plished at the first conference. Advertisements for professional services don't seem to be too terribly complicated."

Lead time for the newspaper would be three or four days. Lead time, of course, is the amount of time necessary to have your copy presented in advance of publication.

Suppose you use the talents of a commercial artist to ensure a well-crafted job. What will he or she do?

The commercial artist takes your written copy, listens to your ideas, and then does a layout. A layout is a drawing that shows, as a sort of blueprint, the placement of the various elements that make up an ad. These elements include what you've already worked on: the headline, subheads, illustrations (if any), prices, hours, location, and the other items that prove to the prospect that it would be worthwhile to take advantage of your talent, time, skill, and knowledge.

The layout serves many purposes, all of them important:

- It lets you and the account representatives of the advertising media see how the ad will appear in print.
- It guides the craftsmen who do the physical work of preparing the ad in the newspaper composing room or other medium. These include the platemaker, the printer, the artist, the bindery person, and others.
- It is the basis for estimating costs of space and artwork.
- It gauges whether the copy can go into the given space.
- It blends all the elements into one place for your eye to judge the advertisement's effectiveness.

Layout artists take the ad through several stages of development as their designs come to fruition. They make thumbnail sketches, rough dummies, comprehensives, and the final layouts or mechanicals. They use certain components in the advertisement, including the headlines, subheads, copy, blocks, illustrations, signatures, trademarks, borders, and rules. These components give the ad appeal to catch the attention of the reader.

For purposes of clarification, I will define some of the terms used in designing layouts. I'm not describing how to do it yourself, because I believe that an amateurish layout does more harm than good to the image of the learned professional. You are a specialist in what you do. I suggest you hire another specialist, in turn, to design a really professional advertisement. The single layout can be duplicated over and over by the media makeup employees with only the components moved around on the mechanical.

The "thumbnail" is a rough layout in miniature.

The "rough dummies" are preliminary sketches submitted to you for approval before the finished illustration or layout is completed. In direct advertising, a model indicating the size, shape, and layout of the finished printed product is made. That won't be the case for you, since you don't sell a product—unless you wish to have a dummy of yourself produced.

The "comprehensives" are layouts prepared to resemble the finished advertisement as closely as possible.

The final layout or "mechanical" is the actual advertisement all pasted up and printed ready to present to the camera; it's camera-ready for publication.

The "blocks" are metal- or wooden-based sections of metal: the plates that create the type and illustrations on paper. Most newspapers are using "cold type," which no longer requires this "hot-type" plate mounted on a block to make the type high. (In broadcasting, a block is a group of consecutive time periods or the same time period from day to day.)

The "illustration" is a picture you might use in a display ad to accompany the headline. It draws the reader's attention to your message.

The "signature" is your name in the advertisement. (In broadcasting, the signature is a sound effect or music that identifies a program or commercial.)

The "trademark" is a word or symbol attached as part of your ad to identify you immediately. It's another form of signature.

The "borders" are rules or designs that surround your advertisement on the printed page. These can also be used as a form of signature.

The "rules" are lines used to separate elements in your printed ad. They also separate one ad from another.

Display ads for sending out the theme of your campaign are more costly than nonvisual ads, simply because you have another talent involved: the artist. I believe, however, that display advertising is twice as effective in attracting the attention of prospects and calling them to respond. Every element in an advertising layout must pay its own way and contribute to the effective communication of an idea. Really pertinent illustrations pay their way more than most other elements in an ad. If you can find the means to use display advertising, do so!

## Successful Use of Classified Ads

The firm of Glaser and Blitz, lawyers practicing in New York City, advertise their specialization in medical malpractice, product liability, and accident cases in the classified section of the newspaper. They say "first consult free" and give their telephone number.

The firm of Siller and Galian in Manhattan does the same thing. They take out a classified ad at the bottom of the front page of *The New York Times:* ". . . experienced trial lawyers specializing in contested divorce, custody, civil and criminal appeals, and tax fraud." Then the phone number is given.

Such ads are perfectly legal; they have no ambiguous fee quotations or questionable claims. They've been well accepted by the public and by the professional associations involved. F. Lee Bailey, licensed under the Massachusetts Bar, and his partner, Aaron J. Broder, licensed under the New York Bar, have been placing classified ads listing only their availability for aircraft-disaster suits. Nobody has complained.

A physicians' group called Medcalls has been advertising 24-hour house calls anywhere in New York City. The fee, not quoted in the classified ad, is $40 a visit.

Such a listing falls well within the guidelines promulgated in October 1977 by the New York State Education Department. They were rules covering the thirty professions under the department's jurisdiction, including medicine, dentistry, and chiropractic. In March 1978, the Appellate Division of the State Supreme Court drew up rules for lawyers' advertising. The two sets of rules differ in some important respects, and this is why more attorneys use the classified pages.

Classified ads do not use self-praise or unmeasurable claims, which are barred by the Appellate Division rules. There is not much room in the classified space anyway to say: "Low fees . . . reasonable prices . . . quality at low cost . . . a responsible attorney interested in your welfare."

The users of classified advertising say it has been quite successful in bringing them business. There are no art costs, and wording is simple, clear, and concise. Lawyers like it because more legal services have been brought within financial reach of poorer people—those who read the classified sections the most. New business is stimulated among those consumers who want services but don't know how, where, or from whom to obtain them. Classified ads conform to the ABA 1976 Code of Professional Responsibility which says that it has an obligation to "facilitate the process of intelligent selection of lawyers, and to assist in making legal services fully available."

The ABA Special Committee to Survey Legal Needs conducted a survey in collaboration with the American Bar Foundation that found 78.9 percent of potential clients do not go to lawyers because they have no way of knowing which ones are competent to handle their particular problems. By listing the areas of specialization in a classified advertisement as do the firms of Glaser and Blitz, Siller and Galian, and Bailey and Broder, this doubt about expertise is dissipated.

**Do you have a problem that requires the services of someone in our field? Send us this coupon, and we'll send you literature that tells you about solutions to your type of problem. The literature is free and puts you under no obligation.**

Name_____

Address_____

City_____State_____Zip_____

Type of Problem_____

_____

**Professional Engineers, Inc.**
**101 Main Street**
**Anywhere, Alaska, U.S.A.**

**Structural Analysis**
**Electrical Systems**
**Construction Supervision**

Sample newspaper or magazine mail solicitation coupon ad. When using this approach, arrange with the publication not to position another coupon on the back side of yours, as this could result in fewer responses to your offer.

*The Alabama Eye Center, P.C.*

Bartholomew Bruce Fang, M.D.

Announces Alabama's First Facility For
IN–OFFICE CATARACT REMOVAL

Kelman Cataract Phaco-emulsification
Lens Implantation
Other Eye and Eyelid Procedures

Medicare and Other Insurances Apply

2266 S. Main Street                      By Appointment
Anywhere, Alabama, U.S.A.           (205) 754–6814

---

## OPTOMETRIC ATTENTION

**Felix F. Gadman, O.D. & Lee B. Failey, O.D.**

**Eyes refracted, Eye exercises, Eyeglasses**

**Dispensing optometrists provide therapeutic
program for home care of the eyes**

| | |
|---|---|
| Refraction visit | $000 |
| Eye exercise program | $000 |
| Eyeglasses—none higher than | $000 |

**No appointments necessary—just walk in**

**Optometric Services, P.C.
449 Main Avenue (at Broad St.)
Somewhere, Florida, U.S.A.
(904) 900–8786**

# WEIGHT CONTROL

## Behavior Modification

Most people who are overweight don't have enough will power or self control over their eating habits. BEHAVIOR MODIFICATION is a step-by-step program that attempts to teach you how to achieve PERMANENT self control over your eating habits. Behavior Modification is designed to help you learn to modify and improve your eating patterns, and to OVERCOME PERSONAL PROBLEMS which may lead to overeating. The goal is to teach you how to lose weight, and keep weight off, not for a month, or a year, but PERMANENTLY. This Behavior Modification program involves no pills, no drugs, no hypnosis, and no dangerous diets. You eat regular food in reasonable amounts. You will be treated in the private office of an EXPERIENCED, doctorally-trained Ph.D. therapist, who is willing to spend a lot of time trying to help you. NOTE: In order to maximize the chances for LONG-TERM success, this Behavior Modification treatment, unlike some others, combines several different behavior therapy techniques and procedures. This should be of special interest to individuals who are able to lose weight but unable to keep weight off. Please phone for further information about Behavior Modification for WEIGHT CONTROL or for OTHER PERSONAL PROBLEMS. You are entitled to detailed description of the Behavior Modification programs, the fees for these professional services, and the qualifications of the therapist.

Calvert F. Vevina, Ph.D.
134 Main Street                    (713) 666–8750
Anyplace, Texas, U.S.A.

SUPERIOR
SERVICE
DENTAL
GROUP

# GENERAL
# DENTISTRY

★ **Cosmetic Dentistry**
★ **Preventive Dentistry**
 **(oral hygiene)**
★ **Orthodontics**
★ **Periodontics**
★ **Endodontics**
★ **Dentures and Partial Plates**
★ **Denture Repairs**
 **made on premises**

*All laboratory work on premises supervised by Dentists and Certified Technicians*

## WE ACCEPT UNION AND INSURANCE PLANS

PLEASE INQUIRE ABOUT
OUR LOW FEE SCHEDULE

Laughing gas used
for apprehensive patients

## SUPERIOR SERVICE DENTAL GROUP, P.C.

44 Main St., Anywhere, Idaho
(208) 545–3231

# 8

# Dealing with
# Advertising Agencies

*There is no such thing as "soft sell" and "hard sell." There is only
"smart sell" and "stupid sell."*

—Charles Brower, President, Batten Barton Durstine & Osborn
advertising agency. Editor & Publisher, *December 7, 1957*

In order to make advertising work for you, how should it be set up as part
of your professional practice? Who does the ad placement or figures out
the theme? Who does the copywriting if you're not good at writing? Who
does the layout or prepares the camera copy if you have no artistic talent?
How much should these services cost? Can you reject ads with the media
once they are printed or broadcast? All of these questions are answered
quickly when you consult an advertising agency. There are nearly eight
thousand of them in the United States. The larger ones employ as many
as three hundred people. The smaller ones may consist of only one person.

So, how do you find and hire a reputable agency where your small
account won't get lost? The amount you have to spend is definitely a factor,
for the agency makes its money mostly by a commission system—payment
from the media with which ads are placed. The ad agency makes its money
in the same way a travel agency does—from the provider of services and
not from the purchaser of those services. It also does market research, helps
in promotion, and assists you in defining your objectives. However, you
frequently must pay for these extra services unless your billings are especially great and the agency is earning a large commission from placing those
billings.

This chapter will explain the commission system and how you can fit into
an agency's stable of accounts even though you have a small dollar volume
of billings. I'll discuss the people with whom you come into contact in
advertising. There could be a lot of them or just one agency account executive who does many jobs. I will define the small versus large firms with

whom you may be dealing, and will suggest the client criteria for selecting an advertising agency.

## THE FUNCTIONS OF AN ADVERTISING AGENCY

For a time after leaving professional practice myself, I wrote copy for a variety of ad agencies as a freelance contractor. I also administered my own tiny advertising business for retail merchants and certain learned professionals who needed promotional direction. I am still actively helping professional persons to promote their sale of services. I have several associates now, but nine years ago, mine was a one-person operation where I performed all of the agency functions: writer, artist, media director, researcher, production manager, broadcast producer, account executive, and billing clerk. I helped the client develop market strategy, planned ads, prepared layouts, and placed advertising with the media. I even sold space for a newspaper that was just getting established, produced radio shows, and published newsletters. My solo operation was not unique, since approximately one-third of the eight thousand ad agencies in this country are one-person businesses.

These valuable experiences taught me the functions performed by advertising agencies in general. Agency responsibility may vary to a great degree. Very few offer services in all media. They tend to specialize. Some devote themselves to counsel on marketing and merchandising procedures. Some marketing agencies just specialize in research.

The American Association of Advertising Agencies (AAAA) offers a seven-point program in the functioning of an agency for its client. You'll benefit from knowing of all the ad agency's duties. An advertising agency:

1. Makes a study of the client's service in order to determine the advantages and disadvantages inherent in the service itself, and in its relation to competition
2. Analyzes the present and potential market for which the service is adapted, as to
   - Location
   - Extent of possible sale
   - Season
   - Trade and economic conditions
   - Nature and amount of competition
3. Knows the factors of services distribution and sales and their methods of operation

4. Knows all the available media and means that can profitably be used to carry the interpretation of the service to consumers. This knowledge covers
- Character
- Influence
- Circulation: quantity, quality, and location
- Physical requirements
- Costs

5. Formulates a definite plan and presents the plan to the client
6. Carries out the plan by
- Writing, designing, illustrating of advertisements, or other appropriate forms of the message
- Contracting for the space or other means of advertising
- Properly incorporating the message in mechanical form and forwarding it with proper instruction for the fulfillment of the contract
- Checking and verifying insertions, display, or other means used
- Auditing, billing, and paying for the service, space, and preparation

7. Cooperating with the client's sales work or dispensing of services, to ensure the greatest effect from advertising[1]

## YOUR LIAISON WITH AN AD AGENCY

On October 18, 1978, I opened my local evening newspaper, *The Advocate,* in Stamford, Connecticut, and, for the first time in my city, saw a one-eighth-page advertisement for dentures and other professional services being offered for sale. This offering was being made by the Cross County Dental Group, P.C. of Yonkers, New York. Yonkers, a bedroom community of New York City, is about ten towns distant from my home—maybe thirty miles away. I was a little surprised that this professional corporation was placing ads so far away from its own home base of operations in the Cross County Shopping Center. I didn't stay surprised for long. I had begun the writing of this book on how to advertise and promote a professional practice, and, without its knowing it, the Cross County Dental Group was carrying out my instructions to the letter. I decided to learn more about the group and so made my investigations.

I discovered that the Cross County Dental Group had been spending an average of almost $2,000 a month for more than a year advertising in the New York *Daily News,* and other local newspapers and shopping guides. The group is composed of young and dynamic dentists, spearheaded by an experienced professional who is fearless. Traditionalists in dentistry who are critical of his group's advertisements don't bother him. He and his associates are practicing excellent dentistry and making money, too, all at lower prices.

Myles L. Sokolof, D.D.S., head of the six-member group, is in charge of approving its advertising concept and placement. He claims that across the board, his group's fees are 30 percent to 40 percent lower than those charged by private practitioners in Westchester County, where Yonkers is situated. Dr. Sokolof says, for example, that dentures for which the Cross County Dental Group charges $175 would cost $250 elsewhere. He concedes that patient volume is the key to the group's success. "We do well financially if we see enough people," he says, adding that since the ads began running, business has risen more than 20 percent each succeeding month. The group is adding on more dental associates. New patients are responding to the ads. Some travel 100 miles to receive their dental care.

This information accounted for the widespread dissemination of ads by the Cross County Dental Group. Sokolof's advertising agency was performing its functions well, according to the AAAA seven-point program. The client had approved the plan presented for distribution and sales of services. Now the plan was being carried out to achieve high patient volume. The same ad has since been repeated in my home town newspaper many times. It takes up one-half a page of the feature tabloid section on frequent Saturdays.

The contact between Sokolof's group and the ad agency is an account executive. He or she serves as the liaison between the client and the various advertising services the client requires. The account representative takes on the responsibility of obtaining Sokolof's acceptance and approval of the agency's campaign plan, individual advertisements, selection of media, and other jobs. He or she may also do marketing research for the group's services and, in fact, probably became thoroughly familiar with all of the marketing and advertising problems of the Cross County Dental Group. If a problem presents itself in the marketing of dental services at any time, the account executive must be capable of researching the difficulty and presenting a solution that will be accepted by the client.

Some of the larger agencies now getting a great number of clients from the professions are having their account executives specialize in particular professions that market their services in similar ways. Dentistry and podiatry are frequently grouped together. Law and accountancy often come under the aegis of one representative. Certain medical specialties such as gynecology, obstetrics, urology, internal medicine, gastroenterology, and proctology do also.

Like the advertiser, the agency has something to sell—the successful planning, development, and execution of your complete advertising campaign. Your account representative is the key person responsible for that success. Not uncommonly, the account executive consults with the agency plans board, a committee composed of heads of certain departments.

### Other People in the Agency

The *creative supervisor* is in charge of copywriting and artwork for your account. His or her job is to convert advertising strategy into actual advertisements. It's a heavy responsibility to write copy, design layouts, or design television commercials that will attract reader or viewer attention. This is a creative process in the purest sense. Creative supervisors deserve much respect if they manage to communicate the desired message and persuade the consumer in your favor.

The *production person* takes over after the creative person does his or her designing job. In production work, plates, mats, camera work, film editing, and sound-track synchronization are carried out. The two types of media, print and broadcast, are usually handled by different production people.

The *media supervisor* plans and buys the scheduled media. He or she follows a media strategy approved by you in consultation with your account executive. The media choices brought to you are worked out by the media supervisor, predicated on decisions that come out of the agency plans board.

The *traffic person* coordinates the progress of advertisements as they travel through the agency from one department to the next. Especially if your agency is a large one, this person is needed to see that the many aspects in an ad's production proceed smoothly. Traffic people set up and administer schedules for on-time preparation.

*Outside contractors* back up the agency's in-house services. They give collateral services as independents and usually don't come into direct contact with clients. There may be an exception made for you, however, if your particular services require the testing of copy ideas or the projection of you as your own TV pitchman. A contractor may be asked to give you counsel and sometimes even undertake marketing-research projects, usually at added cost to you. The agency, on the other hand, may have an expert on its staff who can provide these extra services.

Other outside contractors specialize in the production of television commercials, photo finishing, photoengraving, artwork production, supplying models and other necessary talent to come up with a finished advertisement. These suppliers don't arrive on the scene until the body copy is written, the layout is planned, the storyboard (for television commercials) is decided, and the physical specifications of the final advertisement are approved.

One type of contractor does nothing but test copy. This individual may group advertisements from several clients together and may test them on a single audience in order to save testing costs. A super-subspecialist in testing advertisements is the contractor who does nothing but test the effect of television commercials on an audience.

The tester of the television commercials that were created by dentist Stanley Wasko of Philadelphia proved that Wasko's own pitch on TV was highly effective in promoting new patients' visits. Every week, Wasko is spending $900 for nine sixty-second commercials, where he appears in person as the sincerest of pitchmen. He says that he's about to expand to two more Philadelphia stations—another $900. The ads are bringing in business like mad. In just two months, from the time he began advertising in May 1978, Wasko found it necessary to expand his staff of dental technicians from one to six. He later employed another dentist to handle nondenture work also. And he's about to hire another half-dozen technicians.

The dentures currently sold by Dr. Wasko cost $175; they would go for much more from other Philadelphia dentists—perhaps $500. He says, "I am the only dentist advertising dentures on television, and dentists consider me a pioneer."[2]

## THE VALUE OF AN AD AGENCY

Two display ads published in the *Los Angeles Times* for services provided by local law firms point up the value of hiring an ad agency to do your production work and message placement. The advertisements known as "designer ads" are excellent.

The ad for Loveheim & Cummings, a Los Angeles law firm, shows a man in shirtsleeves wringing his hands while looking straight at the reader. Before him are a variety of law books. The thought-provoking headline says: "REPRESENT YOURSELF . . . AND YOU MAY HAVE SELECTED A POOR ATTORNEY." The illustration and headline engender immediate reader identification. Obviously, they are professionally conceived.

The second ad also uses an illustration for the message of another Los Angeles law firm, Wadsworth, Rogers & Steele. Its significant headline reads, "NO TWO DIVORCES ARE EXACTLY ALIKE." The main winning factor about this advertisement, however, is how the body copy reads. Its message is meaningful—truly professional copy. It says:

Everyone brings something of value to a marriage . . . and they have legal rights which should be protected if the marriage is ended by divorce.
Yet, there's no "standard answer" to the fair and equitable settlement

of a divorce. Each case is unique and can usually benefit from legal assistance that is both experienced and effective.

Divorce is our specialty and our staff devotes full time to divorce cases.

We try to provide maximum protection to the legal rights of our clients and to settle the divorce quickly, with a minimum amount of personal pressure on the people we represent.

Because a divorce proceeding presents a unique set of circumstances, we recommend an initial office conference before beginning any legal work. This gives you a chance to understand how we will represent you . . . and gives us a chance to familiarize ourselves with your individual situation. There is no fee for this initial conference.

If you should decide to have us represent you, all fee arrangements and associated costs will be fully explained before we undertake any work on your behalf. The fees will vary depending on the complexity of the case but fees for uncontested divorces, for example, can start as low as $125.

In a divorce, just as in any other legal procedure, everyone has rights that should be protected. Just call 874–4445 for a private appointment. (References on request).*

This professionally written body copy expresses warmth of understanding, sincerity of purpose, and pertinence to the problem. There is a close identity here with anyone contemplating a divorce. It has a single theme and is absolutely serious in the presentation of that theme. I'm sure you'll agree that the advertisement reflects professional preparation.

It pays to hire the services of an ad agency. Just as the professions recommend that lay people not practice architecture, accountancy, medicine, dentistry, or law, many of the learned professionals believe that advertising, too, is best left in the hands of specialists. The chairman of the Commission on Advertising of the American Bar Association, Roger P. Brosnahan, agrees with the Supreme Court decision that affirmed the Bates and O'Steen claim. Attorney Brosnahan holds, however, that lawyers are hurting themselves when they create their own ads. He affirms that there is no place for amateurism when advertising your professional services.

"We've found that the most effective ads were done by professionals," says Brosnahan. "Advertising is a specialized field that calls for specialists. Lawyers who do their own advertising will probably waste their time and money because they won't adequately determine what they're trying to inform the public of, and they can't define the market."[3]

As for television, the ABA advertising commission chairman is all for using it. He says: "A vast percentage of the public get all of their information from television. So we've got to get our message in the medium."

*Used with permission from Mark Arnold, Adverising Director, Gannett Co., Inc.

Dorothea G. Kaplan, another Chicago lawyer, says: "In another ten years, advertising will be the way most people find a lawyer."

## THE COST OF AGENCY SERVICES

An advertising agency is rewarded in direct proportion to the use that is made of its creative work. It's a "box office" approach, which assumes that the value of an advertisement depends on the size of the audience it reaches. The cost of producing an ad is not how you determine what is paid to an agency.

Yet, you should not labor under any false illusions that you will be getting more for less if you don't allocate much budget for media placement. Most agencies appoint the higher-salaried creative people to produce advertisements for big audiences and higher-priced media. In that way, the cost of production adapts to the size of the audience reached.

The cost of agency services is paid directly by the media in which the ad is placed and indirectly by you, the advertiser, from being charged full price for the time and/or space of the media. It is a "commission plan" that compensates the agency, by the media giving it a discount from the media list price. The agency charges the full price of time or space against your allocated ad budget but pays a discounted price to the media. It keeps 15 percent of your gross billings as its reward. Fifteen percent is the usual media discount.

Commissions from advertising media provide at least 65 percent of income for most agencies. Between 10 and 35 percent of income is derived from other methods of payment.[4]

Extra payments are made by advertisers for certain materials and services, such as engravings, finished art, comprehensive layouts, TV storyboards, producers' services for TV commercials, research, and publicity. Most of the time, the arrangement is cost plus—the price of the materials and services plus 15 percent. This compensates for the agency's specifications for, control of, and completion of the purchase. Sometimes a flat fee is charged. Other times, the advertiser merely pays the exact cost of purchases. There is no standard practice in the industry. Each agency has its own policy. You should learn what it is in advance.

Another source of advertising agency income is the annual retainer—or "professional fee." Under this method, the ad agency turns over to you the commissions granted by the media or credits them against this fee.

Some agencies require a minimum annual retainer and tack onto this the commissions they get, amounting to 17.65 percent of *net* charged.

The agency may charge an hourly rate rather than use the other various methods of payment I've outlined.

An agency has to qualify for receiving advertising commissions. The media pay the 15 percent on gross billings as a *functional discount*—for the agency performing functions that benefit the media. For the media, ad agencies function to:

- Promote advertising as a marketing instrument
- Develop new business
- Increase advertising productivity
- Centralize account servicing
- Reduce costs in the preparation of mechanicals
- Reduce credit risk

All these functions deserve the commission reward. But to get it, the advertising agency has to be "recognized." The individual media furnish this recognition to an agency if it is free from control by an advertiser or medium owner. The agency must also adhere to the figures in the medium's rate card and devote the commissions to developing more advertising. Another test is that the agency must possess adequate personnel and have the financial capacity to meet its obligations. It assumes sole liability for the full performance of its contracts. An agency is supposed to maintain a minimum of 25 percent of its average monthly billing in liquid capital and surplus.

To summarize advertising rates and to make it more practical for you to use this information, let me give you some ballpark figures I've compiled in dealing with agencies.

As mentioned, your agency is billed for the gross cost of the space or time —let us say it is $3,000. On the invoice there is an allowance of 15 percent, or $450. The agency, therefore pays $2,550. Furthermore, if payment is prompt (often within ten days), many publishers give an extra cash discount of 2 percent on the *net:* 2 percent of $2,550, or $51. The ad agency will send you a bill for $3,000 less its cash discount of $51 for prompt payment. You, too, are supposed to pay promptly.

There may be production costs in creating and placing the ad such as artwork, typography, and photostats. For radio or television production, extra costs may be incurred from putting your commercial on audiotape or videotape. The agency will bill you for each additional service rendered by a vendor and tack on its own ordinary service charge of 17.65 percent of net costs or 15 percent of gross costs. Thus, your $3,000 space ad bill may look like this:

| Finished artwork | $ 400.00 |
|---|---|
| Typographic composition | 40.00 |
| Set of original plates | 220.00 |
| Set of duplicate electrotypes | 60.00 |
| Net cost | $ 720.00 |
| Service charge (17.65%) | 127.08 |
| | $ 847.08 |

Knowing the rate charged by the medium in which your advertising agency intends to place your message, the amount of space or time that message will take, and the number of times of insertion, you can figure the cost of the ad. Add to this the cost of production, and you can predict in advance how much your message is going to cost. Frankly, it's not usual for an advertiser to do this. He more often leaves it to the discretion of the advertising agency account executive who is the expert.

It's not uncommon to find professional practice groups spending $30,000 a year on advertising. Solo practitioners most likely spend one-fifth this figure. Service providers with whom I've worked budget about $2,000 to $8,000 annually. One podiatrist who has used my help recently spent $12,-500 for a combination advertising and public relations effort—a full-blown promotion campaign for propounding his skill as a foot surgeon. Billboards were used along with newspaper ads. At the same time he hired me to write some articles which found their way into tabloids. His business is booming! My return alone, including commission and production costs netted me $1,772.45.

## THE SMALL VERSUS LARGE ADVERTISING FIRMS

The large agency will, of course, provide a broad range of services that integrate with its store of talent on hand. Unfortunately, the large integrated agency seldom cares to take on the small advertiser. And most professional practices are likely to provide scant billings relative to the vast advertising budgets afforded by industry. You will probably come to use a comparatively small agency, since it can give you the time and attention needed by an advertiser like you who, in turn, sells time and attention.

A relationship between you and advertising people will be ideal only if candor and frankness prevail. You often have to tell the account executive your private business—office policies for clients or patients, problems with personnel, consumer complaints, backlog of accounts payable, and other intimacies of practice life. Your criterion for selecting an agency is the same as choosing anyone in the professions. Reputation, past performance, referrals, the sincerity projected in an advertisement, and the face-to-face meeting with the agency person in charge will all contribute to your selection.

One final word about advertising agency responsibility: the agency and the advertiser share the blame for any advertising copy that is defamatory, libelous, or slanderous. No untrue statements may be made about other persons, nor may they be held up to contempt. You can't use somebody's name, picture, or statement without his or her consent. Otherwise, it is an invasion of the right of privacy and grounds for action for damages. If an ad exposes a person to ridicule or contempt, or is otherwise defamatory, the publisher, the advertiser, and the agency are all liable, even though standard releases have been obtained.

In the end, advertising agency people who deal directly with your needs as one of their clients must avoid expedient answers to problems. Their job is to try conscientiously to give first consideration to your long-term interests. This expertise is what you are buying. The professionals who run large agencies or small ones know their obligations. Like you, they are facing a countervailing trend due to the new surge of consumerism. Your ads, and everyone else's, have to be based on solid facts—with copy and/or art that is scrupulously honest, thorough, and complete. It is a shared task to be accomplished by you and the agency.

# PART III
## Public Relations and Promotion

# 9

# Your Need for Professional- Practice Promotion

*Once upon a time, there was a little girl who* always *said "Thank you" at birthday parties; who called friends of the family "Aunt" Helen and "Uncle" Jim; and who passed out free cookies the day her lemonade stand opened. When this little girl grew up, she didn't go to heaven. She went into public relations. And learned that what to her had always been unconscious art is now classified as a science—"the engineering of consent"—worth a thousand a week to her and millions in good will to her clients.*

           —*Mary Ann Guitar,* Mademoiselle, *September 1956*

Public relations and promotion are reflected in every thought, deed, and action of the professional person in private-solo or private-group practice. Edwin A. Moll, author of *Sell Yourself Big,* says that any time the professional person shakes a patient's hand, writes a client a letter, makes a significant comment at a community or fraternal meeting, chooses the proper decor for the reception room, even picks the right color tie to go with his suit, or scarf to go with her skirt, the professional person is projecting an image to the observing world. Be assured that this image is being recorded mentally and is part of promotion. It helps to build a professional practice.[1]

You'll agree, I'm sure, that instant success is hard to find. In our world of sophisticated communication technologies, talent and ability are not always enough to succeed. Quality service at the lowest price won't do it all the time. Rather, the public first has to be made aware of what you have to offer.

It doesn't matter that you have built a better mousetrap that comes in a dozen decorator colors and plays stereo music when the mouse is caught. You have to tell people about it before they will buy. The same goes for the selling of professional services. It needs successful promotion.

Before this, learned professionals were prohibited by ethical standards from using some avenues of promotion such as advertising. Business people could sell more mousetraps this way, but not you. Now things are different. Those ethical standards have not been lowered, but they are changed.

Part I of this book informed you about your new freedom to advertise. Professional persons may finally receive mass public exposure with TV commercials, radio spots, sponsored programs, newspaper insertions, billboard ads, and other forms of paid promotion. Amazingly, what has always been available but has not been utilized sufficiently is public relations—the representation and promotion of the reputation of a professional practitioner in the minds of the masses. Most learned professionals do not use free publicity, which brings a person to the notice of the public.

In actual practice, publicity and advertising come under the single heading of promotion, but publicity is not advertising, and advertising is not publicity. The exact difference between them is one of economics. Advertisers purchase space or time from the communications medium—they *pay* for the promotion. Publicists endeavor to obtain news articles, radio features, or other space or time in the media without purchasing them. It is *free* promotion.

In 1967, I ran into a problem with this difference between *paid* promotion and *free* promotion. A book I had authored, *Your Guide to Foot Health,* published by the Follett Publishing Company, Inc., was about to be remaindered. (It has since been reprinted in paperback by the Arco Publishing Company, Inc.) As a last ditch effort to sell books, the Follett Publishing Company advertised the book in newspapers in the Stamford, Connecticut, area where I had been practicing podiatric medicine at the time. My local colleagues sent copies of the ads with a complaint to the Connecticut Board of Examiners in Podiatry. They declared themselves angry about what they considered to be paid promotion. At the hearing which followed, I explained that this was, indeed, free publicity for me. But the publisher had paid for it in the form of newspaper advertising. The advertiser's intent was to sell the remaining stock of books in his warehouse. People who knew me might buy a book I had written if they were told of its availability.

The Examiners in Podiatry made no distinction between free publicity and paid advertising. Their ruling was that I had to dissuade the publisher from continuing the ads. To do so, I was forced to buy up his stock of hardcover books, which I still have stored in my attic. Anybody want to buy a highly informative hardcover book about foot care?

This section of this book deals with promotion of your professional image without paying for it—free publicity. More than ever, public relations and good publicity are available to the professional person, and you have the need and the right to acquire them.

## WHY PUBLICITY?

All providers of professional services have a duty to themselves and to the community at large to make use of available sources of good publicity—to inform the public about what they do in practice.

Why is there a need? Because a lay person cannot judge the architect, osteopath, veterinarian, or other practitioner on the basis of professional competence. There is no way, for instance, to weigh the professional skills and judgment of one psychologist against another. Yet, the community has the right to become aware of a professional person's ability, reliability, competence, and leadership in his or her vocation. Publicizing professional activities is one means by which community members might choose the appropriate expert to fill their professional needs.

Consequently, it follows logically that you ought to apprise the public of how you meet its requirements and maintain the standards set down by your profession and by the authority that licenses you. The community has this need. And you have a duty to fill it.

Gaining confidence and respect for a professional individual's performance from information received in public announcements, the lay person is apt to transfer these impressions and use them as a basis of judging professional capabilities. A potential client or patient will probably seek the services of those who openly inform the public about what they have done, awards received, degrees attained, positions held, research participated in, surveys conducted, conventions attended, courses taken, journal articles published, and much more. All of these professional activities need to be publicized.

Spearheading community relations by joining and working in social, civic, and fraternal organizations also adds to the professional image. The contribution of time, ideas, and effort to these various clubs and groups is a time-honored way to get known. Doing a creditable job in each group helps to make neighbors aware of the professional person's existence. It is proper public relations. But it's slow and has little to do with informing people about your professional competence. There's a faster and better procedure.

You can convince the community of your personal, professional competence merely through media exposure. Be active in your field. Do something worthwhile that will bring you to the attention of your community. Have it newsworthy enough to be given editorial coverage in the local media. You deserve good public relations by getting free publicity. It's a practice-builder and a mass educational device. Everyone benefits from its use.

To repeat, this third section, on the promotion of your professional practice, covers the techniques of public relations and publicity—under the general heading of "free promotion." I will discuss many techniques for building a fine professional image and reaping the rewards that go with it.

## HANDLING YOUR OWN PUBLIC RELATIONS

Besides discovering the cure for cancer or winning prominence in the SALT talks with Russia, what can you do to gain for yourself some decent public relations? In my opinion, the main item of business is to decide what image you want to project, then plan a campaign that will create it. In effect, you can act as your own public relations counselor and get publicity by dint of your own efforts.

Most professional people at one time or another during their practice-lives are going to need or want publicity. They have skill, talent, knowledge, and occasionally achieve some kind of professional service breakthrough, or something else that they want to tell the world about. Many of these learned people cannot afford or do not choose to invest in advertising. If they do it themselves and touch all the media bases, they are able to get free publicity. Not uncommonly, good public relations brings greater returns than do the most expensive ads.

So, what can you do immediately? It's unlikely that, at this moment, some really dramatic professional service breakthrough lies waiting on the horizon. Perhaps you're just a day-by-day plugger, doing your job the best way you know how. Your practice may need a lift by an influx of new clients or patients, but there is no mind-blowing press message to give out to the print media, radio station, or television newscaster. What's to be done?

I suggest that you adopt the philosophy of a good public relations (PR) counselor. His philosophy says that public education and information is an essential function of the management of any enterprise. He believes in telling the enterprise story. He dips into a wellspring of ideas and employs much thoughtful planning. A PR person is the perpetual optimist!

I also recommend the many and varied practices of the public relations counselor. Write pamphlets, brochures, and flyers about pertinent subjects in your profession. Have them printed! Then give these out where your type of service is sought. (In chapter 14, I describe the details of doing this.)

My assumption is that you know how to write readable text, but if you can't, work with a freelance writer in your local area. A number of podiatrists, physicians, optometrists, dentists, chiropractors, and other health care professionals with whom I've worked as promotional advisor have hired my associates or me to write brochures on various foot, stomach, eye, tooth, back, or other human problems. (I specialize in matters of health.) They have had their staff members distribute this print matter in the offices of other health-care professionals, in schools and universities, in public libraries, among factory workers, in banks, and in hospital reception rooms.

It has resulted in people recognizing that these doctors perform certain vital services the people need.

The going freelance rate, according to the American Society of Journalists and Authors, Inc., of which I am a member, is $200 a day or $750 a week, and up. For ready access to a professional freelance writer who specializes in your own area of expertise, contact Dial-A-Writer, Dorothy Beach, managing director, 1501 Broadway, New York, NY 10036; telephone (212) 586-7136. You might also try Editorial Freelancers Association, 111 East 10th St., New York, NY 10003.

Another thing to do is write newspaper and magazine articles. (Chapter 13 explains how to go about getting articles published.) Reprint the published versions with your name, address, and telephone number displayed prominently on them. Distribute these articles in your reception room and in all of your mailings: enclosed with statements, inserted with bills paid, sent as mass mailings to all clients or patients. As described above, they can also be laid out in small stacks in strategic locations where literate people come together. And don't forget distribution through Welcome Wagon or other greeting services in the community.

Engage in public speaking on the professional subjects with which you're most familiar. Good speech making and careful speech exploitation are indispensable parts of successful public relations. (See chapter 16.)

Conduct surveys among consumers and distribute the results to the mass media. Hand out or mail questionnaires to your clients or patients asking some relevant questions that the public at large will identify with such as (if you're an accountant) "What is the most irritating aspect of filing your annual income tax form besides paying out unanticipated taxes?" Find out something astounding and receive attention-getting headlines by publishing the results. (This technique is discussed in the next chapter.)

An example of excellent publicity is a number of highly dramatic headlines that shot across the country over the Associated Press wire. Arthur Colman, M.D., a professor in psychiatry at the University of California Medical Center in San Francisco, described the "Chinese restaurant syndrome" in a letter to the editor of the October 23, 1978, issue of *The New England Journal of Medicine.* He identified the cause of occasional bouts of hyperactivity in his nine-year-old son and fits of rage and depression in his wife for two weeks at a time. Both of these conditions were due to monosodium glutamate, a seasoning common in Chinese dinners and fast foods. The Associated Press picked up on Dr. Colman's letter, and the resultant feature story brought an influx of new patients pounding on the doors of his private psychiatric office.[2]

Receiving headlines, of course, you'll likely confront the green-eyed monster that besets less ambitious colleagues among your fellow professionals —those who don't know how to use promotion effectively to build up a practice. There are bound to be repercussions from other people in your field when you stand out from among your colleagues. It's a caution I have to give you while, at the same time, furnishing ideas for promotion procedures. Personal publicity and professional jealousy among others in your vocation invariably travel together. Spiteful envy among fellow professionals is not uncommon. And they may cause you grief. It's one of the risks of personal promotion.

Still, you alone are able to give yourself the best public relations counseling. No one knows more about your practice than you; no one is more interested in yourself than you. If your imagination is stirred enough, no one can think up more procedures for self-promotion than you. You may be the perfect press agent for yourself. All you need are some ideas that are unique for your kind of profession. The media are waiting for new ideas.

## THE EVER-CHANGING PUBLIC

The American mood is ever changing. The public grows, moves, and people switch from one demographic category to another. Every three seconds of the working day, a baby is born. The equivalent of a town of eleven thousand persons is added to America's population daily. People move! New publics are being created all the time.

As an individual with a message, your job is to identify and establish liaison with those special publics that are interested in what you have to say. Realize that when you speak in the form of a press release, before an audience, over the radio, in a pamphlet, or in some other way, you will be impressing your message on the minds of people in vast numbers of special-interest groups. There are men's groups, women's groups, children's groups, parents' groups, racial and ethnic groups, labor unions, trade associations, professional organizations, religious denominations, service clubs, insurance groups, media associations, safety groups, transportation associations, and many more. The most effective means of impressing your message is to target in on the particular groups that will buy your services.

One way to do this is to focus on the leaders of these separate publics. Work through organizational channels where possible. For example, it is known that women do 85 percent of the nation's buying. The majority of corporate stockholders are women. They are the key members in a family, and usually select the health professionals to whom the other family members go for care. If you're a physician, dentist, physical therapist, naturopath, or other person in private health practice, women form a powerful

150

block of buying power for your professional services dispensed in the local community.

So, how do you reach women, as a group? One way is to disseminate your public relations message through community women's clubs. Combined, more than 45 million American women belong to women's organizations such as the American Association of University Women, the League of Women Voters, the National Federation of Business and Professional Women, and many others. You may learn of the various groups in your area by checking with the local United Fund or business and industry association. For a general reference of all of the nation's organizations see the *Encyclopedia of Associations* edited by Margaret Fisk (9th edition published in 1975). Volume 1 provides extensive information about 14,000 national organizations. Volume 2 lists the same groups geographically, which may be more useful to you for marketing purposes. Other information sources are the *National Faculty Directory* in two volumes that alphabetically lists 400,000 college faculty members, *Public Relations Information Sources* edited by Alice Norton, and *Statistics Sources,* a subject guide to data on industrial, business, social, educational, financial, and other groups. All of these reference books are published by the Gale Research Company, Book Tower, Detroit, Michigan 48226; they may be found in most public libraries.

These groups are also natural outlets for information supplied by you if you are an investigator, politician, professor, psychologist, marriage counselor, pastoral counselor, banker, attorney, accountant, architect, or advisor on other subjects oriented to women. The women who belong to these particular named organizations want to know about their emerging roles in legal affairs, taxes, banking, building, and other fields that affect their lives.

Another segment of the public is the 27 million American veterans. They belong to organized groups such as the American Legion, Amvets, Disabled American Veterans, Veterans of Foreign Wars, and others. Do your professional services involve any part of the veteran population? It is an example of a special-interest group. You can reach this particular group of patients or clients by overtures to the leaders of the local organizations representing veterans' political and economic action movements.

There are also 23 million blacks in the U.S. They constitute about 93 percent of the nation's nonwhite population and 11 percent of the total population. This potential market has definable purchase patterns, a regrettably forced but distinct identity, a specific size, and particular regional locations.[3]

The most effective channels to black Americans are their newspapers, their magazines, their radio stations, their religious leaders, and their black-oriented organizations. U.S. blacks belong to a kind of "nation within the nation," which white people frequently find difficult to penetrate. If you are providing professional services and are black yourself, it would be illogical to ignore this ready-made public that prefers to patronize other black people. Since white-run media still talk *about* the blacks and not *to* them, you will reach their market only by making use of the black organizational and media channels.

I could discuss unions and other groups, but the examples given are just a few of the many segments of the public that are ever changing in the heartland of America. There are at least scores of others that may be open to your personal promotional messages. To reach them, it's necessary to determine your best publicity outlets. These could be local newspapers— daily, weekly, or foreign-language. Perhaps there are shows on your local radio and television stations whose programming would be receptive to your information. A little homework in searching out the best medium to reach your predetermined public will pay dividends. Watch the shows and make some inquiries among their producers. All you need then is to follow the public relations guidelines and publicity practices I will lay down in the chapters that follow this one.

## PUBLIC RELATIONS AND MASS PSYCHOLOGY

In filling your need and exercising your right to professional-practice promotion through free publicity, you will be using mass psychology. From its application, you'll observe results, formulate judgments, and make predictions. These will allow you the means of improving performance in future mass psychological efforts. The result will be even more effective public relations.

So, your initial decisions in employing publicity techniques may be mostly good guesses at first. As you grow in experience in this form of social science, new fairly scientific estimates will come into play. Your predictions of effort expenditure will become more accurate, and return on investment will increase. It's an inevitable consequence of applying mass psychology.

Basically, in promoting your cause, what you will actually be concerned with is *change*. Your wish is to produce attitudinal change in your own favorable direction and then hold onto this change.

To achieve change, you have to communicate in some greater way than in a one-to-one relationship in the business office or treatment room. Look at the word "communication." It is derived from the Latin *communis,* meaning "common." When you communicate, you are establishing something *in common* with others.

The *art* of public communication has now become a *science.* It makes use of situations and circumstances in which the public has an identifying interest. In making use of public communication, you become the *sender* of *messages* that supply information about these situational or circumstantial changes of interest. The middlemen, or *conduits,* are the media people who bring your messages to the public—the *recipients.* These four required factors—(1) the sender, (2) the sender's messages, by (3) the conduits, to (4) the recipients—are necessary for attainment of publicity and proper public relations. They provide the theoretical basis for all the chapters on promotion that follow.

# 10

# Writing and Presenting
# News Releases

*Lady Godiva, one of the earliest and boldest of publicity representatives, had an easy task: all she had to do was to present the bare facts and win her case. Present-day practitioners of the publicity art face a more complicated situation, but there's no need for discouragement.*

*—Herbert Jacobs,* Practical Publicity, *1964*

Getting publicity can be a frustrating undertaking unless you keep in mind that the responsibility of the media is to their readers, listeners, and viewers, and not to you alone. Still, there are times when important events happen to you, and it's important for the public to know about them. Publicizing these events is the way to promote yourself in the most ethical and acceptable manner.

What happens that's significant enough to report? Any number of things:

- You are appointed to a teaching position.
- You deliver a lecture on some aspect of professional procedure.
- You have a paper published in your professional journal.
- You discover some new method of solving a business problem or curing a disease.
- You receive an award for excellence in some professional endeavor.
- You are given a grant-in-aid to pursue research.
- You conduct a survey and make a discovery about people.
- You perfect a different technique to make something work more effectively.
- You have a book published.
- You form a new organization to overcome some handicap.
- You bring together a group of various specialists to render service.

These are activities that make news. Write and present news releases about them for your daily newspaper, local radio station, or regional television station. What you do is news!

This chapter will tell you about publicizing your professional practice by means of issuing news releases (also known as press releases). Before enlightening you on the news-release technique, however, I must caution you about when *not* to use it.

Don't write a release about something that has no news value. If it carries insufficient reader interest for the editor to print or the broadcaster to announce, avoid embarrassing yourself. Don't dilute your efforts by overexposure. It's an unhappy feeling being turned down by the press, and if it happens too often, even really worthwhile and significant events that do occur won't be accepted from you.

It happened to a pastoral counselor of my acquaintance. Every time he moved a chair to a different spot in his office, he seemingly submitted a press release on the event. At first, out of courtesy, the weekly newspaper in his town put in the blurb under "Local Briefs," but then the various editors got to know him too well. They referred to him as the "publicity-hound priest" and took to making jokes at his expense. Defending his actions was difficult to do. I know because I was a feature writer on that newspaper and witnessed the man's inability to take any hint that his continuous news submissions were overdone. Upon receiving them, the editors immediately dropped his press submissions into the "round file."

So before you decide it's time for another press release, take stock of whether it has significance for the reader or listener. Ask yourself, "Does this have news value?" It may not be earth-shattering, but is it news and, therefore, legitimately publicizable?

Practically everybody who has a reason for public relations promotion sends out releases without news or feature value, and nonjournalists can't be expected to know what editors want and don't want. A word of encouragement: KEEP PLUGGING! You never know when something you write is going to strike an editor just right.

Of course, it depends in large measure on which of the media receive your release. This may, in fact, be more significant than the release's content. For example, the following release was sent out by PR director Masa H. Aoki for Organon, Inc. of West Orange, New Jersey, to a wide-ranging list of media and individual editors, local and national:

WEST ORANGE, NEW JERSEY February 26, 1979—Dr. Alan Taylor, a Vice President of Organon, Inc., has been promoted to a newly created position. As Director of Scientific Development he is responsible for scientific advice and strategic input to the business, and will also serve on the Management Committee.

155

The press release went on to tell more of Taylor's new responsibilities (he is a physician active in clinical research), gave his educational background, supplied his photograph, and pitched for the divisions and products of Organon, Inc. There was nothing wrong with the way the release was written or the information it offered, but its news value is doubtful, especially in such areas as Connecticut, where it was received, and among the local and national editors who don't deal with business or medical news. They just threw the press release away. Yet, Mrs. Aoki did her PR job and plugged her client.

There is one more tip I can offer about press releases. After an article and photograph on which you have worked has appeared, send a thank-you to the editor. It cements relations and makes it easier to gain acceptance of your next submission.

## THE NEWS-RELEASE FORMAT

The working press—the reporters and editors who put together a daily newspaper or news broadcast—call publicity releases "handouts" or even "throwaways." You and I may refer to our efforts in persuasion as "news releases," but we also must confess that they are for purposes of free publicity. Hence, the working press cares not a tinker's dam if the written messages we hand out have to be thrown away because of a lack of space or time for reporting the news in them. News releases are considered expendable.

"News" is a story about an event—not the event itself. How well you tell this news story may make the difference between whether it gets printed immediately, put away for release on the date requested, or dropped into the trash basket. The publicity story may be just as deserving of space or time as material flowing from the wire services. In fact, it may be more deserving, since it is about a local citizen—you—but it won't be used unless it has certain editorial qualities.

Effective publicity releases follow a specific format that has been estab-

What's written on the back won't be seen, since news people seldom even *think* of turning over to the other side of a page. Besides, sometimes your words of wisdom will be cut, pasted, and rearranged into different paragraphs. How could something on the back of a page be pasted above something on its front?

2. Single-space your name, address, and telephone number at the top left of the first page. If there must be a release date, put it at the right of the page about one space lower than your identity information. Preferably say: "For IMMEDIATE RELEASE."

3. Your option is to supply a headline or to leave a two-inch space under the release date, so that the editor can write his own headline. Leave margins of up to one inch on both sides for typesetting instructions.

4. Include an identification word or phrase, which is known in the trade as a "slug line," just under the headline space. You'll be carrying this slug line over to the next page—and to the next—if there is any. As an example, the "slug" for the Organon release just described might have been "Taylor Promoted."

5. Try to keep your story short—not more than two pages, if possible. And avoid breaking a paragraph over from one page to the next. End a paragraph at the bottom of the page, leaving about an inch of space below it. Leave more than an inch if one paragraph ends and another that is begun would carry over to page two. Short paragraphs are more acceptable to news readers, anyway.

6. Always keep a carbon copy or photocopy for your files, but never send a carbon copy to the news bureau. A photocopy on bond paper is all right, since it shows equal treatment being given to all competitive news people. A carbon copy says, in effect, "I rate you second!" Also, the carbon smears.

7. Be aware that an ordinary line of typewriting makes two lines of type in an average eight-column newspaper. Four to five lines of average typewriting take up a column inch. Therefore, a five-line paragraph on one of your pages will mean two inches of typesetting in the newspaper. Space is

HOT SPRINGS, Ark., Sept. 23—

Only use a dateline if mandatory, however, because those first few words on the first line of your news story are going to persuade or dissuade an editor to print it or discard it. Editors probably read at least a hundred press releases daily and make up their minds about each in a few seconds. Allow two days' mailing time before the dateline to have the editor receive your release. Count on the postal service taking at least that long. If you are hand delivering the release the day of your dateline, you don't need to leave lead time.

9. The first six words of your story will be the ones that get into the first line of type, so write the news release in the form of an inverted pyramid. The basic news that forms the story's foundation comes first. Thus, put the key information at the top and let the rest of the paragraphs serve to fill in fine details. If possible, in fact, employ the old journalistic technique of answering the "five W's"—who, what, where, when, and why—up front, certainly within the first two short paragraphs.

10. Use direct quotations freely. They are dramatic and give the editor an authoritative peg on which to hang the headline. Additionally, the quotes may pique the editor's imagination so that you might receive a phone call for more quotable information. This could get you a full-blown feature story —perhaps even a photographer sent over to take pictures to accompany it.

11. Make sure your press releases are grammatically correct. Excellent style books include those put out by *The New York Times,* the Associated Press, the University of Chicago Press, United Press International, Ayer Press, and the U.S. Government Printing Office. Follow accepted rules of English. Don't use the U.S. Postal Service abbreviations in the body of the release. And make sure names and places are spelled exactly right.

12. A multipage release should be stapled in the upper left corner, not paper clipped. This is the exception in the general rule against stapling copy in publishing. Paper clips often allow pages to get separated. Certainly avoid any paper clip usage for photographs, as they are the frequent causes of imperfections in pictures.

## HOW TO WORD THE PRESS RELEASE

I have done press-release subcontracting for a large public relations agency based in New York City. New York is the communications capital of the world. It has more public relations counselors, advertising agencies, editors, broadcasters, book publishers, magazine publishers, press agents, literary agents, artists, illustrators, and writers than any other place on earth. One of this PR agency's clients is the Ciba Pharmaceutical Company. That drug company cosponsors a postgraduate medical education series for physicians called "Medical Horizons," which builds good public relations among medical professionals. On October 28, 1978, at a "Symposium on Hypertension" held in Phoenix, Arizona, Norman M. Kaplan, M.D., who is professor of internal medicine and director of the Hypertension Service at the University of Texas Southwestern Medical School in Dallas, described the most common causes of high blood pressure. The two most prevalent factors, he said, involve salt and stress.

This was news! Salt intake and stress exposure are something every individual can control to a certain extent. Control of salt ingestion and stress exposure will reduce the risk of getting hypertension or may even reverse the condition if it has struck. All of us are affected by varying amounts of salt in our food and intermittent stress in our lives. Ordinary people identify with the problem, since almost 25 million Americans are known to suffer from high blood pressure.

It was worthwhile reporting Dr. Kaplan's research studies across the country: good for the public to know, valuable for editors to print, excellent public relations for Ciba, great publicity for Dr. Kaplan to exploit. This is the type of public information most worthy of a press release, and the Medical and Pharmaceutical Information Bureau, Inc., Ciba's Public Relations firm, did a fine job with it.

How is a press release of this type written? What words will most appropriately catch the readers' eyes and hook their curiosity, causing them to read further? Writing with a certain structural style will solve these riddles. Remember, there are two audiences you have to attract. The first is the news editor. Accomplish this and the other audience, general readers, will follow.

The press release is worded in three parts: the headline, the lead, and the body. We'll look at each one in turn.

The headline proclaims the news value of the story. Some editors consider it presumptious for the writer to provide a headline—they wish to make their own. So check before sending out your news release with a headline. Take note that even a reporter seldom writes a headline for his own story.

An alternative may be to provide a one-line summary in the upper left corner of the news release. It's an optional practice infrequently used, but it does serve as a compromise for labeling the press item.

After the headline, the lead opens the message with a single sentence or several paragraphs, depending on how effectively you can focus attention on your item. More than anything else, the lead determines how the rest of the release will be organized. The lead may be straight news, brief and to the point; a long, in-depth report; a feature with some personalities, quotes, descriptions, and other features; or a documentation.

The documentary lead is the toughest, since editors insist that it be adequately documented in the body of the story. The documentary lead constructs the rest of what you've got to say. For example, if the subject is a medical breakthrough by two scientists, the body copy must contain their names, ages, positions, and pertinent quotations relating the facts of their discoveries. There is no better documentation for a story than to quote the story's principals.

The body, as I've mentioned, documents and continues the story. It fills in details and elaborates on the theme. The body, in fact, introduces a second main point, if there is one. However, it often returns to give a final detail on the first point.

It's not easy to arrange wording for a press release. I follow a few self-imposed rules in approaching the task:

- Use short sentences—nothing long, complex, and cluttered.
- Double-check for misspellings, incorrect grammar, etc.
- Identify acronymns and initials.
- Use controlled, information-packed, but colorful language that flows.
- Don't repeat, pad, or be commercial.
- Include active verbs and offbeat phrases; avoid clichés.
- Avoid jargon but explain words if necessary.
- Attribute opinions to those rendering them.
- Don't run over two double-spaced pages, but don't cram a long story either.

Use transitional devices to move from the lead to the body. Moving from thought to thought, your mind doesn't jump, it flows smoothly. In advertising, this is accomplished by the use of transitional words and phrases. For example, suppose you want to write about a divorce action.

*I am happy the case is settled. The plaintiff won too much.*

While these sentences accurately represent your thoughts, they do not accurately represent the relation of those thoughts. Instead, what you really want to say, is:

*I am happy the case is settled, but I think the plaintiff has won too much.*

The omission of a mere *but* causes the whole passage to be obscure. The *but* was your transitional word from one thought to the next that allowed you to end up with something meaningful. There are three ways to use transitional words from the lead to the body or from one thought in the body to the next thought in the body.

First, you can repeat a word or phrase used in a preceding sentence:
*Attorney Clausen was in disagreement with the judge. The judge seemed to side with the plaintiff.*

Or you may use a reference word—a pronoun or demonstrative adjective:
*The result was a clashing of wills between the attorney and the judge. Such a situation made for colorful. . . .*

Third, you may use a transitional expression:
*The conflict between Clausen and the judge continued throughout the trial. Thus it happened that. . . .*

Other transitional expressions besides *thus* are:

For addition: *moreover, further, furthermore, again, in addition, first, second, finally, lastly.*

For subtraction and contrast: *but, yet, nevertheless, still, however, on the other hand, on the contrary, after all.*

Comparison: *likewise, similarly.*

Coincidence: *equally important, meanwhile, in the meantime, at the same time, at the same place.*

Purpose: *for this purpose, to this end, with this object.*

Result: *hence, accordingly, consequently, thus.*

Emphasis: *indeed, in fact, in any event.*

Exemplification: *for example, for instance, thus.*

Summary: *in sum, to sum up, on the whole, in brief.*

Time: *at length, meanwhile, in the meantime, immediately.*

Place: *nearby, beyond, adjacent to, opposite to.*

A good press release writer will be recognized by the skill he displays with using transitional words, sentences, and even transitional paragraphs.

In my opinion—although I have been disputed by more apt journalists—the most convenient, information-packed means of writing a news story in press release form is to mold what's to be said into the inverted pyramid form that I described above in rule nine for story format. Doing this, you separate facts into their diminishing order of importance. To repeat, put the vital stuff on top to take the headline and attract attention. Let the lesser information roll into the story item by item in the likely event that the editor runs out of space or time.

Wire services use the inverted pyramid technique. Feature writers hate it, since inverted pyramid leaves little room for the expression of feelings and the use of language. The technique places a story's climax at the beginning instead of near the end, which is anathema to feature writers.

Nevertheless, we must remember that the purpose of a news release is to report *news;* thus, the pyramid structure is most appropriate.

With the inverted pyramid, you relate the main parts of your news three times—in the headline, in the lead, and in the body of the news account. The disadvantage of this structure is that the recounting may be boring to some readers. But if you write concisely, they will hook into your story quickly and not notice the repetition.

In summary, there is no substitute for a good lead to a news release. The lead is the story's beginning. Journalism stresses the need for it. Writers shoot for it. Editors demand it. They also try for pertinent body copy, the details of an event presented in an understandable context. The body of a story reports the actions taken by the actors in the news. It also quotes the words they say and may include some personal touches about them such as appearance or emotion.

The sample release on page 163 illustrates the pyramid technique. Note the format of the release and the information offered at the top of the page.

## BACKING UP WHAT YOU SAY

Of course, the inverted pyramid is not the only technique for announcing the news. You may lead in other ways:

- Use an anecdote.
- Take the chronological approach.
- Introduce the recollection of some similar happening.
- Start with an interesting quote.
- Show the impact of a forceful personality.
- Apply some other technique.
- Start by asking a question.
- Open with one sentence, several sentences, one paragraph, or several paragraphs.

But however you present your lead, make sure you document your opening in the body of the story. Support your lead in the body copy.

Suppose you are an attorney who has just won a local election. Good publicity will benefit your future programs, and you can show much support from the electorate by announcing the election results. Announce them in the lead but support them by the actual voting summaries plus whatever statements there are that bear on the outcome.

For a winning defense attorney in a criminal case, report the trial verdict

FREELANCE COMMUNICATIONS
484 High Ridge Road
Stamford, Connecticut  06905
(203) 322-1551

CONTACT:  Dr. Morton Walker
(203) 322-1551

FOR RELEASE:  After Thurs., November 30, 1979

Dr. Warren Levin

(blank space left for headline
decided upon by the editor)

WATERBURY, CONN.--On December 10, 1979, at the Second Advent Christian
Church here, Warren M. Levin, M.D., of Brooklyn Heights, N.Y., will
discuss his "Philosophy of Preventive Medicine, Including Chelation
Therapy," to the 300 members of the Connecticut Natural Food
Associates.  The public is invited.

The church meeting hall will open at 1:00 P.M., after the Sunday
service, with a carry-in home-cooked natural-foods lunch, which is the
usual practice of the Conn. N.F.A.  The Association meets six times a
year during December, February, April, June, August, and October.  It
is dedicated to natural life-styles, especially nutrition with unprocessed foods.  Dr. Morton Walker, a medical journalist who is
president of the Conn. N.F.A., says that his membership is extremely
interested in preventive medicine and holistic health.

Dr. Warren Levin is a holistic physician who uses a variety of
nontraditional medical techniques as well as usual medical procedures.
He specializes in nutritional, preventive, and orthomolecular medicine
and is certified by the American Board of Family Practice and the
American Board of Bariatric Medicine.

The Reverend Robert Justus, pastor of the Second Advent Christian
Church on Montoe Road in Waterbury, has urged his congregation to
attend, and to contribute natural foods to the gathering.  They

--more--

must be foods prepared from fresh, whole produce and nothing from a box, can, bottle, or other package.  "If you can't bring an unprocessed dish, bring $3.00 to pay for eating somebody else's culinary efforts," he said.

Dr. Walker said, "We invite anyone interested in learning how to take responsibility for his or her own health to attend.  Dr. Levin's talk will be especially relevant because he is going to tell us about the intravenous injection technique of chelation therapy--a treatment that reverses hardening of the arteries.  I have interviewed many patients who have undergone this procedure and have been informed by them of some remarkable recoveries by its use.  It is nontraditional therapy that unblocks clogged arteries.  People are restored to good health by the doctors who use it."

Dr. Levin, founding member of the International Academy of Metabology, on the Board of Directors of the American Academy of Medical Preventics, one of the governors of the International College of Applied Nutrition, and an active member of the Society for Clinical Ecology and the International Academy of Preventive Medicine, is among only 500 physicians in the United States who dare give the chelation treatment. It is a controversial procedure.  Accompanying the therapy is a change to a healthier life-style, which he will describe.

in the lead but supply detailed narration in the body of the story. Show exactly what was said and how the announcement was made.

Documentation is vital in any news release. There are no rigid rules governing the way it must be written, but you must be concerned with the pertinent facts. Again, back up your lead statements. The editor looks sharply for documentation.

The lead, then, has three particular functions: (1) to grab the reader's attention and hook him into the story; (2) to present the theme or central idea of the story; and (3) to guide the reader into the story. The following are examples of different types of leads, supported closely by documentation:

*The anecdotal lead* starts the story with a bright, applicable anecdote that wastes no space. It should be short, to the point, and carry the reader into the news situation fast. Use an anecdote when it's especially pertinent and will really attract a reader to penetrate deeper into the story.

| | |
|---|---|
| SACRAMENTO, Calif., Mar. 9—Evelyn Collins, a 59-year-old grandmother, had her ruptured appendix removed in a life-saving operation by a surgeon who used hypnosis as the anesthetic. It worked! The patient had no pain. And her recovery has been uneventful. | Anecdotal Lead |
| With her history of heart disease, Mrs. Collins would have been in additional danger by the use of anesthetics. Consequently, Dr. Morton Walker, the famous west coast surgeon who practices hypnosis as a hobby, hypnotized his patient just before having her wheeled into the operating room. | Documentation |
| The case of Mrs. Collins was discussed here over the weekend at the fourth annual meeting of the American Society of Clinical Hypnosis. The Society called on. . . . | Documentation |

*The lead that opens with a question* is used for its thought-provoking effect. Faced with a question, what do you do? You try to answer it! Not being able to answer it, what do you do? You read on to find out the answer! This will draw you into the press release and force you to read further.

BOSTON—Can you honestly condemn fat people for overeating when tempting food advertising is everywhere around us? Would weight control be easier to come by if all the colorful magazine ads or numerous commercials on television omitted pictures of prepared and processed foods? Does advertising create obesity? A clinical psychologist says he has the answer to weight control.

*Question Lead*

Dr. Morton Walker, a member of the staff at Northeastern University, has investigated the collective causes of overeating. The psychologist discovered that pictures of delicious foods produce a salivation effect and endocrine response in the hypothalmus. Saliva in the mouth and hormones rushing to the vagus reflex compel certain people to eat, eat, eat.

*Documentation*

Dr. Walker revealed his findings in a clinical article published in the Journal of Applied Clinical Psychology that. . . .

*Documentation*

There are different categories of leads that give hard news in exposition form. They might be classified one way by one writer and a different way by another. I've listed a lot of them, but these become limited only by one's imagination and skill as a writer. For example, there's the *"deadpan" lead* that totals up casualties in a disaster and pins the news on a source such as the police chief:

NEW ORLEANS, Oct. 15—With forty-five people dead in a bus and truck accident recently, Police Chief Mort Walker revealed his plan for cutting back on traffic flow into the city. There will be no more two-way streets, the Chief said as he faced reporters and alarmed citizens.

*Deadpan Lead*

Since the beginning of the year, 554 residents of this city have died on city streets. Some were victims of head-on collisions like the one between the bus and the truck. These amounted to 12 percent of the auto fatalities. Eight hundred two

*Documentation*

166

cars were involved in crashes that brought injury
or death.

The police commission has ordered signs to be
posted showing one-way streets only, starting immediately. Chief Walker has been pressing for
this policy for two years. . . .

Documentation

*The lead showing the impact of a strong personality* makes the reader
identify with the main character in the news. He or she projects a certain
magnetism, either positive or negative, because of an action, occupation, or
forceful statement. The reader is made to respond emotionally.

MADISON, WIS., Apr. 4—Tall, muscular
Morton Walker, M.D., is a motorcycle enthusi-
ast. In fact, his principal mode of transportation
is the powerful Harley-Davidson he uses to go
from his office to the Medical Center at the University of Wisconsin. There is nothing unusual
about this. However, Dr. Walker's medical specialty is neurosurgery, and many days he is called
back to the surgical service to mend the head of
a motorcycle accident victim who had failed to
wear a protective helmet.

Strong Personality
Lead

Dr. Walker has some strong feelings about mo-
torcyclists' negligence. The neurosurgeon does
wear a helmet when cycling. Failure to do so, he
believes, is a waste of society's medical and
human resources when accidents happen.

Documentation

Of course, many head-injured motorcycle
accident victims die, yielding an ironic result: a
longer life for others, since the young cyclists
who were apparently indifferent to safety measures make "ideal" donors for organ transplan-
tations.

Documentation

*The lead beginning with a quote* is among the easiest to write if the quote
meets certain requirements. The quote must be meaningful, must impart
information not widely known, and must come from an authoritative
source.

MIAMI, Dec. 6—"This city is expanding its tax roles to the tune of $200 million a year, and the only thing that keeps it from being the richest in the nation is the lack of land on which to build," says Morton Walker, a certified public accountant called in as a consultant by the Department of Taxation and Review of the Greater Miami Area.

Quotation Lead

"I have no doubt, as well, that if legalized gambling is allowed to flourish here, the limitation of land won't even be a burden," Walker said. "Atlantic City, New Jersey, has proved the power of gambling for financial rewards. A municipality gains much tax revenue from legalizing it."

Documentation

The accountant documented his presentation with a statistical report of the New Jersey city's experience. . . .

Documentation

Another type of lead puts events in a chronological order. It dates a series of happenings leading up to the main item of interest, which the release really wants to impress upon the reader. Some editors call this lead *the chronological approach.*

JERUSALEM, Dec. 28—First came Herod the Great, around 70 B.C., who was hated by the Jewish people and who built the stone fortress of Masada atop a 2,000-foot plateau. He feared a revolution.

Chronological Lead

Next, Eliazar and his band of Jewish zealots arrived around 60 A.D. They defended Masada against Roman attacks. Finally the fortress fell when the zealots committed suicide rather than be taken into slavery.

Now comes Morton Walker, a Brandeis University archaeologist, who believes he has uncovered the mystery of the architectual wonder that is Masada. Walker, Associate Professor of Mid-Eastern Studies, recently uncovered the water source which makes this high, barren rock so

Documentation

superior as a natural fortress. People are able to live for months without bringing in drinking water and other supplies. . . .

*The lead that introduces a similar event* is a useful technique for introducing professional performance. It's one of the more subtle methods, for it plays down the professional person and limelights what happened to somebody else who benefitted from the professional service. While the previous press release examples were fictional, the similar event release that follows is one that was written for use by the Association for Cardiovascular Therapies, Inc.:

MILWAUKEE, March 22—As had her first heart, the second, or transplanted heart of Betty Anick of Milwaukee had apparently sustained myocarditis, an inflammation of the heart muscle, and it finally stopped beating.

Similar Event Lead

Mrs. Anick received a new heart in an operation on October 21, 1968. She survived a heart transplant procedure longer than any other patient, but she died this morning in Florida, where she had moved a month ago.

Dr. Garry F. Gordon, President of the American Academy of Medical Preventics, said that it's possible the patient would have lived longer if she had undergone chelation therapy, an infusion technique which removes atherosclerotic plaque from the arteries.

Main Point

Dr. Derward Lepley, Jr., who performed the original operation, said Mrs. Anick apparently had suffered ventricular fibrillation, in which the main pumping chamber of the heart suddenly beats irregularly. An autopsy was performed.

Documentation

In events similar to those she experienced before the heart transplant, Mrs. Anick suffered from myocarditis during the eight years and four months after her operation. She survived two years and one month longer than any other heart

Documentation

transplant patient. She had lived a fairly normal
life. . . .

## PRESS RELEASES AND PHOTOGRAPHS

While a few newspapers insist on having photographs taken only by their
own staff members, many do make use of pictured events supplied by
press-release writers. Certainly, studio head-shots are acceptable by all the
media. For television, an action slide or a movie film might be useful, or
the negative of a photo that may be developed into an enlargement for
viewing purposes. The picture has to conform to editorial requirements.

My advice is to hire somebody skilled in news photography to take your
pictures, unless you know the technique yourself. It's different than that
used for portraits. Subjects might be tightly grouped, sometimes with shoulders overlapping. In portraits or group shots, faces alone are usually what
the reader looks at.

In addition to looking in the Yellow Pages for a photographer who
advertises himself as a news photo professional, I recommend that you turn
to the Professional Photographers of America or the ASMP Society of
Photographers in Communications (formerly American Society of Magazine Photographers).

The Professional Photographers of America supplies a free copy of its
directory: write to Frederick Quellmalz, Executive Vice President, Professional Photographers of America, 1090 Executive Way, Oak Leaf Com-
mons, Des Plaines, IL 60018. The ASMP Society of Photographers in
Communications also gives out a free directory. Write to the Society office
at 60 East 42nd Street, New York, NY 10017.

The minimum fee code of ASMP Society of Photographers in Communications calls for a daily minimum fee of $200 for editorial shooting time plus
travel and expenses. However, this is not the established fee that all photographers follow. Prices vary from city to city. In the New York City area,
a usual rate schedule looks like this:

*Publicity photography within the city limits*
Minimum assignment, 3 photos, 2 hours (portal to portal) ......$40
Expanded assignment, 12 shots, 1 roll, B&W, 2 hours..............$55
1/2 day rate, 4 rolls, B&W, 4 hours .........................................$150
Full day rate, up to 8 rolls, B&W, 8 hours...............................$250

*Illustrative photography within the city limits*
Minimum assignment, 1/2 day rate, up to 4 rolls, B&W.........$175

Full day rate, up to 8 rolls, B&W ...............................................$275
Full day rate, up to 6 rolls each of B&W and color ................$400
Advertising photography, Signature Group, B&W minimum ..$600

*Photography beyond city limits or in other cities*
Minimum assignment, 2 hours (portal to portal plus expenses)$100
1/2 day rate, up to 3 rolls, B&W...............................................$175
1/2 day rate, 2 rolls each, B&W and color...............................$250
Full day rate, up to 6 rolls, B&W .............................................$300
Full day rate, 5 rolls each, B&W and color .............................$400

One-column head-shots are inexpensive and always stand a chance of accompanying the printed news release. If available, send one along. Print the identity of the photographed person on the back of the picture at the border with a felt tip pen that does not dig into the image.

For group shots or action shots, a typewritten caption is required to identify the people and what is taking place in the picture. Make your caption brief but clear about what the photograph is showing. Cut a sheet of 8 1/2" × 11" paper in half and affix it to the front of the photograph by pasting the upper part of the paper on the back of the picture. Then fold the captioned sheet up over the photo, so that the typed portion is facing the image. Thus the blank part of the sheet is facing outward. When the editor unfolds the caption sheet, he or she should be able to read the typed portion just below the photograph.

The captioned sheet should contain your name, address, and telephone number as in the news release. Carry or mail both of these to the media in which you wish to be published. As a courtesy to the photographer, in the caption, you might name who took the picture.

Incidentally, if you don't wish to invest in sending along a photograph but do have one available, mention this fact at the top of your news release. The editor might telephone and ask you to send it along for reproduction. This will give you the added opportunity to elaborate further on the story.

# 11

# Launching Your Own
# Newspaper Column

*The market for syndicated material has steadily diminished as newspapers increasingly fill their pages with local news. Such conditions preclude fulfillment of the average writer's fantasy about syndication riches. In fact, there are very few superstars in syndication today. Newspaper syndication has to go hand in hand with other sources of income or whatever your parents left you.*

*—Sidney Goldberg, Executive Editor, North American Newspaper Alliance, February 8, 1979*

Of all the outlets available to you for professional publicity, the regular publication of your own newspaper column will bring in the most clients or patients. Additionally, if you can get the column syndicated, the financial rewards can swell to become even greater than those from daily practice.

My wife and I syndicate a weekly newspaper column through the Trans World News Service of Washington, D.C. The column, "Your New Way of Life," started with repeated submission to, and finally publication in, our local weekly newspaper. It drew sufficient reader interest from people who liked our weight-control and holistic health recommendations so that the newspaper syndicate eventually saw its sales value and took it on. You can do the same thing.

What you write and present for publication to your own local daily or weekly newspaper must have uniqueness, significance, and a certain quality of content in order to be considered worthy of print—something that the editor will decide. All you can do is write as well as possible and plug away with research. Fortunately, some editors will take the time to offer helpful suggestions to aspiring columnists. But don't count on learning more than the bare bones of a newspaper's basic requirements if you make a visit to the editor.

A factor in favor of getting your column into print is that newspaper publishers and editors are constantly on the alert for features of all types written by new contributors. A professional person such as yourself who offers reliable information on a regular basis, could become quite an asset to the newspaper. Since the Bates decision, a general consensus among editors seems to be that they are more receptive to aspiring professional columnists. Any editor wants reliability and expertise in a contributor. You can be the one to supply them, and at the same time help your practice grow through the publicity that goes with getting your professional views read. The steady publication of your regular feature column is a sure-fire practice-builder.

This chapter will tell you how to get your information published regularly —with a decent financial return, or just for purposes of professional publicity. With either (or both), you win!

## GETTING EDITORS TO KNOW YOU

In giving suggestions about getting a feature column into your local newspaper regularly, my assumption has to be that your writing makes sense and is readable, flowing, clear, and tight. You can check if it is. A method exists for testing your ability and to answer the question of whether or not an editor will find what you write publishable. Submit some letters to the editor's column. This technique will raise the editor's (and the public's) awareness of you. It is not used enough by most learned professionals.

In fact, there's no reason not to use the editorial pages exclusively. The page opposite the newspaper's editorials, sometimes called the "op-ed" page, makes a fine place to test your writing acumen and simultaneously produce some good public relations for your practice.

Another way to make the editor aware of your writing ability is to send your news releases to a specific editor, one in charge of making the day-to-day decisions about what's to be printed. It may be either the city editor or the managing editor. Whichever, he or she will be the person to whom you will later be making your pitch for acceptance of the regular column you'll wish to have published.

On the other hand, you may be anxious to provide material in your area of expertise concerning personal care for women, news of business, or aspects of health. This being the case, the women's page editor, the business page editor, or the medical editor would be the better person with whom to establish a relationship. Sometimes it can be helpful to make the personal acquaintance of editors by paying brief calls on them (when they're not closing an edition!) and introducing oneself.

Sending news releases to individual columnists who are writing their views on your local area can be another very effective way to get into the newspaper.

Again, an admonition is called for here: Only send letters to editors, or to the newspaper in general, if you truly have something important to share.

173

Check the idea with somebody in whom you have confidence before sending out the letter. And don't write too often—perhaps once in two weeks is enough. Avoid being a pest by mailing trivial opinions. After a while, they won't be read. Then, you'll never be able to get a regular column published.

## THE SALES KIT FOR A COLUMN

Personal journalism in the form of columns is well accepted in the United States. It marks the development of the individual who has no proprietary interest in the press. He or she merely has a message of value for the reader, which the newspaper recognizes. Consequently, it should be far from impossible to sell the publisher or editor on what you want to say in a regular column.

Among journalists it is said that feature material such as the self-help column—not the news—sells newspapers. Features are designed mainly to entertain—sometimes to instruct. It is the enjoyment and education that readers derive from features that keep them buying the same newspaper day after day or week after week. Look at the *National Enquirer,* a weekly with a circulation of five million across the country. It is dedicated strictly to entertainment and instruction. People read it to be entertained by the oddity of its features. This increases circulation and allows the publisher to charge higher rates for advertising space. From the sale of ad space comes the revenue that enables such newspapers to do business. The same is true for any newspaper.

If your feature column will help to build circulation, it will be welcomed. To get your effort an audition, present your idea with the help of a sales kit. The kit's contents will force you into being systematic and professional as a writer.

Your newspaper column sales kit may contain a variety of items, but chief among them should be the following:

- A personal sales letter to the editor
- Samples of your column
- Letters from other editors that praise your work (if you have any)
- Previously published material of yours in the form of tearsheets or reprints
- Quotations from "fan mail"—preferably the actual photocopied letters
- A resume of your professional qualifications
- A stamped self-addressed return envelope for a notice of acceptance or rejection

On your letterhead, individually type the sales letter to the chosen editor. Write it simply, concisely, sincerely, and to the point, exactly as your column is written. Make statements! Don't ask questions! Avoid giving any impression that you're really an amateur at this business of writing professionally. Your letter may say something like the following:

Dear Managing Editor:

Enclosed are six sample columns of my feature, "Tips for Tired Taxpayers," which I'm offering *The Weekly Sun* on a trial basis.

This type of column is original because it shows how every individual can earn less, keep more, and still stay out of the clutches of Uncle Sam. Your readers will find my recommendations entertaining and highly profitable at the same time. Expect lots of reader mail—letters that I'll reproduce and respond to in the column.

The free test copies of my feature supplied here will—I believe—satisfy you that this material has high reader interest. Use the self-addressed, stamped envelope to advise me of your trial. Together you and I can be the taxpayers' best friends.

Yours truly,

I.R. Service, Jr.
SERVICE & SONS, INC.,
CERTIFIED PUBLIC
ACCOUNTANTS

Enclose about six samples of your feature in manuscript form. If the column has been published someplace else, send along the published versions, too. Six samples of original material should be enough to allow an editor a chance to formulate an opinion of your writing style and reader appeal. Any testimonial letters from readers or editors who have been exposed to your information would be advantageous selling tools. Send them along, as well. And mention these things in your covering letter.

Besides columns printed elsewhere, present previous pieces you've written that have been published. Tearsheets from a national or regional magazine, photocopies of newspaper articles, printed brochures, a book or two, and any other material you have published can help you. There's seldom a case where you'll overimpress a hardnosed newspaper editor.

## PREPARING YOUR COLUMN

The format for preparing your feature for presentation to an editor is slightly different from the press-release format. Customarily, a newspaper column should be about 500 words long, typewritten, double-spaced on

175

white 8 1/2 × 11 bond paper. Type with a black ribbon on one side of the page only, allowing one-and-a-half-inch margins at the sides and one inch at the bottom. Leave plenty of white space for eye appeal and editorial changes. Don't submit carbon copies. (But clean photocopies are permitted.) Make sure there are no typographical errors. Fasten the pages together with a paper clip, not with a staple as is done with press releases.

Estimate the number of words on each page and type the figures in the extreme lower right-hand corner of the page below all copy. With a pencil, encircle wordage figures to distinguish them from the copy. Show a grand total word count at the beginning of the column in the upper right-hand corner. Don't give an exact word count; this is unnecessary—and the sign of an amateur.

Number pages consecutively, beginning with the second page after the cover sheet. Make the cover sheet the first page but don't number it. Use a slug line at the top of the additional pages, which would contain the key word in the title of your feature, followed by your last name. Type "more" in the lower right-hand corner as a sign that more pages are following. On the last page, use either the journalistic symbol "30" or write "The End."

If there are illustrations, mail them in a large manila envelope with a cardboard stiffener so that you don't bend them. Also insert a large stamped, self-addressed return envelope. For a feature column of five sheets or less with no illustrations, a number-12 outside envelope and a number-10 return envelope are suitable. Address the outside envelope to the managing editor personally and write "copy" in its lower left-hand corner. You will have launched your own feature newspaper column by following these instructions. It brings steady professional publicity.

## STORIES TO OFFER IN NEWSPAPER COLUMNS

At the monthly meeting of the American Society of Journalists and Authors, Inc., held February 8, 1979, a number of top-notch speakers who know the syndication story backward and forward explained what kinds of stories to offer in newspaper columns. They also told how syndication really works: the terms of the average contract (not just for the big stars), average fees, the split between writer and syndicate, and what benefits syndication offers besides money. Some of this information has already been given. Other material, straight from the source of syndicate publication, might be valuable for you to have.

For example, John Osenenko, the director of special features for the United Feature Syndicate, described how syndicates were started by an old-time newspaper magnate named McClure (the Bell-McClure Syndicate). McClure had too much material for his magazine and sold it to newspapers.

Indeed, newspapers today are moving to the kind of continuity that comes from a magazine format. Although comics, advice columns such as "Dear Abby," and political columns are staples, they are also, in Osenenko's opinion, stale. Editors don't want them. He believes that to compete with television, newspapers have to emulate magazines and so reach the same audience. Furthermore, he doubted that newspapers are interested in the youth market, since youths wish to read as adults.

Allan Priaux, executive editor of King Features, pointed out some of his syndicate's new projects to illustrate the type of stories to offer in newspaper columns. The newest column for King Features is "People's Pharmacy," written by a pharmacist and based on a book which sold 600,000 copies. After only two months, the column was taken by 100 newspapers.

"It's got legs," said Priaux. "The column's got all the right elements. Everyone takes aspirin and wants to know if it's all right to take aspirin."

King Features developed a CB radio column, and when the CB craze slacked off, the columnist, an engineer, moved to the consumer electronics field—personal computers, home video, and the like. This change is seen as a way of keeping the readership originally attracted to CB.

Even more successful than the "People's Pharmacy" is a column on indoor gardening. A column about psychic phenomena was cited as an example of a King Features failure.

Priaux wants to commission "special one-shot series." His most successful endeavor of this kind has been "Money Power," an accountant/attorney collaboration detailing twenty-five ways to fight the effects of inflation. This was done for a flat fee; the average price for such a series is $750 per paper.

Consumer information columns, money columns such as Sylvia Porter's, and humor columns do well. However, spinoffs are the key to making money from column writing. Art Buchwald makes most of his income from the books and lectures he gives. Ann Landers and Abigail Van Buren are still hustling, although they're are extremely popular columnists.

The problem, unfortunately, is that the number of newspapers is declining. There are no more than 1,750 daily newspapers in America today, which means fewer markets for syndicated columns. Also, the syndicates are selling these papers whole packages, and the column is just part of the package. They get income, but not necessarily the continuity for the columnist that is important to build up his readership. In a package deal, an individual newspaper doesn't have to run the column if the editor doesn't like it. Many columns are dropped by local papers after running only a few months for lack of a following.

Patricia McCormack, Health and Education Editor for United Press International, added to the gloomy outlook for columnists. "We're kind of penurious so far as buying material is concerned," she said. "But we're always looking, willing to look at very excellent, very unusual, very exclusive ideas which, in the writing field, would be the equivalent of the Hope Diamond, for which we would probably pay you ten dollars."

Sidney Goldberg, executive editor of the North American Newspaper Alliance, the Women's News Service, and the NANA Photo Service, said that the day of the high-flying columnist is on its way out. The market for syndicated material has steadily diminished as newspapers fill their pages with local news. However, Goldberg indicated eagerness to receive new ideas, especially those for three- to five-part mini-series (1,000 words per installment) that deal with life-style, leisure, coping, "the kind of article that relates to the individual's problems in keeping home and bank book intact."

Basic payment for one-shot stories is $25 to $50, he said. Mini-series can bring as much as $500. "But if we buy the piece at a set price and find it goes in the market, we'll give the writer a bonus. The last thing we want to do is turn writers off."

He also described contingency deals in which the agreed-upon fee could be increased by a fifty-fifty split of profits if an article or series received an unforseen and favorable response. Goldberg would welcome all inquiries, he said. The column length he prefers is 600 or 700 words submitted three times a week.

## PAYMENT FOR COLUMNS

Realize that publicity is primarily what you're after. An appointment made with you by just one client or patient per month, as a result of reading your column, would pay for your writing efforts. But some people want more.

I believe that anyone who has his or her writing accepted for publication deserves some sort of payment. How can you get paid? Ask for it!

There is a definite schedule of fees charged for features offered by syndicates. The rates depend on several factors, but the main one is the newspaper's circulation, which is usually printed at the top of page one. From a telephone survey I've made among syndicates, here is a per-column rate table designed to give you a general idea of prices paid for newspaper features:

### PRICES FOR FEATURE COLUMNS PER NEWSPAPER

| Circulation | Daily | Weekly |
|---|---|---|
| 10,000 | $ 3.00 | $ 3.00 |
| 20,000 | 3.75 | 4.50 |
| 30,000 | 4.50 | 5.25 |
| 40,000 | 5.25 | 6.00 |
| 50,000 | 6.00 | 6.75 |
| 100,000 | 7.00 | 7.50 |
| 150,000 | 8.25 | 9.00 |
| 200,000 | 9.00 | 10.50 |
| 250,000 | 10.50 | 12.50 |
| 300,000 | 14.25 | 15.00 |
| 500,000 | 18.00 | 21.00 |
| 1,000,000 | 30.00 | 30.00 |

When in doubt as to prices to charge, you may wish to specify "payment at your usual rates." Other factors besides circulation may prevent the daily or weekly from adhering to the recognized rate schedule for features. Variable conditions could involve the newspaper's franchise for a particular feature, its financial status, general economic circumstances of the region, the type of column offered, its size and length, the number of illustrations, wordage, your reputation as an authority, and other factors.

If the managing editor likes your column and the readership it has drawn, get him or her to sign a confirmation of your agreement—an order form. The following is a suggested contract to offer:

John Hardnose, Managing Editor
*The Weekly Sun*
Main Street
Someplace, U.S.A. zip

Dear Mr. Hardnose:

This confirms our agreement that your newspaper will publish the free test releases of my newspaper feature, "Tips for Tired Taxpayers," beginning (date).

At the conclusion of the trial period, the rate for this feature will be $_____ for each column, to be published weekly.

This confirmation protects you against sale of the above feature, for as long as you continue to use it, to any other newspaper within a radius of _____ miles of your newspaper.

In accordance with your instructions, future copies of the column will be sent to you _____ days before publication.

Your agreement to use this feature may be canceled at any time. I request that you send me at least one checking copy of each edition of *The Weekly Sun* in which my column appears.

When payment is not made in advance, bills are payable on the tenth of the month for material used during the previous month. Make checks or money orders payable to _____.

Cordially yours,

I.R. Service, Jr.
SERVICE & SONS, INC.,
CERTIFIED PUBLIC
ACCOUNTANTS

You can make excellent money by syndicating your column. Syndication is the ultimate dream of most newspaper and magazine writers. About 12,000 daily and weekly newspapers are published in the United States. Imagine the financial remuneration if you got published in just 1 percent of them at an average payment of $6.00 per column. Ann Landers—the nation's most widely syndicated columnist—is published in 50 percent of the daily editions, at an average rate of $10.00 per column.

There are two ways to get syndicated. Do it yourself or sell your column to a newspaper syndicate. Self-syndication is a full-time job, something that would dilute professionals' efforts in practicing their learned professions. It is also a very expensive venture, but it is done frequently. Writers may self-syndicate at first, and then, after acquiring a quantity of column clippings from a number of purchasing newspapers, offer their assured market to a newspaper syndicate. The market is built into the package they sell, and the syndicate sends its sales people out to beat the bushes for more newspapers to buy the feature.

To learn how to self-syndicate, read the book *The Road to Syndication*

edited by W. H. Thomas and published by Talent Information Press of New York City.

Newspaper feature syndication is a major industry that grosses about $95 million annually in sales of feature material to newspapers. Syndicates sell columns, comic strips, stories, articles, art, verse, fillers, and cartoons. Feature syndicates don't sell news, but specialize in distributing feature material exclusively.

Some are owned, operated, or controlled by privately held newspaper groups. While most syndicates operate independently, many are one-person syndicators selling their own output.

You can procure the names and addresses of syndicates by referring to the two directories, *Syndicated Columnists* and *New Bureaus in the U.S.* (each $20), published by Richard Weiner, Inc., 888 Seventh Avenue, New York N.Y. 10019. Furthermore, check the *Annual Directory of Syndicates and Features,* published by *Editor & Publisher,* 575 Lexington Ave., New York, N.Y. 10017.

Newspaper directories will provide you with the names of editors and addresses of newspapers if you're self-syndicating. See: *The International Year Book* published by *Editor & Publisher,* the *Directory of Newspapers and Periodicals* published by N. W. Ayer & Sons, Inc., and the *National Directory of Weekly Newspapers* published by Weekly Newspaper Representatives, Inc. Most of these directories may be found in your local library.

# 12

# Getting Your Book Published

*Writing a book is an adventure; to begin with it is a toy and an amusement, then it becomes a master, and then it becomes a tyrant; and the last phase is just as you are about to be reconciled to your servitude—you kill the monster and fling him . . . to the public.*

*—Winston Churchill*

Much image building comes from writing and publishing a nonfiction book in the area of your expertise. By a publisher's efforts to sell your thoughts to the masses in book form, you'll have little trouble packing in patients or clients. And in the bargain, the book may make you some money.

Look at what happened to Robert C. Atkins, M.D., of New York City. His book, *Dr. Atkins' Diet Revolution,* has made him a millionaire four times over. It was first published in hardcover by David McKay Company, Inc., in September 1972 and went through nineteen printings by April 1973. For five months following its initial publication, the book was in constant short supply.

When I was newsletter editor for the New York Chapter of the American Medical Writers Association I interviewed Dr. Atkins' editor, Eleanor Rawson, who was then McKay's vice-president and editor-in-chief, about the phenomenal success of the Atkins book. She said, "I learned that pre-publication publicity is enormously important. It was what produced this all-time best seller. We dug very hard to get Dr. Atkins to tell exactly what happens inside the body with the use of his diet. Then, *Vogue* magazine published an article about the diet and civilians lit up our switchboard with query calls.

"Do you know," Mrs. Rawson added, "that *Dr. Atkins' Diet Revolution* had the fastest rate of sale in nonfiction books? It sold more than fifty thousand hardcover books a day." Atkins receives 15 percent of the hardcover retail sale price as his royalty.

The Bantam paperback edition was published in September 1973, and by January 1977, it had gone through twenty-four printings with more than four million more copies in the hands of revolutionary-minded dieters at $1.95 apiece. It's still selling well and bringing Atkins royalties—not counting the annual income he makes from vast numbers of patients stepping over his threshold.

I recently visited Atkins' office in Manhattan. Its walls are covered with original paintings of the old and new masters, and the rooms are plush, spacious, packed with patients waiting to see the famous author. They were begging him to put them on his revolutionary diet at a first-visit fee of $250. During our interview, Atkins said, "The waiting list for new patient appointments always numbers in the hundreds."

Not only that, in collaboration with Fran Gare, who co-authored two best-selling cookbooks with Dr. Atkins, he has put together a company consisting of food technicians, stylists, cooks, researchers, and writers. The company, called Nutri Plan, Inc., does nutritional food development and produces articles and books about its research. It also acts as a literary agency for other learned professionals with book ideas.

Furthermore, Atkins turns out his own brand of vitamins and minerals, which he markets through his own chain of "diet revolution" weight-reducing and nutrition salons in various cities.

Why did Robert Atkins write the book on dieting that has brought him so much fame and fortune? In 1973, when he was called before the Senate Select Committee on Nutrition and Human Needs, he said: "With the success a vast majority of my patients were enjoying, I sincerely felt the public should be allowed to benefit in the same gratifying way as my private patients. In no way did it seem fair to withhold this opportunity to solve such a frustrating problem as obesity from people who would never be able to visit my office. And so I wrote the *Diet Revolution.*"

This chapter will be a practical guide to producing a book about something you do professionally. It will be a tested approach to selling the full-length book, either by yourself or with the aid of a collaborator. Dr. Atkins, for example, had collaborators on the two main books that made him famous and rich. The second one is *Dr. Atkins' Super Energy Diet* co-authored by Shirley Linde.

In all fairness, I should point out that most nonfiction books published never sell more than five thousand copies.

This will be a realistic show-and-tell chapter that lays out the processes for preselling your book idea to an editor, the promotional benefits, and more. A great deal of good public relations accrues for the professional person who writes a nonfiction book. The benefits relate to image-building publicity, which includes public appearances, invitations to lecture, potential institutional appointments, broadcast and print interviews, and requests for magazine articles. A published book is your entry ticket to the big time.

## SELLING YOUR BOOK BEFORE IT'S WRITTEN

How is it done? What is the procedure to be followed in selling a nonfiction book written by someone unknown to publishing professionals? How can you sell a book that hasn't even been written yet? How do all those plaudits and publicity that go with book publishing come about? I will answer these questions in this chapter, although I won't be discussing writing techniques and style. Learn how to write in courses you may take or have taken in journalism and English.

You can presell the idea for a book before you actually start writing it. An outline and/or a query often are enough to sell a nonfiction book without your writing even the first page of the manuscript itself.

I will first discuss the submission of a query letter. Select a publishing house that has already shown its interest in your field of expertise. You'll know this by the titles on its backlist, which you can learn by seeing the current catalog or checking your local library for a copy of *The Publisher's Trade List Annual.* Write a brief descriptive letter to the single selected publisher—or to many publishers, since you don't have to confine yourself to one. Multiple submissions of a book idea are accepted if you inform the publishers they are competing for the idea against other houses. Explain the subject and your qualifications to write on it. The sign that you really have a topic for a book is your ability to summarize the subject in just one sentence. Perhaps make this summary your first sentence of the query.

At any rate, one or two single-spaced typewritten pages would be of sufficient query length. Describe yourself in an informal, friendly, lively writing style. Show your familiarity with language. Use contractions but not slang. Talk naturally. Give editors all the data—make them look up and say, "Hey, maybe this author's got something!"

Your query letter should contain seven elements:

1. Say who you are and why you should be considered a potential author for this publisher.

2. State the basic idea of your book in its briefest possible form—a single sentence will do, as I mentioned.

3. Tell why your proposed book is different from others on the same general subject. (Check the subject guide to *Books in Print* at your library to get a list of the competition and to make sure that the book you want

to write hasn't already been written.) State the facts that make your book new and fresh.

4. Say who you think the potential readers will be and why they will want to buy the book. Help the editor visualize how the book might be advertised if published.

5. Give details about the book's structure and character and what you are going to say in the body. Draw a word picture of how the book will be built—its tone of voice.

6. Present some facts. Convince the editor you know how you're going to do your research, the needed sources available, and how you'll meet the problems of approaching these sources. Make it known that you're aware of what research represents.

7. Offer to send a more complete outline and maybe a sample chapter, with no obligation. Ask the editor for an action or decision.

You say that you aren't able to say all of the above in a one- or two-page letter? Then write another page. However, keep the letter as short as you can.

If your query strikes a responsive chord, the editor will probably suggest changes in structure, approach, and tone. He or she may contact you by return mail or by a telephone call. Editors usually want to see your chapters and outline, if they are available. If not, you may need to produce an outline —whose structure will likely change from what you first envisioned.

In writing the outline (also called a "proposal"), the going may be tough because you must see the book as a whole. An outline is the framework on which you build the book, but it does change during the actual writing of the manuscript. Editors know and accept this. An outline may include from six to sixty pages. Keep in mind, however, that the more informative it is, the better an evaluating editor likes it.

Some editors have declared that longer outlines bring a larger advance against royalties. I haven't found this to be true. It's the subject matter that captures an editor's imagination, the reputation of the author, and—mostly —the salability of the book that determine the size of the advance payment.

The book outline may be your rough guide that maps out the general order of chapters and their content. Or, it could be a deeply detailed plan, explaining almost exactly how the text will read. I have sold outlines of both types. Some of my annotated outlines have been so detailed that I've used them for manuscript copy. I research my subject studiously and know in advance almost all of the material to be included in the book before I submit its outline. Hence I'm able to use my actual proposal words as part of the manuscript. That was the case with this book.

I don't recommend writing a book-length nonfiction manuscript before you have a publishing contract. It could be an awful waste of time. Some subjects don't lend themselves to publication. Some aspiring authors who are experts in a professional vocation just write too poorly. Subjects that have a hard time getting sold by themselves shouldn't be burdened, as well, with writing that may need much revision. Let the editor judge the quality of your writing by reading your outline and not the whole book.

## GETTING THE DECISION TO PUBLISH

Most publishers like to go with authors who have performed well in the past. It's natural for them to try to reduce their investment risk. But unpublished authors do eventually find a market for their words and move themselves out of the unpublished category.

Book proposals may be submitted directly to the editors, or maybe they are sought out by the editors. A friend of an editor may recommend a manuscript. The editor may meet a scholar at an academic convention who suggests a subject. Or a publisher might learn that a prominent professional person plans to write a book, and make an offer on it. There may be a magazine or newspaper article that suggests a full-length work, and the article writer may be approached. An editor might think up an idea for a book and commission the appropriate person to write it. Another professional may have heard about an editor through some form of publicity and go to that person with the subject matter in mind.

Agents can be very useful. I now use the services of an excellent author's agent for my books. The Richard Curtis Literary Agency of New York City has sold eight books for me from either query letters or outlines. I have also sold five others on my own.

There are approximately ninety literary agencies in the U.S., most of them in New York City. They range from one-person shops to organizations with a dozen or more agents. They actively submit publishable manuscripts, outlines, or queries to book publishers.

Briefly, a literary agent conducts negotiations with a publisher for sale of your proposed book. It may be a complete manuscript, or it may be nothing more than an idea set down in a letter to the agent. If the agent sells the book, he or she takes a 10 to 20 percent commission of the royalties as payment for his effort. If you're not yet a selling author, the agent may request a reading fee ranging up to $100 for books and stage plays. This is to ensure some compensation for the time spent with your manuscript.

But once you're a selling writer, an agent will be glad to market your books. There should be no service charges (except for something special such as messenger delivery of a manuscript to the publisher), although some literary agents do continue to charge for reading a manuscript, and add more if an evaluation is given.

Not many literary agents handle nonfiction articles and short stories. The commission is apparently not enough to warrant the marketing time and expense. Consequently, a reading fee of around $25 may be requested for working with such a piece. The royalties on book sales are greater than those on magazine articles.

My advice is to sign no exclusive contract with an agent. You should be free to sell your general output on your own while the agency markets specific manuscripts you've assigned to it. Otherwise, no matter what you sell on your own, the agent will have a commission claim on the material.

There are two sources for lists of literary agents: The Society of Authors' Representatives, 101 Park Avenue, New York, NY 10017 and the Writers Guild of America, West (agents who handle TV and film material), 8955 Beverly Boulevard, Los Angeles, CA 90048. A third source is the "Authors' Agents/Literary Services" listing in the current annual *Writer's Markets* published by Writer's Digest Books, 9933 Alliance Road, Cincinnati, OH 45242.

In 1962, when I began to plan the writing of my first book, I had no author's agent. I was a practicing doctor of podiatric medicine who wrote merely as a hobby. My idea was for a book about some health care of the feet. I responded to a letter published in the *Writer's Digest,* a magazine for beginning writers. Lou Zara, a newly appointed editor-in-chief of the adult trade division of the Follett Publishing Co., said he was looking for book ideas. I queried him just as I have described.

Zara replied by telephone and asked me for a fully developed outline. A month later I sent it to him. Three months later, I was in Washington, D.C., attending the Fiftieth Annual Meeting of the American Podiatry Association. I had just received the podiatry profession's highest award, the gold medal in the William J. Stickel Annual Awards for Research and Writing in Podiatry—the golden anniversary award. I also received the silver medal for a scientific exhibit depicting my research.

It was a banner moment for me. Just as I was leaving the podium after having accepted the two medals and accompanying cash remunerations, a bellboy walked into the dining room and handed me a telegram. I have it still; it was from Lou Zara. He said, "I WANT TO BUY YOUR BOOK. AM PREPARED TO MAKE AN OFFER. CONTACT ME IN NEW YORK AT YOUR FIRST OPPORTUNITY."

The decision to publish is arrived at in one of two ways, depending on the policy and size of the publishing house. Because of their position in management or seniority in years or specialized knowledge, a couple of people in the company may have the right to buy a property without consultation of colleagues. This doesn't often happen. Usually decisions to make an offer for the book come from the members of an editorial committee. It's a collective decision. A particular editor on the committee may get really enthusiastic over a book project. He or she creates an upbeat atmosphere for an affirmative committee decision.

A nonfiction contract may be offered on the basis of book sales potential, which is discussed by this committee. Some firms hold formal meetings around a conference table where an editor proposes a pet project. It will be approved or rejected by the editors or by just the management alone, even with their not having read the outline. The idea may be appealing or repulsive. The editor promoting it, who has a known track record, may swing the decision in the book's favor. The way an idea is presented could be beneficial or could sink it like a lead weight. The factors for deciding to bid on a book are variable.

## BOOK PUBLICITY AND THE PROFESSIONAL PRACTICE

Would you believe it? Less than 60 percent of adult Americans have ever read a book, according to the American Library Association. And only about half that percentage have ever *bought* one, says the American Association of Publishers. Yet in 1977, 520 million paperbacks were sold and 400 new paperback titles were published each *month!* If a disproportionately small percentage of the population buys or reads them, why write books? Because the people who are book-minded are the intelligent, higher-caliber individuals who also make use of professional services.

For the professional service provider, book writing has tremendous public relations value. A vast amount of good publicity goes with having your book published.

Who reads your book, how many read or hear about it, who sees you on television talk shows or hears you on the radio—these are vital points for any author. The effects of book publicity on a professional practice are fabulous.

Don't be impatient with the lengthy publishing process, however, for the results of your effort may be a long time in coming. From the time you sign the publishing contract to the time you hold a finished book in your hand can range from six months to four years, or more. In my own case, Lou Zara's telegram arrived in July 1962. The publication of my opus didn't take place until November 1964.

While not every book lends itself to publicity, many do. The publicity department of the publishing house goes to work to stir up interest among the public and to stimulate sales. Such publicity is excellent for any professional practice—it brings clients and patients seeking services.

Yet sometimes an author may not be suited to publicity, and it's rather difficult for a public relations person to say, "You may be a good writer and an excellent dispenser of professional services, but you're a rotten speaker." You have to look at the situation realistically: If you can't get a point across orally, you should not go on radio or television; nothing can kill book sales faster than an inarticulate author.

Ideally, the public relations director of the publishing house will have read your book and instantly be inspired with marvelous ideas as to how to promote it. That's not the usual way publicity comes about. You wrote the book—and it's up to you to sell it.

Bring quotable phrases to the attention of the publicity people. Show them special angles. If you were interviewing yourself, what questions would you ask? Write them out! Maybe you feel authors shouldn't have to do this. They shouldn't, but they do if there's going to be good publicity for them.

The only thing a publisher's publicity department is going to do is send out press releases soliciting reviews of the book in the form of an author's interview. They will send review copies and wait for responses from program directors or show producers. Once they are scheduled, the public relations director will budget some expense money to send you on tour. It will take time out of your office, but the exposure is worth it. Go!

If you do get booked on radio or TV shows, be aware that the people who are going to interview you have probably *not* read your book. Provide them with questions to ask you. They will appreciate it, and you will get across the points you want to make. If it's a TV show, watch the show in advance, if you can. Become familiar with the approach of the interviewer. See how the guests look on the screen. Learn about camera angles. Insist that the public relations person give you all important details. Know, for example, whether someone will be applying makeup; if nobody will, you may wish to devote some thought to it yourself. Arrive in enough time to get ready for the appearance. Know how long you'll be on the air—don't attempt a thirty-minute presentation in eight minutes.

For a morning show, you're often asked to arrive at 7:00 A.M. when you're actually scheduled to go on at 8:45 A.M. Be prepared to wait!

Guest spots are not paid for by the publisher or by you. You are a source of free entertainment for the show. In a couple of cases, as I recall my own experience, the show paid for my airfare.

The promotional benefits of getting published at that time were glorious for my podiatric practice. I appeared on network television during the first three months of 1965. I was invited to tell about foot care on the nationally telecast Mike Douglas show. There, I diagnosed the bunion difficulties of Patrice Munsel, a popular opera singer, in front of a viewing audience from Maine to Florida to California.

I had guest spots on network programs such as "The Price Is Right," "To Tell The Truth," and on other local TV shows in smaller cities. Before millions of viewers, the master of ceremonies asked, "Will the real Dr. Morton Walker please stand up?"

I shared the spotlight with Dr. Benjamin Spock at the time he was leading a "ban-the-bomb" movement. I also appeared on various television programs with Elvis Presley, and with Ray Walston of "My Favorite Martian" fame.

I was the guest authority on at least two dozen radio talk shows in Chicago, Boston, Philadelphia, Cleveland, New York, Washington, D.C., Pittsburgh, Atlanta, Hartford, New Haven, and others.

I was possibly the best-known podiatrist in the United States at the time. I loved it! My Connecticut colleagues, I later learned, detested it. And the public? They brought their foot troubles to me by the droves.

While a few thousand people bought copies of my book, *Your Guide to Foot Health,* many telephoned my office directly for foot-care appointments. They came not only from the Stamford and New York metropolitan areas but also from Florida, New Hampshire, Illinois, Texas, and other states. In fact, some wealthy patients hobbled onto planes from distant cities for quick appointments with me. They repeated these trips, week after week, until their care was completed. For others, my staff reserved motel rooms and the patients stayed in Stamford for periods of time.

Today, fourteen years after those public appearances, I still get letters and long-distance telephone calls from people wanting to come under my care. I haven't practiced in ten years. Where possible, I refer would-be patients to other podiatrists or orthopedists in their own cities.

As a direct result of my book's publication, I became a consultant writer for a number of magazines. More than 150 articles on foot care written by me were published in a four-year span. These I reprinted for distribution to patients. Now, podiatrists around the country are buying packs of these reprints for distribution to their own patients. I wrote and edited my own newsletter on foot health, too. I will describe the procedure of how you can do this for yourself in chapter 14.

Radio Station WSTC, in Stamford, Connecticut, invited me to broadcast my own sponsored daily fifteen-minute radio show on foot health. It not only brought patients to my practice but also paid me a commission from payments by sponsors for commercials. I will explain how to manage a broadcast column for yourself in chapter 15.

In conclusion, book publicity can be gratifyingly extensive for the professional person who has a message. It is stimulated by the selling efforts of the publicity department of your publishing house. You assist where possible. If the department personnel take a fancy to your book, the amount of exposure you may experience is unlimited. The content of what you've written, new ideas you expound, may influence society and change the lives of people in a lasting significant manner. Then, they surely will get to know you and what you do professionally. It tends to come about by itself, abetted by good publicity that accompanies getting your book published.

## SUBSIDY PUBLISHING WITH A VANITY PRESS

Depending on anticipated investment, the average publisher will reject a book manuscript if the assured first edition sale is less than 4,000 to 8,000 hardcover or trade paperback copies. I mentioned earlier that most nonfiction books don't sell more than 5,000 copies. The result is that many commendable works won't be published at all without the author's investing money and time in subsidy publishing.

You have a choice! Either become your own publisher and take on the myriad details involved, or turn to one of the vanity presses that does the job for you, at a fee.

Some famous people have subsidized their own book productions. Fanny Farmer paid for her cookbook in 1896. Henry David Thoreau subsidized publication of *Walden.* Ernest Hemingway privately published *In Our Time.* Stephen Crane paid for publication of his first novel. Mary Baker Eddy supplied the money for *Science and Health.*

Under the subsidy publishing programs offered by "vanity presses," manuscripts are turned into books. One sees advertisements for the services of these vanity presses in many publications. The magazine for beginning writers, *Writer's Digest,* finds them a rich source of revenue.

Upon answering one of these ads, you'll quickly receive literature about the program. If the publisher meets your needs, the next step is for you to submit your manuscript. It will be acknowledged as received and turned over to the editor assigned for reading and review. In approximately two weeks you will get a comprehensive report without charge, telling you of the publishability of the book. Needless to say, almost all manuscripts are publishable, since you pay the subsidy house to do it. The question is, can you afford it?

The amount of your investment in publication is determined by the length of the manuscript, the number of illustrations, the quality of binding, the quality of paper, typographic selection, other edition specifications, and what the traffic will bear. You get a 40 percent discount on the retail price. Of course, you will probably buy most of the books, to give away or to resell. Thus, you pay all production costs, give the vanity press its administrative fee, and give it an additional profit on the sale of books to you. Are you prepared to make such an investment?

Besides cash, you'll be putting out time. There are contract arrangements, editorial conferences, publicity conferences, and proof checking. You may also be involved in the artwork for a book jacket.

Remember, as a professional your real underlying requirement is promotion of your practice. It's your main source of income, recognition, prestige, and satisfaction in life. Consequently, your book should really be published for two reasons: publicity and advertising. Writing in the *Saturday Review* perhaps two dozen years ago, Norman Cousins said:

> It isn't true that the only thing a good book needs for its success is to be born. Bringing a good book to life is an exciting and demanding affair. Good books have died virtually still-born for want of air and light and constant attention. First of all, the fact of a book's existence must be made known to the nation's book reader. A book needs the widest possible discussion in the reviewing media of the country—whether magazine, newspaper, radio, television or public platform. It needs window space, counter space. More than this, it needs the bookseller's personal support.[1]

Take note that books produced by vanity presses usually do not get reviewed, get very little advertising, hardly any publicity, are seldom sold in book stores, and are virtually still-born. The only way such a book will bring you the rewards of authorship is if you spend more money, time, and effort in promoting the book yourself.

Of course, this is not unreasonable since the book's promotion is an excellent excuse for self-promotion. It has become an accepted technique, recognized even by the various professional associations.

How much does subsidy publishing cost? The going rate today is about $6,000 for two hundred published pages. In a discussion with Edward Uhlan, President of Exposition Press, Inc., a subsidy publisher in Hicksville, New York, I was almost persuaded that this was the way to go—that was before I tried to sell on my own. I decided not to make the $1,750 investment he was asking then, and I'm glad I did not. The rewards of authorship came without my paying because I had a message and sufficient talent to deliver it. Do you?

# 13

# Creating Your Own Public-Education Literature

*The most essential gift for a good writer is a built-in, shock-proof shit detector. This is the writer's radar and all great writers have had it.*

—*Ernest Hemingway,* Paris Review, *Spring 1958*

Do you own the kind of instrument Ernest Hemingway says you should have? It will come in handy to create your own public-education literature, as you'll soon see from the information in this chapter.

Disseminating knowledge acquired in your professional occupation by writing magazine articles is a potent way to educate the public and promote your practice. There are three models of writers—the never published, the sometimes published, and the often published, according to Robert Hays, head of the English Department at Southern Technical Institute, Marietta, Georgia. Hays admits that part-time article writing is no smooth interstate highway to riches. Bumping along the cobblestones, however, can bring you rewards from article writing in several ways you may not have imagined.

The detection tool touted by Hemingway comes into use in collecting those rewards. Here is what comes from article writing:

*First,* of course, you get paid for your piece by the magazine editor who wants to publish it. It's not easy to get bylines and checks, yet it's done every day by learned professionals who freelance on the side as part-time writers.

*Second,* your biography is often part of the article—maybe your photograph, too. Editors are anxious to show their readers that material printed in their magazines is bylined by experts. Professional background lends authenticity to the piece, makes it more useful, and also lends prestige to other articles in the same publication. The magazine builds you up as an expert.

*Third,* you can tear out sheets containing your article and use them as credits for getting published again in other magazines. This may put you into the category of the "often published," which brings greater financial and promotional returns. Tear sheets of prior publication are the means used by writers to get more assignments. They show that you deserve to be assigned a writing job when approaching an editor who does not know you. Tear sheets also demonstrate how you might style the next article. And they are useful for leverage in getting more money for an individual piece.

Clipping bureaus will give you reprints of your articles used in newspapers around the country which came from wire services. They'll also supply clips of your published press releases. To make sure you get them, send copies of articles and releases to the bureau you've employed with information about where the material was sent. The cost for employing a clipping bureau averages $50 per month plus 25 cents per clipping. There are just two national clipping services available, but at least one hundred others that give comprehensive specialized service such as clips in the black community, medical news clips, or financial news items. You can find a complete listing, the minimum period for a contract, and rates for all the clipping bureaus in the United States and Canada by referring to Richard Weiner, *Professional's Guide to Public Relations Services,* Third Edition, (New York: Richard Weiner).

*Fourth,* having articles published puts you in a position to be spotted by different editors in a variety of places. They read competitive magazines to get new ideas and to find new writers. An editor might jump at the chance to contact you, without your need to solicit an assignment. Editors really do look for working writers—especially members of the learned professions willing to share their knowledge with readers. In the lesser-known magazines like trade and professional journals, the market is wide open. Francis Smith, retired editor of *Southern Engineering,* frequently issued a letter asking for articles from professional engineers. Unfortunately, Smith has said, "I always ask would-be writers, 'What have you written?' Too often, they answer, 'Not anything, but I want to be a writer.' " Having a published article that an editor sees will leave no doubt that you are a working writer.

*Fifth,* and most important in relation to your ultimate goal of promoting your professional practice, what you write can be reprinted. The reprints are excellent for distribution to clients or patients or to those prospects you want to make a part of your practice. They are promotion pieces. Judicious use of article reprints will effectively bring consumers clamoring at your door for an opportunity to have you solve their problems.

## WHAT IF YOU ARE NOT A WRITER?

Up to now in this chapter, my assumption has been that you write well enough to get published. But what if you aren't a good enough writer to be published? Perhaps, no matter how you try, there's no way to gather any credentials as a writer—but only enough rejection slips to paper the walls of Grand Central Terminal. How are you going to make up reprints illustrating your professional knowledge? Get other journalists to write articles or broadcast programs about you. Call a press conference!

This was the technique employed by Herman Tarnower, M.D., of Scarsdale, New York, in publicizing his new "Scarsdale Diet," the latest dieting technique making the rounds. Dr. Tarnower, a cardiologist and internist, received five thousand letters a month from all over the country and around the world, directly as a result of a press interview he gave a *New York Times* feature writer in July 1978. The journalist wrote a story about all the people in affluent Scarsdale, a Westchester County suburb, who were on the Tarnower diet. The article's title was "The Scarsdale Diet: If It's Friday, It Must Be Spinach." A wide readership was assured by putting "diet" in the headline. Americans spend $100 billion a year in quest of thinner selves.

The physician followed this up with publication of the Scarsdale Diet in the September 1978 issue of a women's magazine with readership of more than eight million; it carried the headline: "Dr. Tarnower's Super-Diet— Easiest Diet Ever!" In large type was the claim that you can lose up to twenty pounds in fourteen days. It's likely that this article writer attended the same July news conference as had *The New York Times* writer.

By the end of the same month, another headline shouting from the front page of a popular supermarket-checkout tabloid said: "How to lose fourteen pounds in fourteen days." The waiting list of patients seeking Tarnower's services became as long as a piano roll.

With collaborator Samm Sinclair Baker, who is an exceedingly successful author with thirty books to his credit, Tarnower delivered the manuscript for a book that was published in November 1978. It was a medium-sized book, which was an extraordinary accomplishment, since his vast array of new patients on the diet follow directions written on a single sheet of paper. He explained, "It was very easy to get a whole book out of it."

Tarnower's book includes several variations on the original Scarsdale Diet. While there have been warnings in the press that the diet might be risky for some people, the book hit the best seller list early in 1979. It provides an economy plan for people who can't afford to live in Scarsdale and eat steak twice a week and lamb chops once. The book also offers gourmet variations, international cuisine, and a vegetarian version. "There are five chapters right there," the doctor said.

With Baker's help—and Samm is an expert who co-authored all of Maxwell Stillman's best sellers—more chapters cover simpler diets for various medical problems such as diabetes, ulcers, high blood pressure, congestive heart failure, diverticulitis, and constipation. Tarnower admits that his advance payment on the book was "nice and juicy."[1]

## IS YOUR STORY IMPORTANT?

Needless to say, you must have something important to share with the press. The embarrassment to you, waste of time for reporters, and potential harm the press could do, in turn, might be devastating to your image and practice. My advice is to focus on subjects where you know the major problems in your field that affect ordinary people, and that you have some valuable answers for solving those problems. Speak the public's language. Study yourself, your background, and your situation to decide about what you know best. Explain to full-time freelancers and members of the working press significant aspects of the chosen topic. Give feature writers or news reporters the information to produce a story that makes the public turn full attention to those writers' printed or spoken words. This will get you public relations coverage.

But suppose you're unsure of the significance of your story. Maybe you suspect it has meaning only to you or to fellow professionals in your specialized field. What are you going to do to avoid potential embarrassment?

Create a simulated press conference. It's a unique approach rarely used in the public relations arena. I recently had the privilege to be one of two news people who experienced the simulation for a professional consulting engineer.

Jerry Goldberg, the executive vice-president of one of New York City's leading public relations agencies, telephoned me with an ordinary and yet extraordinary request. "Are you free for lunch next Monday, November 6, 1978?" he asked. "Would you come here to the city, and participate in a simulated press conference—not the real thing? We just want to see if our client has a good enough story, and as a favor, we ask that you let us bounce it off your brain. OK?"

He explained the particulars, and I agreed to attend. There could be a feature-length article for *Omni* magazine in what Goldberg's client had discovered, I thought. I believe in exposing myself to any opportunity. Besides, I was curious to be part of this little experiment anyway. I went and listened to the story of a new discovery of an old problem in mathematics.

While on a commercial flight from New York to Salt Lake City, an engineer-physicist, to whom I will refer only as "Dr. J" for reasons that will become obvious, read an article written by Harold M. Edwards in the

October 1978 issue of *Scientific American*. It was about the last theorem of Pierre de Fermat, a seventeenth-century French jurist and mathematician. Within seven minutes of finishing the article, Dr. J claims, he solved the theorem," a problem that mathematicians had been trying to unravel for three hundred years.

A CBS-TV associate of television newsman Walter Cronkite named Gary Shepherd and I, the only two journalists invited to Dr. J's luncheon, listened to his overly involved technical explanation. We ate our lunch in the President's Room of the Chemist's Club as this scientist wrote many mathematical equations on a blackboard. After listening for two hours, I stopped the fellow. I had reached the saturation point.

I asked him the questions any feature writer must answer before he embarks on an article. I said, "Dr. J, how is finding this last equation of Fermat going to affect the lives of ordinary people? What benefit will they gain from learning this information? Will they identify with the theorem you have discovered? What will it take to put the theorem into practice? When will its benefits accrue? How soon will they show up and bring people a return? Why should ordinary people have this information? How much will it cost them if they act on it? Where should they begin to use it? Can they understand your discovery?"

Dr. J was unable to answer any of these key questions. Their viable answers would provide the reason for giving press interviews. No answers meant one thing. He did not have a story suitable for presenting at a real press conference. Gary Shepherd backed me up. We agreed that we listened longer than ten minutes only out of courtesy to our hosts.

My recommendation was that the engineer-physicist should prepare a scientific paper for publication in a journal devoted to mathematics. He has now done this and submitted the paper. He has also published on his own a booklet called "On Fermat's Last Theorem," in which he attempts to answer the dozen questions I asked. I believe that the simulated press conference and my brutal questions have saved Dr. J from experiencing embarrassment by unnecessarily calling in writers and reporters.

The man is a brilliant scientist and a nice person. I was glad to help him avoid inestimable damage to his own and his consulting firm's image. He told me recently that he now believes himself ready to call a real press conference.

This simulation of a press conference is not a bad idea—anyone can accomplish it. Moreover, it could be an entertaining and valuable way to spend an evening. Try it out on friends and professional associates. Bounce your brainchild off these people before you face the "lions" of the press. Make sure to answer the dozen questions I've offered.

## HOW TO SET UP YOUR OWN PRESS CONFERENCE

Not everyone has a public relations counselor, so it might be advantageous to know how to set up your own press conference. The principal sources of news, in fact, are the highly individual press interviews given by people with newsworthy items for public information.

There are no rules for a standard press conference, no script for a standard story, and no way to predict what questions will be asked by reporters. Everything is the same today as in the time of Jonathan Swift. Press conferences can take unexpected turns that often yield surprising results. Most of the time they are gratifying, if you are prepared with valuable material and have a valid claim to headlines.

What may you expect in return for your preparation? Usually, fair treatment. Obviously you cannot hope to influence the kind of stories that go out. Having something newsworthy to report, you're bound to attract a certain amount of favorable public notice. Yet, the normal practice of using both sides of the story, favorable or unfavorable, applies, since reporters are not obliged to give their host special consideration. Just keep in mind yourself that publicity is "information with a purpose."

Send invitations to your press conference to press agencies and syndicates, as well as to your local press people. Depending on how much money and effort you're willing to put into sending the invitations, there is no limit to the number of organizations you can invite. Send out your invitations about three weeks before the event. Schedule it for a midmorning time, as it enables you to reach the evening TV shows. They require several hours to process their films. You'll also reach the next morning's newspapers, which often have greater circulations than evening newspapers. Note that the big four, the *Los Angeles Times, The New York Times, Chicago Tribune,* and *Washington Post* all are morning newspapers.

Plan your press conference for any weekday but Friday. Saturday's newspapers are the thinnest and have the smallest circulation, so a Friday conference may not appear in print. Sunday is a worse day for a conference; Saturday is the worst of all. Monday may be poor because reporters may be recovering from the weekend and catching up on stories. Therefore, the three midweek days appear to be the best for setting up your press conference.

Before setting the exact date, check to see if something else of magnitude is going to compete with your news. At least query your local convention bureau, chamber of commerce, trade association, and other organization to learn what are their plans. Ask a reporter what invitations he's received for your date.

Follow up your invitation with another mailing one week before the press conference. Remind the media of your forthcoming event. Invite them again. You can do this by telephoning, but there may be too many calls to make without knowing who is assigned to cover your story. When I worked as a feature writer for my city's weekly newspaper, my editor assigned me to accept the press conference invitation of a consultant engineer to the Stamford Sewer Commission. Before the conference, the engineer's office telephoned to remind the newspaper of the event. Another writer took the call and adopted the assignment as his own without asking anyone. The result was that two of us covered the story. The editor was disgusted with the wasted manhours and refused to print anything that came out of that press conference. A written follow-up might have been better.

Use a "tip sheet" format for your invitation. It should provide the who, what, where, when, and why of the press conference. Include the date, time of day, location, and travel instructions, if applicable. Invite photographic coverage.

At the conference, have all of your props at hand for photographing. A photographer will want to get in and out quickly. Try to accommodate photographers by removing drinking glasses, cigarettes, pained expressions, and anything else you wouldn't want in pictures.

Make sure the room is large enough to hold a crowd. Have enough seating. Still, don't be shocked if few show up. A recurrent nightmare of people holding press conferences is that no one will turn up for them. Publicists have even joked about forming a company called "Bodies Incorporated" which would supply people who look like reporters to turn up at news conferences.

## TWENTY-SIX PRESS CONFERENCE TIPS

With all factors affirmed and possessing information everyone wants to know, there are some precepts to follow in handling a press conference. Richard Conarroe, the president of Walden Public Relations, Inc., of Westport, Connecticut, prepares his clients for their press interviews. He has written out the step-by-step planning guide for professional people.

Conarroe told me in an interview: "It doesn't matter whether you are to be interviewed by a small trade magazine or a major newspaper; by a group of reporters or just one; whether the reporter initiated the interview or someone in your company did; whether you've got good news to report or bad." In all cases, the rules for planning and handling a good press interview are the same.

1. No matter how gratifying the prospect of the interview might be, avoid getting into a situation where you are not going to know what you're talking about.

2. If more than one person in your practice is to be interviewed, separately or together, make sure your stories are going to match.

3. Plan the time and place of the interview to your own advantage: over lunch to explain some written material the press person already has or at your office if you're going to dig into records and references.

4. Before they arrive, alert the staff that press people are coming. Make your interviewers feel welcome from the start. Have your receptionist greet them by name. See them as soon as possible. Take no telephone interruptions.

5. Anticipate questions and have answers ready for them in advance.

6. Save awkward interviews by taking the lead if the interviewer stumbles, runs dry, or fails to have proper questions at his command.

7. Be ready with additional story ideas if reporters are just fishing for something—anything—to write an extra feature. Plant the seeds for the next story, if you can.

8. Since publications are overloaded with material, be ready to sell your story, not just tell it. Make it identify with the common man; the writer must see your story as important in his reader's life.

9. Check the audiences of the publications interviewing you. Focus what you say to their self-interests. Read the articles. Never insult the press people by revealing that you're unfamiliar with the media they represent. Maybe have copies of the publications lying on your desk for the interviewers to see.

10. Don't make the press conference a monologue. Ask the reporters if you're telling them what they wish to know. Give an answer to a question, and wait for the next one. Let an interviewer talk if he wants to.

11. Try to slant the story in the direction you desire. If the reporter has a preconceived notion of how he intends to treat the topic, find out what it is in order to help him report accurately.

12. Don't speak "off the record." Nothing is ever off the record, for if a writer wants to use something you've said, he or she will use it. Why should anyone keep your secret?

13. If you don't have the answer to a question, say so! Seldom are people 100 percent informed on a subject. However, promises you give to supply more information by a given date must be kept.

14. Give short, terse, quotable quotes using colorful words. Speak idi-

omatically and pack lots of meaning into a few words. Don't use technical jargon even if the interviewers understand you.

15. Tell the truth in a press conference, since a lie is invariably found out and makes everything else you said invalid.

16. Give reporters, especially feature writers, anecdotes, case histories, pertinent stories, and other examples of declarative statements.

17. Suggest additional sources of information to your interviewers such as reference books, periodicals, other experts, and reprints of your previously published papers.

18. Watch out for tricky questions similar to "Have you stopped beating your mate?" Say that you don't understand the question.

19. Explain the negative side as well as the positive side of your news. Diminish the unhappy information if you can, but don't try to hide it.

20. Don't let your public relations counsel answer questions that are directed to you. The PR person is not the expert from whom quotes can be taken.

21. If your material is unavoidably technical and not easily understood, offer to write out the important details and deliver them to the reporters. (If possible, do this in advance.)

22. Don't give inside information that violates the disclosure laws. Watch that you don't invade a client's or patient's privacy.

23. Avoid giving information exclusively to one reporter, especially if it's some earth-shaking announcement. Make up a press release and give out the news to anyone who wants it.

24. Try to get attention for your story with photographs or other illustrations. Make graphic material available for use by the interviewer. Don't expect to receive it back.

25. Don't demand to see the story before it goes into print. Simply ask, "Is it your policy to let me see the story you are going to write before it is published?" Be polite and you may get to make needed changes. Be tough and you'll get nothing!

26. Don't render unsupported personal opinions. Wherever possible, give facts, statistics, case histories, and other hard news. Then dress them in colorful, human interest stories.

These twenty-six tips for handling yourself during a press conference are tailored for the professional person. Such interviews offer fine opportunities for publicity and the later public-educational literature that evolves from reprinting the published articles.

## YOUR LITERATURE AS YOUR CALLING CARD

Let me again warn you that some of your colleagues won't appreciate your promotional efforts, especially if they are not oriented to this sort of thing themselves.

I remember in January 1963, when an article of mine with the title, "What You Can Do About Corns," was published in *McCall's Magazine.* It was the first time any podiatrist had ever been published in a nationally distributed women's magazine. I described in the article how a foot doctor provides relief for hard corns, soft corns, blood corns, nerve corns, and seed corns. These are troubles that plague many women in this country.

My former colleagues in Connecticut did not see the advantage of educating the public to help itself. I received personal criticism from fellow podiatrists for telling women how to relieve their corn problems and that shoe pressure caused them. They failed to see the great public relations value of alerting the public to the fact that doctors of podiatric medicine treat toe troubles of this type. Instead, they were critical of my describing the corn as having a central eye, or root, that causes pain. They disliked the word "root," and this is all I heard from them.

For years, several dozens of articles I have written and have had published in national and regional magazines have been reprinted thousands of times and purchased by hundreds of podiatrists. They use them as mailing pieces, statement stuffers, reception room literature, general educational material, and also for their personal promotion purposes. Professionals who use my articles in this way recognize that in many cases the article promotes the profession as well as the podiatrist distributing the foot health information. I will explain how to do this with your own professional literature for the public in chapter 14.

To make educational literature your promotional calling card, have your name and location included on it. I print the podiatrist's name, address, and telephone number on available white space of the reprints I supply. He distributes to his patients a variety of these articles, which describe the individual foot troubles he treats. They bring him business.

*The American Chiropractor* magazine does the same thing. Eric C. Watson, D.C., of Erie, Pennsylvania, publisher of this magazine—it is sent under controlled circulation to thirty thousand U.S. chiropractors—has hit upon a "different" plan for chiropractic promotion. He prints a journal for the education and entertainment of the doctor of chriopractic. But then he does something more.

Chiropractic is the fastest growing health-care profession in the world and the second largest in the United States. *The American Chiropractor* is a magazine specifically designed to appeal to the professional and avocational interests of these practitioners. Articles on travel, leisure, and nutrition comprise the bulk of this full-color periodical. I am a contributing editor.

What is unique about Watson's publication is that an additional magazine is bound into the book by saddle stitching. Each month, an extra thirty-two-page detachable insert covers the topics of nutrition and chiropractic philosophy in lay terms for the education of the chiropractic patient. Half a million patients are exposed to this publication daily, for this is the number of people visiting their chiropractors each day. The patient-readership potential is eight million monthly, according to Watson.

The subscribing doctor has his name, address, and telephone number printed on the detachable insert, which he may acquire in far greater numbers. A chiropractor buys these monthly health bulletins in lots of fifty and distributes them for patient education. Each lay-person booklet is the practitioner's personal goodwill messenger.

In chapter 14, as I said before, I shall describe the direct-mail selling of your professional services, using article reprints, brochures, pamphlets, and a newsletter published by yourself. There is no limit to the goodwill to be derived from these promotional messengers.

# 14

# Promotion and Direct Mail

*The professional man must develop lines of continuing communication.*
*This is a means of maintaining contact with the patient or client throughout the year or until professional services are again needed. It is a service which indicates that the professional is interested in the welfare of his patient or client.*

—*Edwin A. Moll,* Sell Yourself Big, *1966*

Irving L. Straus, president of Irving L. Straus Associates, Inc., a specialist in communications for nonprofit organizations and public relations for professional corporations, spoke to me of how he had developed lines of communication with the clients of an accounting firm in trouble. Straus described how he had helped to enhance the faded image of Seidman & Seidman, Inc.

Seidman is viewed as the eleventh largest accounting company in the United States. This firm saw its professional reputation take a nose dive when one of its clients was investigated by the Securities and Exchange Commission.

"I had to mitigate the Equity funding mess," Straus told me. "And then I participated in Seidman & Seidman's practice development program to overcome the bad public image that remained."

"The Equity funding mess" involved a financial institution whose officers perpetrated a computer theft and stole millions of dollars. They made up life insurance policies for people who did not exist and then paid off the policies when the imaginary policy holders were killed off. This went undiscovered for years, even by the company's accounting firm, Seidman and Seidman.

Among the things Straus did was to use direct mail for "reprints of meaningful articles . . . forwarded to a select list of members of the financial community across the nation who would have special interest in the [accountancy] corporation."

Straus' direct-mail technique can be employed by any person who provides professional services. You need only follow the advice he gave to members of the American Society of Association Executives. He wrote in *Association Management:* "Perhaps the best way to start investigating media potentials is just to look around the office. There may be enough information in that new brochure to make an interesting article for the local newspaper. What about that speech the director [you] made in Washington or Florida? It could be excerpted and sent out to some selected trade magazines. Does anybody know how many contributions the association [you] made to worthy causes this year, or last? What about those questionnaires and surveys sent to members [clients or patients] or other persons this year and last? They probably contain a wealth of facts and statistics of high interest."[1]

## DIRECT-MAILING YOUR PUBLISHED ARTICLES

In chapter 13, I recommended several ways to get articles written about you and published in the print media. My suggestions also included that you should educate the public by writing your own articles for publication. By now, it could be that the press conferences you've held and the magazine and newspaper features you've written have netted lots of educational literature about the professional services you provide. There is no better public relations than to have favorable mention of what you do published in a popular magazine. It's the aim of any publicist to get his or her client "ink" in the press in this way. Being your own press agent, it's possible you have done an excellent job for yourself.

However, you shouldn't stop there! It will pay dividends to go the extra mile and reprint your best publicity material. Turn these magazine and newspaper articles into direct-mail reprints. Distribute them to a mailing list consisting of your present clients or patients, prospects whom you anticipate could be patrons, feeders of referrals, and others whom you judge to be of importance to the growth of your practice. Send them also to other members of the press. It is not unlikely that a feature article about you that has been reprinted will stimulate the writing of another newly published article.

Realize that particular people—those whom you would consider "key" individuals—are significantly more important to the health of a professional practice such as yours. They may include the corner pharmacist for a health-care professional, the president of a construction firm for an architect, certified public accountants for a tax attorney, family dentists for an oral surgeon, or satisfied customers for a stockbroker. And for all learned professionals who require occasional promotion, members of the press are always "key" individuals.

While you may do a superior job of getting the press mentionings you're after, the primary audience—these "key" individuals—are likely to miss them. The logical reason is that a superabundance of literature in the form of books, magazines, newsletters, mail, newspapers, press releases, brochures, pamphlets, reprints, labels, directories, and other items remain to be read. All of us are buried daily under a snowstorm of paper.

Still, you have a message that you really want to impart. It should be read by others, and it's incumbent on you to make the attempt. At least, give the "key" individuals a chance to read it, absorb it, and act on it—or discard it.

The way to spread your message of service excellence (remember, rules of advertising professional services don't let you say you're superior to anyone else) is to photocopy the published piece exactly as it appears.

On my visit to the office of Walden Public Relations, Inc., in Westport, Connecticut, the business manager, Ronald R. Conarroe, showed me the technique his firm uses for clients. Walden reprints a small quantity of a client's articles by the low-cost offset method. The client uses the reprints as enclosures with letters or other mailings going out of his office. In turn, the client may continue this reprinting and sending out as many mailings as are required.

Doing this for yourself, you can deliver reprints to your mailing list of patrons with a brief covering letter. It might say simply, "Recently some of the work that comes out of this office was discussed in a popular publication. Perhaps you read the article. In case you did not, I am providing you with the enclosed reprint. I thought you would be interested to know of the services I supply, which are mentioned here."

More than once, a mailing of this nature will find its way into the hands of a feature writer. Then, as I suggested, there may be another article to reprint.

## MAKING BROCHURES FROM REPRINTS

The Walden business manager also told me: "Some professional firms go a step further and make their reprints more elaborate and attractive. There are many ways to do this; adding color and some form of attractive design is perhaps the most obvious. One of our clients, a research engineer, had a feature story about his services in *The New York Times*. Instead of making an unadorned reprint, he printed an attractive two-color folder, with the feature story reprinted inside and the cover of the folder prominently featuring the logotype of the *Times*. Although first printed many years ago, this reprint folder continues to be used year after year as a soft-sell mailing piece and handout for his engineering firm."

In practice as a former podiatrist, I used to reprint articles I had written on foot problems, which were published in trade journals and national magazines. I wrote a lot of them. They covered the whole gamut, the one hundred or so foot troubles that doctors of podiatric medicine treat. I selected perhaps twenty-five articles covering the most common ailments to reprint. They were distributed by my receptionist to patients newly entering my practice. An envelope of articles accompanied by my office policy for patients and services was handed to them for their information and education.

Those foot-care reprints were spread far and wide around the community. My patients often distributed them to friends or relatives as illustrative text describing what they were being treated for. Or, a reprint covering the complaint would be given to somebody who had that problem.

These reprints invariably brought me more patients. I know, because not infrequently, strangers walked into my office for an appointment, carrying the reprints in their hands.

Of course, my former Connecticut colleagues were upset by what they considered "advertising." Handing out literature that I had written just wasn't done, they said. It was condemned as self-aggrandizement, whether the recipients were my patients or not.

The podiatrists became particularly irritated when I took to mailing reprints to patients as a form of appointment recall. Having written an article about almost every foot problem for which there was therapy, it wasn't difficult for me to send the appropriate reprint to a patient who had not had a foot-health checkup for a long time. After all, I knew very well what the person's foot condition was since I had made the diagnosis.

My direct mailing of reprints was an influential way of getting prior patients to reappoint. Other podiatrists outside of Connecticut recognized this as an excellent adjunct to any foot-health public relations program. They saw that it permitted them to rifle-shot their foot-treatment messages to the people they wanted to reach most—their nonreturning patients. Consequently, a lot of podiatrists reprinted quantities of my pieces. Today, I do it for them!

Actually, I have to do it for them, since I have permission to reprint, and they do not. Reproducing a magazine article without the publisher's permission is a violation of copyright law. It's usual to acquire the publisher's agreement in writing before making a reprint for public distribution.

## Don't Forget Unpublished Articles

Transforming *un*published articles into attractive brochures is something to be considered, too. I have a recommendation for salvaging your words of wisdom from bygone times. Look over the unpublished pieces you have stored in the attic and self-publish them as descriptive brochures. Perhaps they weren't good enough for payment and publication in a magazine, but they may be just right for distribution to your own clients or patients.

The differences between reprinting a feature magazine article and producing your own brochure are twofold:

First, a piece published in a magazine under the aegis of an editor has its control taken out of your hands. The editor decides what the article should say and how it must be written, in most cases. Printing your own brochure, you take over total control of the text. You're exactly on target with the information you want disseminated.

Second, a magazine offers wide distribution of your message although maybe not to the immediate audience with whom you wish to speak. The brochure, on the other hand, targets directly on the prospects for your services. (True, it does not give you anywhere near the same kind of broad distribution.)

My five tips for self-publishing brochures that produce impact include the following:

1. Publish information that talks about matters considered important by prospects for your services. Don't discuss what interests you alone. Check your files and see the sort of problems that bring people to you seeking help. These are the items they want to have explained.

2. Keep your descriptions short, clear, and precise. Make one word do the job of three. Absolutely avoid professional jargon. Speak plain English in print.

3. Make your brochure look different from anything used by competitors. Have it designed by a professional in the printing field. Include illustrations. Remember that an excellent piece of educational literature is your personal image builder. It is a messenger that recruits prospects and sometimes turns them into consumers of your services.

4. A good design technique is to use large type. Write in short blocks of copy. Put captions under photographs or drawings you've included, and employ these illustrations as often as is reasonable.

5. Realize that the physical appearance of your brochure is going to give an impression, at least at first, of the kind of services you dispense. Don't be skimpy about the paper quality, the artwork, the logotype, the typography, the print, the size, or the number of pages. Try to have this com-

municating piece of print establish the style or personality of your practice. Don't let it create more confusion than enlightenment.

## PRINTING AND HANDLING YOUR LITERATURE

If you're going to be your own publisher and mailing service, certain mechanics can save wasted money, time, effort, and emotional stress. Nothing is more upsetting than to put your whole self into a promotional piece and have it arrive from the printer for mailing, filled with errors. A little knowledge of type measurement, format, type style, illustrations, printing rates, bulk mailing rates, and other aspects of publishing will prevent frequent frustrations.

Type is set by machine today, and you can choose a type style from books the printer has on hand. He should offer advice, show you samples, and help you choose. The type selected, remember, may become part of your image —a logotype—that people will immediately recognize as representing your office. Type size will provide easy or difficult reading: I recommend that you not go below 12-point type, even though it takes up more space. It's better to write less and print larger for easier reading.

The printer will also have a paper selection. Your paper may also become your logo—try to print on a quality texture, finish, good weight, and grain.

The printer becomes an all-important person in the life of a publisher. His skill and cooperation determine whether the publisher's job will be tough or easy. You'll be looking for a printer who can attain the "unattainable triad," price, speed, and quality, in the same production job.

How do you find such a printer? Sometimes you can trace the printer of a particularly attractive piece of printed matter you have seen. Or, you might want to get competitive bids from reliable suppliers. In any event, seek out a firm which for one reason or another is willing to do the work at less than standard rates but at higher than standard quality. A skilled production specialist can get top quality at a reasonably low price. Speed may or may not be sacrificed. The quality printer will cut his price to take a job that can be done in spare time, and this means that he can't be rushed.

Selecting from a Yellow Pages list of printers without knowing their production quality and pricing is risky. Would you choose your doctor or lawyer this way?

Get quotes from a few printers, remembering that rates may change quickly. Inflation, the ever higher costs of paper, different paper qualities, the format of your job, the typographic qualifications, the printer's overhead, the number of pieces, the number of illustrations, and a dozen other factors determine a job's quoted rates.

209

The printer will help you with design or do the designing himself for a fee. Only you know your talent in that more artistic area. The price of a design may cost from $25 to $100, or the printer may throw it in as part of the job. Design, of course, means layout and paste-up. See the section on advertising for more information on this subject.

Don't mail your brochures, articles, newsletters, press releases, or press conference invitations by first-class mail—it's too expensive. Instead, acquire a bulk mailing permit at the beginning of the calendar year; it enables you to mail your material for the next twelve months at the lower, third-class rate.

Third-class bulk mailing demands that you pay an annual fee of $40 for permission to pay postage of only 8.4 cents per piece, provided at least 200 pieces are mailed. For fewer pieces, you'll have to resort to first class. Furthermore, you're asked to use a postage meter for third-class bulk mailing rate, or you'll have to pay another fee.

Without a meter, you must get a permit number for a one-time fee of $30. The permit, therefore, will cost the annual filing fee for bulk mailing of $40 and the permit number fee of $30, a total of $70. This will give you the opportunity to show your envelope saying: *Bulk Rate U.S. Postage Paid (city name) Permit Number. . . .* All bulk mailings will cost you just 8.4 cents per piece for the year thereafter.

I have some recommendations for handling direct mailings that I've culled from the Addressograph Multigraph Corporation, Pitney Bowes, Inc., and *Boardroom Reports:*

- If the piece is not representative of your best image, don't handle it.
- Monitor your mailing list and delete obsolete names.
- Attempt the lightest weight mailing possible.
- Check your scale's accuracy.
- Mark the class of mail plainly.
- Use postage meters if you can.

For two directories that show mailing services and list supply companies refer to *The Reporter of Direct Mail Advertising* and the *Directory of Mailing List Houses.* In them you may find a mailing service that will do your mail handling for you.

## THE ALL-IMPORTANT NEWSLETTER

There's an even better way of keeping lines of communication open with consumers who have used your services once or twice and may want to use them again. A simplified newsletter, which serves no other purpose than to keep your patients or clients informed, is a superb means of keeping in contact. The newsletter should be just that—a four-page letter filled with *news!* Let there be no commercialism involved. Have it tell the latest developments taking place in your professional field, especially as those developments affect the consumer.

This steady form of patron communication will keep your name and services in front of people. Furthermore, by reporting the latest trends in your profession, you may open new avenues of interest for your services.

If you're imaginative, you won't find yourself lacking information to fill a newsletter. Material may be gathered from professional journals, intra-professional bulletins, newspapers sent from product and service suppliers, convention and meeting handouts, and other professional sources. You can also write your own editorials.

Indeed, some syndicated services write newsletters for the professions specifically to give out to clients or patients.

One of the companies that do so is Newsletters Unlimited, The Newsletter Clearinghouse, operated by Howard Penn Hudson. He handles part or all aspects of newsletters, from creating them for you to mailing them for you. Contact Hudson at 44 West Market Street, Rhinebeck, NY 12572; telephone (914) 876–2081. Get costs quoted directly from him.

The *Standard Directory of Newsletters* lists more than 6,000 newsletters in 200 categories. You'll be able to select the format you wish from seeing some of them, but none are free newsletters or house organs of the type you may wish to publish for clients. To see samples of these check the *Gebbie House Magazine Directory.*

Not only that, there is a *Newsletter on Newsletters* available for $36 a year. It's published by Thomas Gilgut, Jr., Wynkoop Lane, P.O. Box 128, Rhinebeck, NY 12572; telephone (914) 876–2713.

If you produce your own newsletter, paying the costs of design, artwork, printing, folding, etc., you will spend in the vicinity of $140 for 1,000 copies of a four-page edition, not including postage and the envelopes you may stuff it into.

Martin Rosenfeld, an independent career agent—a life underwriter—working out of the White Plains, New York, insurance offices of Bernard Mayer and Marvin Meyer Associates, makes use of the services of a newsletter syndicate. The syndicate is a central clearinghouse of financial information that gets published as newsletters for insurance, banking, and brokerage distribution.

Rosenfeld's firm dictates the newsletter's format and edits its content. In an interview, the life underwriter explained what he wants in his newsletter.

"We try to include items of interest to our clientele such as current tax laws, new court decisions, social security provisions, financial legislation, and other topics relating to financial advising, in general," says Rosenfeld. "We send it monthly to clients, counselors, accountants, attorneys, bank trust officers, and other professional advisers. We hope to gain prestige, awareness of our firm, and referrals to us for insurance services and other financial services."

The newsletter I receive from Rosenfeld is printed on a rich-looking, off-white bond paper of fine quality with navy blue ink. Mailed first class, it has a clean format with a lot of white space and contains the Bernard Mayer Associates location and phone number. While Rosenfeld adapts the editorial matter to his clients' needs, the back of the four-pager does contain a disclaimer that says:

> This publication is issued with the understanding that we are not engaged in rendering legal, accounting, or other similar professional services. The services of a competent attorney should be sought in connection with any legal or tax problems covered by this publication, and your accountant and trust officer should also be consulted on pertinent matters.
> Filed NASD [National Association of Security Dealers]. In the opinion of counsel, this publication complies with the SEC statement of policy.
> If you have friends to whom this publication would be of interest, we would be glad to make a subscription available to them with our compliments.

One more thing, your production of the newsletter is an event by itself. It's worth publicizing. Certainly send your newsletter to editors of appropriate publications. Perhaps a wire service writer or freelance writer could get some feature material out of it and give you credit as a result of its use. Some professional people merchandise their newsletters to the press by sending out news releases on the contents of each new newsletter edition. This practice engenders curiosity and requests come in from editors to see the whole newsletter—a valuable contact for inducing a bigger story.

## YOUR "SUBSCRIBER LIST"

When you distribute your professional message through print or broadcast media, by paid advertising or free publicity, you can be reasonably certain that a sizable percentage of your potential audience will neither read nor listen to your presentation, much less actually come to you seeking your services. However, when you choose to send your professional story by mail, messenger, or telephone, you can exercise greater selection and control.

By carefully picking the names on your list, you can do a test mailing and reduce the risk of wasting time, money, and effort.

Sending to a broader list, you can direct your brochure, reprint, or newsletter to particular individuals and make them true prospects for the services you have to dispense. There is very little guesswork with direct-mail solicitation.

In fact, it's a form of promotion that is unique because it eliminates most waste circulation. Direct mail can accomplish a specific objective to achieve a designated purpose. It is the most effective, inexpensive, and practical form of promotion if you have a clear definition of your market and know how to target on it.

Consumers respond to direct mail most enthusiastically, since it:

- Creates the opportunity for telephone follow-up by your office personnel
- Brings the prospect to you with an inquiry
- Delivers background or educational material to present to clients or patients
- Solicits return responses by enclosing a survey form
- Permits you to conduct professional research by means of surveys and questionnaires made among consumers of your services

The benefits of well-prepared reprints, brochures, and newsletters are easily stated. These benifits are:

- *Good personal calls,* on paper, to prospects and patrons
- *More economical,* relative to person-hours spent, than other forms of promotion
- *Extremely efficient* in getting across the particular message you wish to impart
- *Attention-getting;* they call for action from the client or patient. Recipients may throw away your mailing piece, but before doing so, they will have gotten your message and have it planted in their subconscious
- *Able to create a demand* for your services
- *Enlightening* as to how consumers can increase their application of your talents
- *Stimulative* of new-prospect contacts among those who had not heard of you previously

- *Keep your mailing list accurate* and up to date. Wrong addressing sees your direct mail returned

To receive these benefits from distributing educational literature by direct mail, this is what you should do:

- Dispense a service in demand by the people on your mailing list.
- Develop the most attractive proposition possible: in price, payment terms, and quality of service.
- Provide a mailing piece with impact by having it pleasing to the eye and meaningful to the mind.
- Present your story with sincerity, believability, and simplicity.
- Compose your mailing list of definite prospects for your professional services, or key people in a position to refer others.
- Test the mailing on a small group before sending it out wholesale to a large one.
- Time the arrival of the mailing piece to a favorable period as described in chapter 5.
- Offer to answer questions on anything that arises from the prospect's reading of your literature.

# 15

# Your Own Broadcast Show

*Television is now so desperately hungry for material that they're scraping the top of the barrel.*

*—Gore Vidal, July 20, 1955*

*. . . I hate television, I hate it as much as peanuts. But I can't stop eating peanuts.*

*—Orson Welles,* New York Herald Tribune, *October 12, 1956*

A lot of the same approaches used for the print media work for the broadcast media when you're attempting to get free promotion over the airwaves. The broadcast media, that is, radio and television stations, are more oriented to solicitation by personal contact than they are to impersonal letters. Thus it often is possible to get an appointment for a radio or television interview program by means of a telephone call or an in-person visit. This chapter will describe the technique for getting invited as a talk-show guest on the broadcast media.

Radio and television stations use the "talk" format, which refers to all kinds and styles of content: hard news, telephone conversations, play-by-play sports, editorials, serious interviews with prominent persons, and informal interviews with passersby. Many radio stations program talk during the daytime and shift to music through the night; other stations program in just the opposite patterns.

As a person who provides serious professional services, you would want to be part of a dignified interview program, day or night. Studies have shown that the viewer or listener to talk programs, once involved, gives closer attention to what comes over the receiver than does the listener to music. Listening to serious talk that imparts valuable information is akin to attending educational classes. Rather than sitting in a classroom, however, the listener's knowledge is gleaned in the comfort of his own living room or in the captured environment of automobile travel. Broadcasting, therefore, is a worthwhile undertaking for any promotionally-minded learned professionals who want to inform consumers of their specialized training.

Suppose you get it—appear on the broadcast—and turn out to be a big hit. You experience an influx of clients or patients, and the station receives much positive feedback. The station manager or the program producer lets you know of your success. What do you do then? Make the attempt to get on the same show again, of course.

Perhaps you aspire to have your own program on local radio or television. You can do that, too—with a little luck and a lot of persistence.

On the pages that follow, you will learn how to acquire your own broadcast show or how to manage guest appearances on a regular basis. A lot of people who provide professional services back at the office also are important national or regional figures in the glamorous field of broadcasting.

## GETTING ON RADIO AND TV

How do you get invited to appear on radio and television in the first place? The procedure is less difficult than imagined. There are probably a lot of programs you would like to appear on as a guest expert. Choose your desired program. Then call the program producer or the person whose sole function is to book the program's guests if it's a major show. For a lesser show, it may be the individual interviewer whom you should talk with.

How do you know who it is? Two ways: check the credits broadcast at the end of the program. If there are none, go to one of several directories available that contain this information. A good reference source for television programs is *TV Publicity Outlets-Nationwide,* published by Harold D. Hansen. It's a loose-leaf binder crammed with information about twelve hundred television programs, with revisions made twice a year. For radio, see the *National Radio Publicity Directory,* Peter Glenn Publications. It has over two thousand interview programs described and gets updated every six months as well. Possibly find these in your municipal library, or you might have access to them at a public relations agency.

Even better than a telephone call is your personal visit to the program producer for a discussion and demonstration of your value as a guest. Bring your credentials in the form of a resume, exhibits, press notices, any books that you've written, and other items. Be yourself—but without overdoing it; project wit, charm, and a winning personality. These are the characteristics looked for in broadcast guests. You don't have to be attractive to the eye, but this helps, too.

The afternoon of October 12, 1978, I taped a segment of "The Joey Adams Show" heard over radio station WEVD in New York City. Our discussion centered around my new book, co-authored with Abram Hoffer, M.D., Ph.D., *Orthomolecular Nutrition: New Lifestyle for Super Good Health* (Keats Publishing, 1978). It describes no-junk nutrition and supplementing your diet with vitamins and minerals. Joey Adams's program producer, Sharon Nichols, suggested that this would also be an excellent topic for the "Gary Null Show" on WMCA. The WMCA radio station was just two blocks away from where we were speaking together. Nichols told me whom to see over there, and I decided to give it a try.

Adria Isenmeyer, Gary Null's program producer, listened to my pitch, evaluated my personality as I spoke, took my credentials, and said she would let me know if I might appear. Two weeks later, I received her telephone invitation to be a guest for one hour of the program's two-hour time period. On December 7, 1978, on the "Gary Null Show," I gathered some excellent prepublication publicity for one of my newest books, *Total Health: The Holistic Alternative to Traditional Medicine* (Everest House, 1979). Gary and Adria have since invited me to return for additional appearances.

Another way to get on radio and television is to follow the direction taken by Marshall Mandell, M.D., an allergist practicing in Norwalk, Connecticut. Among other talk-format programs, Dr. Mandell wanted to appear on the "Sherrye Henry Show" broadcast daily over WOR-Radio, New York. Along with a letter of explanation, he sent Henry a quantity of his published articles reprinted from medical journals. His is a unique treatment approach for counteracting patients' allergies of an environmental nature. He uses methods of clinical ecology and is one of only two hundred practitioners in the country utilizing this new science.

After a week elapsed, an interval in which Sherrye Henry or her producer had an opportunity to look over his material, Mandell telephoned. It was just the right time because he got the invitation to appear. Mandell has since written a recently published book on clinical ecology called *Dr. Mandell's 5-Day Allergy Relief System.* He is quite promotion-oriented, for he understands that good publicity is the way to popularize his medical specialty. "I'm after exposure," he told me. "It's the only way to inform the masses about the science of clinical ecology. Publicity is the best way to spread my message."

Mandell had chosen the correct hour to make his telephone call. The radio and television people who book guests tend to be more harassed at certain times of the day. This harassment is not necessarily the hour when the program is about to go on the air, as many programs are taped. Consequently, you should choose your times for producer contact, in person or by telephone. A way to do this is to check with the station and find out if the producer can be disturbed. Honestly declare yourself as a potential guest who has an entertaining and educational message that would go well over the airwaves.

## Press Agents Can Help

Marc Lemshen, a New York orthodontist, turned to publicist Bambe Levine to help get public exposure for a vital message he wishes to share. Dr. Lemshen has a practice consisting of 50 percent adult patients, and he wants people to know about getting their teeth aligned even in later life.

"He is not your typical doctor in that he is very modest," Bambe Levine told me. "Many doctors have enormous egos and think you're going to get them on the Johnny Carson show right off. They also want to build their practices or get in the various 'People' columns. Perhaps their mothers wanted them to be doctors so badly that they never had time to play. Other doctors really think their lives are more fascinating than ours, and the world should know this fact.

"Dr. Lemshen is not like this. He believes he has a real medical story to tell. He wants to explain to the adult world that it is possible to straighten crooked teeth if this problem has been neglected in childhood."

The first thing Bambe did was figure out a technique of getting to Lemshen's target audience. She interviewed him for several hours—asked every conceivable question concerning the practice of orthodontics in general and Lemshen's procedures in particular.

The publicist went on to do independent research. Putting this together with Lemshen's transcribed interview, she wrote a four-page press release. In it were included some human interest case studies. She showed Lemshen's skill as an orthodontist by describing how he solved dental problems.

This release was sent out over a broad media market, accompanied by an exceedingly well-written pitch letter, which closed with the statement: "I will call you in a few days to determine your interest."

Some newspaper editors, radio commentators, television programmers, magazine writers, and the wire services picked up immediately on Levine's extra pitch when she made the follow-up telephone calls. She got her client interviewed on WOR-TV, a WOR-Radio feature-beeper show (a broadcast telephone interview), and on "Eyewitness News" television, "Good Morning America" television, WHN-Radio, WNEW-Radio, "The Bob Grant Radio Show," and other broadcast media.

Of course, Lemshen received much coverage in the print media, as well. For example, *New York* and *Cosmopolitan* magazines prepared articles featuring his orthodontic techniques. *Family Health* has commissioned him to write two articles: one on the psychological aspects of wearing braces on teeth, the other on cosmetic dentistry. The latter is a thousand-word story that's part of a column called, "Ask Your Dentist."

A press agent does more than just send press releases and book programs. He or she must spend a lot of time in following up the mailing. The booking is scheduled, and the professional person must be informed.

In the case of Howard Bellin, M.D., of New York City, Bambe Levine managed to get "Midday Live" to do a live-remote television broadcast of him performing a facial operation. Dr. Bellin is head of plastic surgery at Mother Cabrini Hospital in Manhattan. Bellin's patient was quite willing to appear on camera before, during, and a few weeks after the surgical procedure, to show the excellent result of the facial procedure.

The publicist also put together a lively debate on radio between two of her physician clients. It is legal and acceptable for ophthalmologists to do plastic surgery for the removal of skin pockets under the eyes. Norman Stahl, M.D., of Brooklyn, New York, the inventor of an operation for interocular lens implantations, for which he wanted publicity, does this plastic facial procedure, too. Bambe Levine pinned together ophthalmologist Stahl and plastic surgeon Bellin in a "two-for-one" client appearance that proved quite successful. They argued the greater skill and worthiness of their separate professions to perform the plastic surgery on sagging eye pockets. They vied for the same consumer dollar and made a big hit over the radio.

I suggest that your reading of chapter 17 will give you a great deal of information on how to use the full range of press-agent services. They are more extensive in scope than most people imagine.

## BECOMING A REGULAR GUEST

On August 24, 1978, my wife and I were making a guest appearance on WSB-TV in Hartford, Connecticut. We were to be interviewed live on "Newsday," a news and features television program. One of the guests with us was Ralph Nader's sister, and the other one was Hubert "Hoppy" Hopkinson, D.V.M., who is director of the West Hartford, Connecticut, Veterinarian Clinic. The veterinarian was interviewed just before us and went on camera accompanied by a cockatoo, a Siamese cat, a skunk, and a gerbil. He discussed these animals and described them as making excellent pets. It was an adorable, lively, and entertaining segment of the television program.

Afterwards, "Dr. Hoppy," as the veterinarian has been nicknamed by his clinic staff, his clients, and the TV station people, drove Joan and me to a nearby restaurant where we were meeting friends for lunch. On the way, he told us that such media appearances were usual occurrences for him. His guest spots take place regularly on Hartford's "Newsday"—about every eight weeks. He has appeared six times and always gets an enthusiastic audience response.

"Yes, I do receive some patients from my TV appearances," Hopkinson said, "but more amazing are the telephone calls. Even those people who have their own veterinarians ask me for advice about their pets. I do what I can to help with suggestions, and animal patients are taken to various veterinary clinics for follow-up care."

"Dr. Hoppy" has a winning way! He is warm, outgoing, obviously concerned, loving of pets, and courteous to their owners. His personality comes across on the television screen similar to the way the writings of James Herriot grab hold of your heartstrings. Herriot is the British veterinarian who wrote *All Things Wise and Wonderful* and other best-selling books that express love and compassion for all animals.

How can you become a regular guest? It's not easy! Persistence and charm are the keys. Perhaps a look at the *modus operandi* of psychologist Wayne Dyer will give you a hint.

You may know that Dr. Dyer wrote a best-selling book, *Your Erroneous Zones.* His publisher, Lew Gillenson, was also my publisher for *Total Health: The Holistic Alternative to Traditional Medicine.* Gillenson told me how Dyer opened doors for himself long before his book was known—in fact, Dyer is largely responsible for the popularity of his book. He became a one-person public relations campaign and became a regular guest on national television and radio shows, on the lecture circuit. Thousands of people pay to hear him at Carnegie Hall. He has written a second best seller, and now he has his own nationally syndicated television show: He has become the psychologist to millions.

Gillenson said he had not realized at first that Dyer's book was so valuable. Only about 5,000 books were shipped to the stores. But the psychologist applied his professional knowledge to turn people on to him. "His attractive, interesting, incredibly energetic, charming, mesmerizing personality, plus his dedication—even to quitting his job in the psychology department of St. John's University and going out on the road in his station wagon full of books with his wife and dog—put the book on the best seller list and the author in the category of millionaire," said Gillenson.

The publisher put up $50 a day for the first month of Dyer's tour. Within two weeks they were out of books in Cleveland. He received invitations to appear as a regular guest on numerous TV and radio shows. It happened strictly because of his pleasing personality and the common sense he espoused. He had a message people wanted to hear.

Running out of adjectives to describe the tall, easy-going, likeable man, Gillenson finally described him as "a strange cat, who can walk into local newspapers and local radio stations and be just so nice ('I'd like to tell you my story . . .') that all America was curious to meet him. He was all over the women's pages in every newspaper all across the country," said the publisher. He's become the male Joyce Brothers.

To become a regular guest, therefore, you have to use tact, charm, perseverance, friendliness, and verbosity. And you must have something important to offer. These winning characteristics in an appointment with a program producer will get you your first guest appearance. The rest is dependent on your finding the opening to use your winning ways. Thus, it's not so much who you know or what you know, but how you apply some personality attributes. These may be yours naturally or you can cultivate them. It's strictly up to you.

## PRODUCING YOUR OWN SHOW

The economic necessity for station specialization and the need for a different image may open an entry for your own talk program on radio or television. The 1978 issue of *Broadcasting Yearbook,* which is the electronic counterpart of *Editor & Publisher,* lists more than two hundred stations in large and small markets, which program some form of talk as a major portion or as *all* of their daily schedule. You may be able to produce your own broadcast show on one of these stations, or create the demand for it in your local community. Your program might become good enough to be syndicated.

In 1975, there were 107 AM radio channels available on standard broadcast frequencies assigned to 4,483 stations. On FM, 100 channels are open to 1,098 FM radio stations. Surely with all the needed programming of these many stations, you have a chance to produce your own program. But how do you do it? What do you need? Byron G. Wells, a veteran radio executive, advises:

> You're going to need many things before you even get close to going on the air—things like aspirin, money, aspirin, patience, aspirin, money . . .
>     After a while, if your programming is good, if the advertising comes in, and if you get a few lucky breaks, the show may start to pay.[1]

To persuade a program director to take you on as a talent, there are at least five items that have to be in your inventory of characteristics:

1. *Your program theme.* This is probably the easiest characteristic to acquire, since it will come out of your professional expertise. You know

221

already what the lay person requires. Your knowledge can fill that need.

2. *Your camera or microphone poise.* The ability to act with poise comes with confidence in yourself and mastery of your subject. The American psychologist and philosopher, William James, described poise before there were cameras or microphones to have poise in front of. He said, "Action seems to follow feeling, but really action and feeling go together; and by regulating the action, which is under the more direct control of the will, we can indirectly regulate the feeling, which is not.

"Thus the sovereign voluntary path to cheerfulness, if our spontaneous cheerfulness be lost, is to sit up cheerfully and to act and speak as if cheerfulness were already there. If such conduct does not make you feel cheerful, nothing else on that occasion can.

"So, to feel brave, act as if we were brave, use all of our will to that end, and a courage-fit will very likely replace the fit of fear."

3. *Your ability to sell show time.* Commercials have paid the way for broadcasting since 1922, when WEAF in New York aired the first advertising message as a source of revenue. This is true for commercial radio and television today, except for cable and pay television. You may be the talent, but not infrequently you are the time salesperson, as well. Your program has to pay the station to have it continue on the air.

4. *Your ability to stand up well in the ratings.* As a program producer and talent, you're open to be rated against other shows on other stations in similar time slots. How will you stand up to those ratings? You have to hold your audience and provide the medium for your advertisers to sell more goods and services. It's something different from merely selling your own professional services.

5. *Your program's viewer value.* While it's true that radio and television are glamour media, they should have educational value, too. When he was chairman of the Federal Communications Commission, Newton Minow, in speaking of television programming, said: ". . . You will observe a vast wasteland." Any station, whether it's making money on your program or not, will want your broadcast to have value of content for its listeners or viewers.

All of these attributes have to be part of your presentation when you attempt to produce your own broadcast show. You must sell yourself! You may be able to display such characteristics by means of an audition. Or, you may make such a hit and get vast audience response by appearing initially as a guest on some other show. It depends solely on the talent hidden within yourself.

I appeared as a guest expert on a talk show over Radio Station WSTC in Stamford, Connecticut, during the spring of 1964. It was about six months before my book on foot health was published. Listener response to the program was voluminous. I spoke on patient self-help for all kinds of foot problems, and listeners jammed the station's phones with questions. Jay Johnson, the radio personality who conducted the show, asked me to return for a repeat performance. He had requested my guest appearance initially because I had relieved his wife of the same sort of foot troubles I later spoke about over the air.

The next month, with listenership increased as a result of Johnson's advance promotion by "promos," repeated announcements over the air, the number of calls were even greater. The station manager, Julian Schwartz, took note of his station's overloaded switchboard. He asked Johnson to invite me again.

After the following month's guest spot, Schwartz called me into his office and quizzed me about my acumen with broadcasting. In fact, I didn't realize I had any. I was just answering questions on foot health that I thought people had a vital interest in. Both circumstances were true! People were anxious for information, and I had communicative skill to give it to them.

Schwartz said I could have my own five-minute weekly program if I would get a sponsor to pay for the time. I approached a shoe store owner on the subject. He thought it was a superb idea to buy commercial time on a foot-health program.

In a couple of months, other advertisers lined up for sixty-second commercial spots on my show. Schwartz gave me five five-minute time allotments, one for each working day. Then the publicity from my newly published *Your Guide to Foot Health* broke, and my radio show *really* became popular. As the number of sponsors grew and letters from listeners piled into my postal box at the station, it was essential to furnish me with additional air time. The Federal Communications Commission wouldn't allow more than one sponsor for each five minutes of programming. My show, therefore, increased in length and in number of days steadily, until I was on WSTC-AM for fifteen minutes a day, six days a week. This continued for five years. Of course, my practice grew enormously. I felt myself really reaching people with my foot-care messages. It gave me tremendous satisfaction to know that my advice had value and my words carried weight. I found myself enjoying mass communication more and one-to-one podiatry practice less.

My professional colleagues in Stamford and environs hated every minute of my daily broadcasts. They complained to the Federal Communications Commission, to the Connecticut Podiatry Association, to the Connecticut State Board of Examiners in Podiatry, and to the radio station manager.

One of them frequently followed me around on Wednesdays, which was my usual day off from practice. It was the only opportunity I had to visit sponsors to get their commercial changes. Sometimes, I wrote their messages. I didn't broadcast the commercials myself. A female announcer was hired to do that.

The podiatrist who followed me asked the advertisers not to sponsor my programs, and some did drop their spots. They explained that they didn't want to offend anybody in Stamford.

Another former colleague had his cousin tape-record my programs every day. The podiatrist listened to a week's quantity of tapes for anything unprofessional, unethical, incorrect in treatment, or self-aggrandizing that I might say. After five years—more than 1,500 programs—he finally was able to bring to the Connecticut Podiatry Association, the recording of my voice saying that some of its members were archaic in their thinking. I had been referring to the fact that self-help information is held back from a foot suffering public. As a group, the professional association officers brought charges against me before the State Board of Podiatry Examiners. They sent letters indicating this fact to Julian Schwartz. His reaction was to take me off the air, even though he was loath to lose revenue and listeners for the station.

It was after this blow that I actually left the practice of podiatric medicine, although I had prepared for the event nearly two years before.

## SYNDICATING YOUR PROGRAM

An independent station needs to produce or procure at least 5,064 hours of programming a year. It isn't physically or economically possible for the independent, in either radio or television, to create that much talent time. Each month, the station requires approximately 370 hours of videotape or audiotape programming that it purchases or gets free from outside sources. It operates about fourteen hours a day, or almost 422 hours per month. The networks and syndicates supply the extra programming, besides what is performed live at the station.

While the network with which the local station is affiliated supplies much of the broadcast material, the stations also buy "off-network" programs. The sale and distribution of "off-network" talent is provided by syndication companies. Through careful selection, a station even in the remotest part of the country can present outstanding talent.

A syndication company may be a giant such as Fred A. Niles Communications Centers, Inc., in New York City, or a one-person operation such as Helen Hall Productions, also in New York. You, too, can syndicate your own program and become a talent company. You might try what Helen Hall has done.

Now in her tenth year of successful nationwide syndication to five hundred radio stations each month, Helen Hall has broken her program away from Fred A. Niles Communications Centers and formed her own firm. She has hired a staff of three assistants to produce a worthwhile show. Helen gives coverage of theater, books, fashion, special events, and interviews with celebrities and other newsworthy personalities. The whole program runs three minutes in a magazine concept.

The taped commentaries are made for individual stations, to program one each weekday, or as inserts with news, or at the end of usual programming when there is a time gap. Her three-minute inserts are similar to the fillers at the end of a story on a newspaper page when white space is left over.

"The Helen Hall Show" goes out on two twelve-inch discs (records) each month. There are six programs "cut" to a side. An accompanying "cue sheet" tells the station who is the guest on each cut of the disk. The station, in turn, sends Helen comments about what sort of guests it would like to hear in the future. Payment is derived from sponsors who record "editorial features" about products, services, points of view, and other public relations messages. It is an open presentation and not subliminal.

Off-network syndicated programs on television and radio have found favor with many audiences around the country. Syndication is available to anyone with time, patience, money, and talent enough to stick it out until he or she gets well established. Then the program carries itself as a feature in demand. Perhaps this is a broadcasting technique you would want to try for yourself. It affords publicity and an eventual financial return.

# 16

# Special Events
# and Speaking Engagements

*Fill your mouth with marbles and make a speech. Every day, reduce
the number of marbles in your mouth and make a speech. You will
become an accredited public speaker—as soon as you have lost all your
marbles.*

—*Brooks Hays,* New York Herald Tribune, *June 15, 1960*

Enough has been said in many other books and by other people about
community relations for purposes of public relations. It's too basic, too
elementary for this particular book. You should make community activity
one of the first orders of business before opening yourself to other forms of
promotion. I'm going to drop the subject now, expecting that you know
something about it already. This chapter has much to say instead about
taking part in special events and accepting speaking engagements. What
you do to improve your community is the obligation of any civic-minded
citizen.

## BECOMING KNOWN

Problems you confront in gaining public awareness and acceptance of the
services you render can be overcome in part by performing unselfish acts
in the community interest. Your aim, ultimately, is to become a "thought
leader" in the city, town, village, neighborhood, or other area of influence
—the place where you're selling your services. You may become the one
who proposes the plan to save money on the main boulevard's Christmas
decorations. You could be the person who spearheads the United Fund
drive or puts forth effort to conserve the environment.

In building public relations through community relations, you have to
make it your business to become linked with contributions to community
improvement projects. Lay your effort on the line on behalf of civic and
fraternal activities. The community parent-teacher's association offers excellent opportunities for you to make people aware of your presence.

226

Bond issues, school taxes, local referenda, public works, and other matters call for speaking out by professional persons, you among them. Your work in a civic organization can create the atmosphere that opens the door for an invitation to speak about these matters—and about matters relating to your profession. I will have more to say about speaking engagements for providing the public with professional information a little later in this chapter.

Furthermore, don't overlook the importance of working in your own professional association. Such activity can play a part in the total public relations buildup of your practice. Referrals can come from fellow professionals. And projects of the professional society that you participate in are quite likely to be reported in the local media more than any ordinary civic effort. Editors like to publish reports on the events of professional societies.

Moreover, don't forget that your spouse is a distinctive participant in your community relations. His or her endeavors on behalf of the practice may be momentous. They can be great public relations builders, too.

## THE PUBLICITY REWARDS OF SPECIAL EVENTS

Most news about certain people does not just happen—it is created. The instrument those people use for creating news is the special event, ranging all the way from getting the mayor to make a proclamation to leading a parade, running a contest, opening an exhibit, or something else that lands on the front page. In some way, the project they undertake splashes into the consciousness of the public. The splash is planned—to attract attention. It's an effective ploy to pull in business. Unfailingly, observers of the event are stimulated to action by ideas conveyed by these subtle promoters. The public gets caught up in the dynamic event and moves in the promoters' direction.

This is a smart and honorable way to make people aware of your existence as a vendor of professional services. Not uncommonly, your occupation will be broadcast or remarked on in a reporter's coverage of the event. And to make sure that people know who you are, what you work at, and where you're located, there are measures you can institute to make sure the news gets out.

Robert R. Rinaldi, a podiatrist in Stamford, Connecticut, took steps to make his name known around the whole of Fairfield County. He planned his approach for more than a year, and it paid off handsomely for him and for many of his fellow podiatrists in the state.

Rinaldi volunteered to be chairman of the tenth annual Columbus Day

Road Race that was run in Stamford on Sunday, October 8, 1978. He made the Stamford Running Club the tool of his personal publicity. The club did the work, and Rinaldi got the glory—and a vast new influx of foot patients, especially runners.

For six months before this big event, posters were mounted on walls around the city. Advertisements taking up one-third of a page were run in the city's daily newspaper, and announcements were broadcast over the radio. We have no television station in Stamford, but broadcasts announced the race on other TV programs that I heard about.

The posters and ads announced the Connecticut AAU Fifteen Kilometer (9.4 miles) Championship and Open Road Race. On all the posters, over every broadcast, and in each newspaper ad, Rinaldi had his name, doctorate, and address listed at least twice. His office was the mail drop for the Stamford Running Club. Its members laid out the course, kept records of participants, distributed entry numbers and T-shirts, and performed the other tasks.

The race was jointly sponsored by the Region One of the American Podiatry Association, which includes foot doctors in the six states of New England, and Champion International Corporation. The two organizations put up money for T-shirts and advertising. Also assisting were the local Marriott hotel, the Stamford YMCA, the Stamford Running Club, and the Board of Recreation of the City of Stamford. A half-dozen members of the American Academy of Podiatric Sports Medicine supervised a free "run clinic" before the start of the race, which was excellent publicity for all the podiatrists. I was one of the 444 entrants who attended the clinic, ran the race, and finished it. To me, the event was the classic example of a publicity stunt that brought big dividends for its promoter.

The blustery day of the race, Rinaldi ran the proceedings. While everyone else wore shorts, sweatshirts, and sneakers, he stood out in contrast. Rinaldi dressed his short, pudgy frame in a long, black, sleek leather coat, bell-bottom trousers, chukka boots, and a little peaked, Greek fisherman's cap. The speech he delivered to the crowd of anxious runners was masterful. The radio reporters recorded his remarks. The press photographers crowded around snapping pictures.

The publicity for this road race was fabulous. Several articles and photographs appeared in the newspaper the next day, and radio broadcasts reported the results a number of times. A lot of people raced to be first that cool Columbus Day, and in the end, there actually were two winners. Roger Moffat led the field with a time of 49 minutes, 11 seconds, for the whole distance. And Robert Rinaldi won first place for the quantity of new business brought home to his group podiatry practice.

## THE NUTS AND BOLTS OF STAGED EVENTS

Almost every village and town has its own special occasion when it goes all out to make a whopping success of some staged event. This is a time in your community when you should get into the act and take charge of one of its aspects. Such an event is wonderful for the exposure it affords. Crowds fill the streets or auditorium. People shed their routines and sometimes their inhibitions. They have a universal desire to witness and participate with others in public affairs. There is eagerness of young and old to acquire knowledge, have experiences, and enjoy the pleasures of seeing, hearing, and participating in an exhibition. The crowds, action, lights, color, and motion of a special event are the foundations on which every promoter's dreams are built. My suggestion is that you be a promoter of your cause.

As it was for the Stamford Running Club, it's necessary for you to get the assistance of heads of corporations, clubs, institutions, city departments, and associations. These are the community leaders who can give official sanction to your special event. Get them behind you. The pitches you must throw at them to receive cooperation are the following:

- The event will create goodwill for the particular organization the community leader represents.
- Because of the event, citizens will gain understanding of and enthusiasm for a necessary community project.
- The event will dispel misconceptions in the public's mind—notions that have interfered with progress.
- The event will give people in the community personal contact with their leaders.
- The event will allow taxpayers an opportunity to see their tax money bringing them some joy.

Your pitch to the press to bring in publicity should be made a couple of months in advance of the event. A press conference is the way to deliver the news. Distribute news releases then, giving the event's time, the place, the program features, the purpose, and the names of featured guests. Additionally, distribute releases by mail or in person to all surrounding media. Send along captioned photographs of guests as well. Be sure to include your own picture.

Follow up these publicity pitches a few days before the event with more press releases and photographs, and add information about parking arrangements, refreshments, statements by guest speakers, and a mayoral proclamation. Get your picture taken with the mayor by paying for the photographer if you have to.

Immediately preceding the starting time of your event, give a press preview. Make sure to get in some good quotes of your own.

When there is a media budget supplied to you for the event, place advertising on local radio, on television, and in newspapers. Send out direct-mail invitations. Make sure they're received by the "key" people who sometimes send you referrals. They'll be reminded to send more.

Before leaving the subject of publicity derived from special events, there is one precaution I feel compelled to offer. It's a problem inherent in putting all your eggs in one basket. The eggs can get broken! When an event doesn't work, when hardly anyone shows up, as with the annual Veterans Day celebration in my city, you're left with egg on your face if you've been the primary spark behind setting off the event. Also, you will have wasted an awful lot of valuable time.

So the precaution I am giving is that you evaluate the event before you decide to become associated with it. Think of the hard work, the brainstorming, the releases to write, the people to cajole, the telephone calls to make, the time away from your office, and the many other aspects of loss that may arise from a failed undertaking. Weigh all this against the potential worth of the publicity that comes from running a really fantastic special event. Then decide whether you will or won't participate in full. In summary, only do the tasks for a special event if you're sure it's got an excellent chance of doing well, or if it's simply the best way you can see of getting lots of free publicity.

## SPEAKING ENGAGEMENTS: INVALUABLE CLIENT/PATIENT BUILDERS

In contrast to your appearance before thousands or millions on local or network broadcasting, there is special public relations value in direct, face-to-face contact with prospective clients or patients numbering in the dozens or in the hundreds. Local speechmaking and lecture tours will bring almost immediate results in consumer appointments for your professional services.

And if speeches are effective patron producers, seminars, round tables, and other meetings people pay to attend are even better, if you are a featured speaker. It does not mean that you can turn a seminar into a vociferous sales pitch for your services. It does mean that the audience has a chance to observe you, note your confidence, hear your command of the subject, observe your ability to think quickly, mark your judgment, be convinced of your ready knowledge, experience your pleasing personality, and generally be impressed by other attributes you may possess. The meeting is likely to turn into a self-serving program just because you are an exceedingly competent professional person.

Your acceptance of a speaking engagement will turn out to be a highly effective and the least expensive medium of public relations communication. Your giving a speech informs selected publics about your professional services. It's an assured way to get prospects into your office.

If invitations to speak don't come spontaneously, go after them. Telephone, write, or personally put the arm on the person in charge of programming for the organization that has your targeted audience. Find out the program chairperson by asking a member of the organization. To get invited as a speaker, you must not be shy. Remember, the object is to promote yourself in order to promote more business.

There are all kinds of ways to give oral communication for purposes of public relations. They include lectures, persuasive speeches, round-table conferences, panel discussions, question-and-answer discussions, oral testimony, informal conversation, demonstrations, and dramatizations.

Of them all, formal and informal lectures giving information from your professional specialty are the quickest way to get new business. The response may be so fast that you'll be making appointments on the spot. Lectures educate people at once about what you know, what you do, where you do it, and more. Lecturing is the best way to give out factual information, make announcements, and furnish instruction.

In all that you say, however, never be blatant about your own superiority of services. Instead, turn your attention to the self-interest and emotions of the listeners. Correct misunderstandings, exchange ideas, and where possible during a question-and-answer period, make it a two-way flow of communication. Give the public an opportunity to express its views, discuss grievances, and get educated according to your point of view.

This two-way discourse is the actual method of turning a lecture into a less formal round-table discussion. My recommendation is that you do just that. It's one of the most effective methods of projecting the warmth of your personality and displaying your personal interest to people who might buy your services in the near future.

You can receive professional assistance in perfecting your skills for delivering speeches. To contact one of the many agencies that provide such services, see the heading "Public Speaking Instruction" in your local Yellow Pages.

### The Lecture Circuit

There are plenty of places for an effective speaker to get astounding returns from publicity. You can also get paid for your words. The instrument of your fame and fortune will be a lecture bureau, which does the booking, collects the fees in advance of your scheduled lecture, and splits with you on a fifty-fifty or other equitable commission basis.

Your main job is to carry on research, collect source material, practice an entertaining delivery, and be prepared to go on the road for some heavy dispensing of knowledge.

This chapter is not going to tell you how to perform dramatically in making a speech. You can acquire that skill from a public-speaking school. My aim is to get you thinking in terms of using speaking engagements, including lecture tours, as tools of practice promotion.

Your effectiveness as a public speaker is dependent not only on your ability to deliver the talk in an entertaining way but also on your having something worthwhile and interesting to say. Only you know what the subject must be.

I suggest that you could sign yourself onto the roster of a lecture bureau. Have your interview with the bureau management, give your speech in a scheduled audition, and enter the lecture circuit. Wherever you travel, when you return to the office, patients or clients from those places will have called in advance for appointments. Your waiting list will be long and lucrative. This is the way it is with lecture touring.

The following are national lecture bureaus looking for new talents who will be sent on tour around the country:

Keedick Lecture Bureau, Inc.
Robert Keedick, President
475 Fifth Avenue
New York, NY 10017
(212)683–5627
Also a branch in San Francisco

W. Colston Leigh, Inc.,
1185 Avenue of the Americas
New York, NY 10036
(212)865–8430
Also branches in Chicago and
San Fransisco

The Handley Management
Martin A. Forrest, Director
50 Church Street
Boston, MA 02116
(617)542–2479

American Program Bureau, Inc.
Robert P. Walker, President
850 Boylston Street
Brookline, MA 02167
(617)730–0500

Richard Fulton, Inc.
Richard Fulton, President
850 Seventh Avenue
New York, NY 10019
(212) 582–4099

National Speakers Bureau
John Palmer, Director
222 Wisconsin Avenue
Lake Forest, IL 60045
(312)295–1122

Harry Walker, Inc.
Harry Walker, President
350 Fifth Avenue
New York, NY 10001
(212)563–0700

Public Affairs Lecture Bureau
Ann Weinreb, Director
109 E. 42 Street
New York, NY 10017
(212)679–6050

Lecture bureaus also exist throughout the country, and many are constantly on the lookout for new people who have dynamic messages that will attract large audiences. To contact one of these bureaus, see the heading "Lecture Bureaus" in the Yellow Pages.

Bruce Barton, the famous head of Batten Barton Durstine & Osborn advertising agency, said, "In my library there are over ten thousand volumes of biography. They all tell the same story. More men have achieved success by their ability to speak than through any other skill. Speakers have always ruled the world. The wise thing to do is to join them."[1]

Other than the grueling routine of traveling from one city to the next, the life of a speaker on tour is rather gratifying. You're treated like a celebrity! The late Dave Alber, a well-known press agent, offered the following advice for the treatment of celebrated speakers:

If the celebrity has to use air or railroad transportation, send him his ticket in advance (first class, needless to say—and don't tell him to buy his tickets and you'll reimburse him). Call the celebrity a day or two before the event to remind him. Meet him at the airport or station—in a limousine, not an ordinary car. Take him to the hotel where you've made reservations, then send a responsible representative or go yourself to pick him up. Assure him that you will return him anywhere he wants to go after the event. Tell him what time he is wanted, and make sure that his appearance takes place close to that time—don't have him sitting around for hours waiting to be called on.[2]

Obviously, you don't have to pay your own way. Rather, you do receive a fee ranging from $300 to over $2,000, depending on the part of the country and whether it is a "one-shot" or part of a tour. The fees generally include travel expenses.

The speakers bureau of the American Society of Journalists and Authors,

233

Inc., charges a fee of $350 plus expenses for each of its twenty members who give lectures. I am one of them. My talk on underwater adventure and professional scuba diving brings me sparse income, simply because I prefer not to be away from my desk more than three days out of the month; otherwise, I could be a full-time lecturer on the college circuit. Hundreds of speakers are available including professors and other academics. You can be one, as well, if your professional message has high relevance for an audience. While my speaker's bureau takes just 10 percent commission from my booking fees, most lecture bureaus take more. Some work on a fifty-fifty split with you.

Without question, you have to prepare your own speech and have at least a little experience. The experience may come from speaking to clubs, groups, and service organizations at home. Then you can take your talk on the road. Success comes with good preparation. Follow this formula:

- State your idea.
- Accentuate your idea.
- Illustrate your point.
- Wind up the talk.

Maybe he didn't realize it at the time, but this is the formula used by Lincoln when he delivered the Gettysburg address.

Begin with an anecdote that's relevant to the subject matter and deliver the whole talk within one hour. You may stand still for a question-and-answer period for another twenty minutes. Your job will be done after that.

## YOUR OFFICE IMAGE

What sort of first impression do you make? Is it a professional image that you project?

Step outside the door of your inner office. Go into the reception room, look around, and answer these questions: Is the decor in keeping with a dignified, modern reception area? Are the magazines current? Are your personnel superior representatives of your profession? Do they dress properly and groom themselves well? Have you done everything possible to make your waiting patient or client comfortable? Is there anything you can improve to enhance the first and last impressions your image projects to patrons?

What I'm leading up to is that no matter how capable a professional you are, no matter how much you spend on advertising, in the end you will be judged to some degree on these outward appearances. They make up part of your image. During the time that you are performing your services, you will have the best opportunity to sell yourself and your profession. This includes the time the consumer waits in your reception room.

Passive promotion by methods of professional-practice management and patient/client contact is the most subtle form of public relations. This is a truth that most professional people know, or should know, instinctively. Yet all too often they overlook the significant roles played by such items as office stationery, the telephone manner of a receptionist, the effectiveness of a recall system, the ways bills are collected, and other things. These have a total effect on one's image being projected to the public.

I am not going to linger here on forms of passive promotion employed in the management of a professional practice. All of us realize they leave a lasting impression. Just remember, your image is a reflection of what you are—perhaps more important, of what people think you are. My only suggestion is to enhance this image at every opportunity. With the proper image, and with the inborn and learned skills you possess, you are destined to build your practice and sell yourself in the bargain. Of course, it doesn't hurt to boost one's image with participation in community relations, special-area events, and speaking engagements. They, too, are excellent forms of practice-building promotion.

A last word: When you open your own professional practice office, you have the satisfaction of knowing that your success is entirely due to your own efforts. But you do have full responsibility for the consumers who come for service as well as for the management of the practice. This responsibility may weigh heavily, depriving you of needed rest and vacations, of time with your family, of opportunities to do postgraduate work. You need plenty of stamina because in addition to running your practice, you do have to involve yourself in promotional activities to help build your practice.

For many a professional, opening one's own practice is the culmination of a dream of several years' standing. Still, my last bit of advice in this chapter is to do some personal public relations within yourself. Take stock of your physical, emotional, mental, and spiritual needs, and fill them. Give yourself sufficient time to enjoy living. Nothing is as important as pursuing a healthy life that brings happiness, fulfillment, and joy. Appoint yourself time for those kinds of activities, too, a necessary interval of diversion for continued success.

# 17

# Employing
# a Public Relations Agency

*I have found it [public relations] to be the craft of arranging truths so that people will like you. Public-relations specialists make flower arrangement of the facts, placing them so that the wilted and less attractive petals are hidden by sturdy blooms.*

—*Alan Harrington,* Life in the Crystal Palace, *1959*

The publisher of *Public Relations News,* Denny Griswold, defined the job of a public relations agency. She printed the definition on cards and distributed them throughout the industry, which, incidentally, is evolving into a profession. Griswold wrote: "Public Relations is the management function which evaluates public attitudes, identifies the policies and procedures of an individual or an organization with the public interest, and executes a program of action to earn public understanding and acceptance."

About two hundred thousand men and women in the United States engage in the performance of public relations duties for clients.

The two thousand or more public relations counseling firms in the United States offer a variety of services. A growing number, in fact, have expanded their helpful activities to include professional-association management, graphic arts, advertising, sales promotion, and client representation in projects related to civic, social, cultural, political, educational, and public affairs. Also, they are doing opinion and historical research to use as tools in other tasks. Some are specializing—for example, in financial relations, nonprofit associations, and in the learned professions themselves, now that the Supreme Court has opened this new source of PR clients.

The Education Committee of the Public Relations Society of America has developed eight major job classifications of public relations work. Knowing these classifications will help you to determine how best to use your PR agency. The following is what the public relations agency does to earn its fee:

- *Writing.* Reports, news releases, booklet texts, radio and TV copy, speeches, film sequences, trade-paper and magazine articles, product information, and technical material.
- *Editing.* Employee publications, newsletters, shareholder reports, and other management communications directed to both organization personnel and external groups.
- *Placement.* Contacts with the press, radio, and TV, as well as with magazine, Sunday supplement, and trade editors, with a view to enlisting their interest in publishing an organization's or a client's news and features.
- *Promotion.* Special events, such as press parties, convention exhibits, and special showings; open-house, new-facility, and anniversary celebrations; special day, week, or month observances; contests and award programs; guest relations; institutional movies; visual aids.
- *Speaking.* Appearances before groups and the planning requisite to finding appropriate platforms; preparation of speeches, organization of speakers' bureaus, and the delivery of speeches.
- *Production.* Knowledge of art and layout for the development of brochures, booklets, special reports, photographic communications, and house periodicals.
- *Institutional Advertising.* Advertising a company's or client's name and reputation through purchased space or time. Close coordination with advertising departments is maintained and frequently the advertising-public relations responsibility is a dual one.
- *Programming.* The determination of need, definition of goals, and recommended steps in carrying out the project. This is the highest-level job in public relations, one requiring maturity in counseling management.

Despite the institutional advertising mentioned above, advertising and public relations are distinctly different. While both may be dedicated to selling your image and your services, public relations is an "invisible sell." It is the "engineering of consent" for purposes of building goodwill through the communication of information to the people through various media. Public relations professionals try to effect a two-way formal and informal exchange of ideas between you and your various publics. They aim to mold favorable public opinion on your behalf.

You don't have to do your own public relations. The talents of public relations professionals are at your disposal if you choose to pay for them. Your greatest single advantage of having a public relations counselor in your employ is your opportunity for objectivity. The PR person can stand apart and judge what is best for the building of your image. He or she offers you constructive criticism and then acts on it.

## YOU AND THE PR COUNSELOR

The process of engaging in public relations with an agency includes four basic functions that are furnished by the assigned account executive and his or her group of backup personnel. The PR counselor does the following:

1. *Researches and listens.* The PR account executive probes your opinions, attitudes, and reactions and evaluates the outflow. In effect, he or she determines the problem to be overcome and the obstacles which have prevented this problem from being solved previously.

2. *Plans and decides.* PR counselors chart a course by bringing their ideas to bear on clients' present policies and programs. They may suggest policy changes involving entirely new programs or additions to existing programs. They come to their conclusions strictly objectively and sometimes make difficult decisions.

3. *Communicates and presents.* Public relations professionals explain and dramatize the chosen course first to you and then to your various publics. They lay out the procedures to follow for a viable PR program. They execute the procedures. Then they document what was done.

4. *Evaluates and analyzes.* PR people take all the facts known about the results of a PR program and analyze them. Measurements are made. PR professionals evaluate the public relations value that came from program activities and tell you of the true effectiveness of each of the techniques employed.

The five points to be explained by the PR counselor for any client before, during, and after the process of engaging in a public relations program are:

- The problem
- What we can do
- What we did
- Why we did it
- The results

As a public relations agency client, these explanations are as important for you as the others. In carrying out their functions, PR counselors move steadily forward in the preplanned program. They see it as one whole, continuing process so that your professional-image promotion takes place in the best possible light. This is the objective for the PR counselor and for you, as the client.

## WHERE THE PR AGENCY TAKES YOU

The number of public relations techniques is limited only by the imagination of the PR counselor involved. Some of the more elementary promotional paths your PR agency may have you pursue—with its active assistance—might include the following:

- Establishing a dialogue with local and regional press and editors so that they know of your existence.
- Providing the press with some input (opinion) on news and developments relative to your profession. This is done to assist them in any writing they might be doing on the subject of your profession or on you as the subject.
- Writing articles or opinion pieces on topics of interest relevant to your profession. These should be issues of interest to the population at large.
- Arranging your availability to appear on local and network radio and television, and before groups and organizations when topics related to your profession may be involved. The counselor perhaps will suggest topics to the broadcast media for their airing consideration.
- Joining local organizations, civic groups, social clubs, professional societies, and other associations. The PR person may recommend programs and events where you can make a material contribution and receive recognition for it.
- Arranging your availability to academic institutions in your community such as schools, colleges, business schools, universities, and the like, to lecture, teach, or give of yourself in other ways.
- Offering tours and/or visits to your facilities to give the opportunity for interested persons or groups to sit in on certain aspects of your business and business day.
- Involving you in your community in general and making an effort to be visible. The visibility thus gained will measurably enhance recognition, stature, and lead to an increased tempo in practice development. The objective will always be in the forefront of your PR activities—to enjoy a "presence" substantially above the competition in your field.

239

You, in turn, are expected to keep the PR agency informed of your practice changes, as well as developments in your profession. This will enable your PR counselor to prepare and disseminate news and feature information to the appropriate media.

## A Case Study

In chapters 2 and 6, I described the groundbreaking advertising activities of the Denture Center. The dynamic entrepreneurial dentist behind this clinical facility is M. David Isaak of Jersey City, New Jersey. He runs a dental clinic in Jersey City and two in New York City. Dr. Isaak is not using advertisements as the sole means of developing his practices. Public relations appearances and publicity of all kinds are being integrated into his total promotional program. In fact, in 1979, he is opening eight new centers in Michigan, five more in the New York area, and he is moving into California and Texas. He holds exclusive rights to the name *Denture Center* in sixteen other states. Isaak appears to be the new "Painless Parker" of the 1980s.

I spoke at length with the account executive in charge of Isaak's Denture Center account at Lobsenz-Stevens, Inc., a leading public relations agency in New York City. Charles M. Prins explained that the public relations program undertaken by Lobsenz-Stevens for Dr. Isaak and his denture centers was directed toward:

- Calling media attention to the new dental procedures he developed in which upper and lower dentures can be provided in a single four-hour visit at roughly half the cost an individual practitioner would charge for the same service over a period taking close to eight weeks.
- Establishing Dr. Isaak as a spokesman for the dental profession.
- Reflecting this dentist's views on various subjects dealing with dentistry.
- Projecting him and his work in geographic areas outside the New York metropolitan area.
- Alerting various segments of the population to this practitioner's activities. These segments include corporations, ethnic groups, senior citizens, the indigent, the middle class, and other publics.
- Attracting ultimately more patients to Isaak's services.

Charlie Prins told me: "The Lobsenz-Stevens company believes it has succeeded in elevating public awareness to the Denture Center operations.

Perhaps the best indication that this is so occurred at the end of October 1978 when—as a result of an appearance on the WOR-Radio Bob Grant program—Dr. Isaak received more than five hundred telephone calls from listeners.

"Our media targets for the Denture Center," said Prins, "continue to include publications and electronic media in its immediate geographic area; trade publications and in lay health-care, medical, retirement, business, and science publications; publications reaching opinion leaders and decision makers, as well as the mass media.

"The media response has been highly enthusiastic," Prins continued. "Not only have there been stories on the single-session denture fittings, but also on the fact that Isaak's clinics provide all services—at top quality— at fees far lower than those charged elsewhere. As a result of these media placements, the Denture Center clinics have received several thousand new patients who have been alerted to the dentist's activities."

Isaak has received publicity in major women's magazines, the "in-flight" publications of the various airlines, Sunday supplements of both local and national coverage, the wire services, major newspaper syndicates, major news magazines, family feature pages of major daily newspapers, and travel and leisure-oriented magazines.

In the main, the media interest has been obtained through one-on-one conversations by the Lobsenz-Stevens account executive with editors and radio program producers. In addition, much print material has resulted from the sending out of news releases on Isaak's work that have been reprinted in their entirety.

The public relations efforts have been directed toward building up Dr. M. David Isaak as the "logo" or living representative of a chain of Denture Centers around the United States. The dentist is stressing on his media appearances that just because he has lowered his prices to the public, his is not a "schlock" operation. He provides quality service. Dental ethical codes require that he do this through publicity only, since making this statement in advertisements might place Isaak's license to practice dentistry in jeopardy.

## SELECTING A PUBLIC RELATIONS AGENCY

The usual way to select a public relations agency is by the referral of a satisfied client, the same way most of your consumers come to you. The Counselors Section of the Public Relations Society of America suggests that the following questions be asked by you in selecting an agency:

241

- What is the professional competence and background of the agency's principals?
- How much of this experience has been in areas of importance to your particular professional field?
- Can you see their client list and talk with selected members on that list?
- How long have these clients been served by the agency?
- What is the agency's rate of client turnover?
- What is the agency's general reputation?
- Does the agency adhere to the Public Relations Society Code of Ethics and are your assigned counsel's integrity and professional standing above reproach?
- Who among the agency's principals and staff will be working on your account?
- What are their qualifications, special training, and background as related to your needs?
- Does the agency make speculative presentations—advance programming of your needs at no charge to you?

The PR firm you finally select should not represent a client with conflicting or competing interests to yours, without express consent to do so given by both the competitor and by you. Nothing the counselor learns about you and your business can be disclosed to your disadvantage. A client/counselor relationship of confidentiality must prevail. Keep watch that your agency does not engage in practices that tend to corrupt the integrity of channels of public communication. It could reflect on your own image and produce a bad press, even if the practice is not of your doing or desire.

If you have no source of referral to a public relations agency, help is available in selecting one from at least two places. One is the Public Relations Society of America, 845 Third Avenue, New York, NY 10022. Telephone (212)826–1750. Ask to speak with the person in charge of administration.

You may also contact the International Public Relations Association, 110 William Street, New York, NY 10038. Telephone (212)233–7650.

Of course, you can always try your luck by selecting a PR firm listed in the Yellow Pages of your own city.

## HOW MUCH DO YOU PAY?

More than $3 billion in fees were paid in 1977 to PR counseling firms, not including expenditures for internal corporate departments. Nonprofit institutions also invest in public relations, and their budgets are excluded from the 1977 figure.

One of the rules in the Public Relations Society Code of Ethics is that a PR counsel should not propose to a prospective client that the counsel's fee be contingent on the achievement of certain results. However, there is no accepted standard amount that is charged for public relations.

When I asked Charlie Prins to give me a range of PR fees, he was unable to do so. Prins said, "It wouldn't be fair to anyone even to offer a ballpark figure. It all depends on whether the client wants local exposure or national exposure. The fee could be in the hundreds. It could be in the thousands. The price varies with how much service is expected and what kind of placements are wanted by the client."

Based on my experience and information I've received from a variety of souces, I can supply some ballpark fees charged by public relations agencies. For instance, James O. Stallings, M.D., a plastic surgeon who practices in Des Moines, Iowa, does highly creative and innovative cosmetic and reconstructive work on patients. He hired the Lobsenz-Stevens Public Relations Agency, the firm for whom Charlie Prins works, to help publicize his surgical skill and a book to which he contributed, *The New You,* about plastic surgery. His co-author, Terry Morris, told me that Stallings paid Lobsenz-Stevens $4,000 a month to spread his message. I was called to interview Stallings in January 1977, the year the PR agency had him as a client. My freelance effort was just one of a hundred or more media representations by other writers for the plastic surgeon. Stories about him were published in a couple of dozen national magazines, and many radio and television shows had him as a guest.

Spending $48,000 a year for public relations is not unusual when you go with an agency and want an all-out program. Half the effort naturally costs less of a fee, although probably more than half of $4,000 a month—maybe $2,400, since you have to take into account startup costs of an initial program. Of course, smaller agencies supplying fewer services charge less. You may be able to get away with spending $1,000 a month for a good, consistent, local program undertaken by a public relations firm.

Determining a fee based on a fixed percentage of either sales or profits used to be done, but nowadays this kind of figuring isn't applicable. Advertising, entertaining of consumer referral sources, point-of-sale techniques, and other marketing methods don't permit the client or the counsel to make any allocation of benefit from publicity. Public relations brings too intangible a return.

Public relations counselors will make a determination of your needs and then tell you the cost of employing their services. They decide this based on your specific objectives. First, they make a study of your public relationships, learn of your PR goals, and estimate the cost of the program that finally comes out of these investigations. Because the results are incapable of being anticipated or perceived in any palpable way, you have to go by the firm's past performance for others. That's where those questions recommended by the Counselors Section of the Public Relations Society of America are applicable. You should ask them of the prospective PR counselor.

If the cost of attaining your objective is excessive in relation to the expected benefit to be derived, you might consider a revised objective. Ask for another quote from the counselor predicated on modifications in the program. Realize that compensation of a public relations agency varies with the work to be undertaken, the time involved, and the salary remunerations of the personnel required.

The fee may be established as (a) a fixed monthly retainer, (b) a retainer plus monthly billing for actual time on an hourly or per-diem basis, (c) or a base fee billed monthly, to which are added charges for services performed beyond the retainer. The agency usually bills for out-of-pocket expenses at cost, and the expenses are exclusive of the fee. You may be quoted a single fee on special, short-term projects, and there could be an allowance asked for expenses.

Per-diem rates most often cover the salary of the account executive, along with a share of the overhead. There may be an extra fee to coordinate the salaries of staff specialists working on the assigned project. Added in may be the cost of outside contractors when they have your assignment to fulfill. It takes the skill of a true cost-accounting specialist to figure out a realistic public relations fee to quote the client.

# 18

# Epilogue

*If a man is good in his heart, then he is an ethical member of any group in society. If he is bad in his heart, he is an unethical member. To me, the ethics of medical practice are as simple as that.*

—*AMA President Elmer Hess, M.D.*
American Weekly, *April 24, 1955*

*Those professionals who have spoken out, within and beyond their organizations, have too often been demoted, ostracized, discharged, or suppressed when in fact, they frequently may be heroic figures.*

—*Ralph Nader, January 27, 1971*

We've come to the end of this book—you in reading it and I in writing it. It's time to say a final word about the learned professional's use of advertising and promotion.

Admittedly, there are two criticisms that can be made of these practices now being employed by the person who works in the learned professions.

First, it may be pointed out that advertising campaigns and public relations programs have already cluttered our choked channels of communication. Industry, business, retailers, wholesalers, manufacturers, and other entrepreneurs frequently bury the public under pseudo-events, false bargains, cut prices that are elevated prior to their cutting, phony phrases that confuse rather than clarify, and other nefarious actions dedicated to fooling consumers into purchasing more and more of what they don't want and cannot use. Why add another four million to sixteen million professional practitioners to this burgeoning group of public-message purveyors?

Second, excesses of advertising and promotion have corroded our communication channels with cynicism and "credibility gaps." We have become a public of nonbelievers. More often than not, we accept that only half the projected message—or less—is true. Obfuscation and obscurity have become the normal implants of media. We shrug off what we are told over television, radio, or in print as "clever advertising" or "sharp public relations." Why give out more words that serve to blur rather than clarify, or in general serve to debase the exercise of communication?

While it is true that we no longer are a nation of innocents, we do not reside in a state of anarchy either. We have standards. Because of our standards, one line of reasoning will serve to answer both criticisms and all questions relating to why the learned professionals should be allowed and even encouraged to advertise and promote their professional practices.

I ask critics to consider the professional person as an individual and the professions as a whole.

Willard Hurst, a noted legal historian, pointed out that "no abstract logic has created the concept of the professions." Instead, "practice and experience in making society function have led to the definition of some occupations as professional, and have from time to time, determined which ways of earning a living should fit the professional category."[1]

The professional person has certain characteristics, which were described in part in the first chapter. They bear repeating in this last chapter. The learned professional has:

- A defined area of competence
- An organized body of knowledge of some consequence
- Self-consciousness
- Controlled entrance into his field by some supervisory committee of his peers
- Continuing education
- Support of research
- Aid in the education of competent replacements
- Independence[2]

Do the professional people suddenly lose all these attributes when they begin to advertise and publicize? No! An enduring profession is built upon something more substantial than self-pleading. Advertisements and publicity don't tear down the structures of professionalism. They do, in fact, strengthen its foundations. Opening the professions to public scrutiny by the use of advertising and promotion is in fact applying an acetylene torch to the watertight bulkhead that lies between professional practitioners and the society in which they operate. The professional person is finally coming out from behind a false mystique that has been allowed to surround most of the learned professions. Advertising and promotion are blowing away the smoke screens.

The four horsemen of calumny—fear, ignorance, bigotry, and smear— are galloping madly about within the very fabric of the highly competitive circles in which professional people move. They suffer from petty jealousies and stab-in-the-back ethics among themselves. They preach righteousness when in their individual hearts they seethe with envy of their fellow professionals. Much progress is held back by intraprofessional fear of criticism.

I've been asked by clients who purchase my promotional services how they should react when they are stung by the criticism of their professional colleagues. They question how they should handle complaints about their advertisements or promotional activities. They wonder what to do if a fine is levied or a hearing conducted by the professional association involved. "What are my rights?" they ask. "Do I need a lawyer?"

Paradoxically, the answers can only come from the individual professional associations themselves. They make the rules and see that the state board of examiners enforces them. Consequently, I do not give direct replies to my clients' questions. I only explain what I did when my ethics and professionalism were castigated. I left the profession and turned full time to writing, advertising, public relations, publishing, research, and organizational representation. I made no appeal; I just left. I'm happier doing advertising and promotion for others. Maybe you would prefer to get legal counsel and fight back. The law says now you can.

Advertising and promotion, by their very use, are stimulants of progress. They give professionals incentive to try for new breakthroughs in their fields.

The growth of strong professional associations reflects the efforts of practitioners to wrap themselves in pseudo-status. Indeed, professional associations have proved themselves to be no more than glorified lobbying groups dedicated to greater financial gain for their members. The public's welfare is seldom included in their thrusts in the direction of professional change.

Rather, the skill, concepts, knowledge, training, compassion, and talents possessed by the wide variety of professional persons in associations are served better by public information about these people and their services. This is accomplished by employment of techniques of advertising and promotion.

The point made in this book is that the public and the professional are better off with honest advertising and promotion. From the mutual interest of individuals and institutions, a new philosophy has arisen. It is called "freedom of information." All of us have a right to get information and to give information. In my opinion, we should thank divine providence and the wisdom of the Supreme Court for the Bates and O'Steen decision.

# Notes

## Chapter 1

1. James A. Reynolds, "How Soon Will Your Colleagues Begin Advertising?" *Medical Economics,* February 23, 1976.
2. David Green, "Dental Advertising: Where in the World Will It End?" *Dental Management,* November 1977.
3. Richard Severo, "U.S. Controls Urged for Funeral Industry," *The New York Times,* June 19, 1978.
4. Ibid.
5. Wesley J. Liebeler, "Why the F.T.C. Wants Price Advertising," *Optometric Management,* August 1976.
6. Deborah Rankin, "Taxes and Accounting," *The New York Times,* June 20, 1978.

## Chapter 2

1. "Medical Journal Prescribes Physician Directories," *The Advocate,* September 2, 1978.
2. John Carlova, "What Would It Take to Make You Advertise?" *Medical Economics,* July 12, 1976.
3. Robert E. Gehrman, "Learning to Live with Advertising," *Dental Management,* July 1978.
4. "Is Advertising Laying an Egg? Lawyers May Be More Interested in Solicitation," *American Bar Association Journal* 64 (May 1978):673–74.

## Chapter 3

1. Richard L. Peck, "Do the Yellow Pages Make You See Red?" *Medical Economics,* August 22, 1977.
2. David Green, "Will It Really Pay to Advertise?" *Dental Management,* May 1976.
3. "Two Dentists Face Grilling," *The Advocate,* September 15, 1978.
4. "Dentists Fight Illegal Advertising Charge," *The Advocate,* September 16, 1978.

## Chapter 4

1. Raymond A. Bauer, "The Obstinate Audience: The Influence Process from the Point of View of Social Communication," *American Psychologist* 19, 322 (May 1964).
2. Joseph T. Klapper, *The Effects of Mass Communication* (New York: The Free Press, 1960), p. 92.
3. Walter Lippmann, *Public Opinion* (New York: Macmillan, 1922), p. 36.
4. Albert T. Poffenberger, *Psychology in Advertising* (New York: McGraw-Hill, 1932), p. 202.
5. James A. Reynolds, "How Soon Will Your Colleagues Begin Advertising?" *Medical Economics,* February 23, 1976.

## Chapter 5

1. Howard D. Hadley, "Newspapers vs. Television—Which Is the Better Buy?" *Media/scope* 2 (November 1958): 31–34.
2. Stan Luxenberg, "For Billboards, the Signs Are Bullish," *The New York Times,* June 25, 1978.
3. Gene F. Seehafer and Jack W. Laemmar, *Successful Television and Radio Advertising* (New York: McGraw-Hill, 1959), p. 102.
4. Richard P. Jones, "A Look at the Future of Radio" (address before NBC Network Radio affiliates, December 4, 1962).

## Chapter 6

1. Charles Brower, *Editor & Publisher,* December 7, 1957.
2. Joseph Serian, "The Case for Contact Lens Advertising," *Optometric Management,* March 1977.
3. Michael Halbert, *The Meaning and Sources of Marketing Theory* (New York: McGraw-Hill, Marketing Science Institute, n.d.), p. 110.
4. Richard M. Baker, Jr., and Gregg Phifer, *Salesmanship, Communication, Persuasion, Perception* (Boston: Allyn and Bacon, 1966), p. 21–46.

5. Philip H. Dougherty, "Blue Cross Stressing Self-Medical Care," *The New York Times,* April 13, 1978, p. 68.
6. John Kenneth Galbraith, *American Capitalism* (Boston: Houghton Mifflin, 1956), p. 70.
7. Robert K. Merton, Marjorie Fiske, and Patricia L. Kendall, *The Focused Interview* (New York: Columbia University Press, Bureau of Applied Social Research, 1952).

## Chapter 7

1. Charles F. Adams, *Common Sense in Advertising* (New York: McGraw-Hill, 1965), p. 35.
2. Ibid., p. 68.
3. John W. Crawford, Advertising, 2nd ed. (Boston: Allyn and Bacon, 1965), p. 120.
4. John Caples, *Tested Advertising Methods* (New York: Harper & Row, 1947), p. 89.
5. Steven Brill, "TV Pitchman for Cut-Rate Legal Advice," *Esquire* 89:87–88, 1978.
6. Victor O. Schwab, *How to Write a Good Advertisement* (New York: Harper & Row, 1962), p. 27–29.

## Chapter 8

1. Frederick R. Gamble, *What Advertising Agencies Are—What They Do and How They Do It* (New York: American Association of Advertising Agencies, Inc., 1963).
2. "Ads Start to Take Hold in the Professions," *Business Week,* July 24, 1978.
3. Quoted in Steven B. Roberts, "A New Breed of Lawyer Born of Advertisements." *The New York Times,* November 26, 1978.
4. Ira W. Rubel, "Rubel Spells Out Agency Operating Facts to Dispel Visions of High Profits, Easy Living," *Advertising Age,* December 9, 1957.

## Chapter 9

1. Edwin A. Moll, *Sell Yourself Big* (Chicago: Topaz Books, 1966), p. 72 & 73.
2. Daniel Q. Haney, "Psychiatrist Finds Chinese Food Additive Can Make People Unhappy," *The Advocate,* October 23, 1978.
3. D. Parke Gibson, *The $30 Billion Negro* (New York: Macmillan, 1969), p. 41.

## Chapter 13

1. Marian Burros, "The Scarsdale Diet: A Sure Fire Diet, or a Shortcut to Kidney Disease," *The Washington Post,* October 16, 1978.

## Chapter 14

1. Irving L. Straus, "Pointers to Help You Get Your Message Across," *Association Management,* June 1972.

## Chapter 15

1. Byron G. Wells, "How to Start Your Own FM Station," *Hi-Fi/Stereo Review,* September 1965.

## Chapter 16:

1. David Guy Powers, *How to Say a Few Words Effectively* (Garden City, NY: Nelson Doubleday, Inc.), 1958, p. 3.

2. Dave Alber, *The PR Reporter,* October 12, 1964.

## Chapter 18

1. Willard Hurst, "The Professions of American Life," *Public Relations Journal,* August 1957.
2. "Hallmarks of a Profession," *Public Relations Journal,* July 1968.

# Glossary

**Account executive** (or account representative): Advertising or PR agency executive responsible for management of a client's campaign or program.

**Agate line:** A space one column wide and 1/14 inch deep; used as unit of measurement in classified advertising.

**Billing:** Total amount of business of an advertising or PR agency. (Can also apply to classified advertising.)

**Bindery:** Plant where books or magazines are bound.

**Body copy:** The actual text, as opposed to headlines and other display matter.

**Boldface:** Type heavier and thicker than the rest of the type with which it appears.

**Borders:** Rules or designs marking the edge of printed matter.

**Box ad:** Display ad with border. Not run alphabetically in classified advertising, but premium display rate is usually charged.

**Bullets:** Solid circles used to head off paragraphs or other items on lists in text, to focus readers' attention.

**Closing date:** Publication deadline for submitting material; can also apply to final editing or actual reproduction.

**Cold type:** Erroneous but widely used term to describe offset and other reproduction methods that don't use cast-metal type. Correctly used, it refers to typewriters and other keyboard machines.

**Column inch:** Unit of measure for printed matter (primarily in newspapers) one column wide, one inch deep.

**Comprehensive:** A layout designed as closely as possible to the final reproduction.

**Controlled circulation:** Circulation limited by publisher to a particular readership; there is usually no charge for controlled-circulation material.

**Display:** Matter set on larger or different type, to distinguish from body copy. Can include artwork.

**Double half-column:** Two adjoining half-columns used for a single advertisement.

**Filler material:** Brief item of information to fill in extra space on a column or page.

**Film editing:** Cutting and arranging movie or TV film to give a story continuity and dramatic effect.

**Format:** Shape, size, and general makeup of printed matter; general organization and style of a radio or TV program.

**Frequency rates:** Classified advertising rates determined by number of insertions used within a given period (often 12 months) following date of first insertion of contract period.

**Hot type:** Metal type.

**Layout:** Designer's plan of an advertisement or other printed matter.

**Live-remote broadcast:** Untaped program originating outside TV or radio studio, often in another city.

**Local rates:** Classified advertising rates based on placement of ad in a newspaper edition delivered only to a particular zone of coverage, such as a suburban edition. These rates are generally lower than those for insertions in a metropolitan edition.

**Logotype (logo):** Single piece of type carrying one or two words (e.g., the name of a newspaper or a trademark), or other identifying symbol.

**Makeup:** Arrangement of text and artwork into columns or pages for reproduction.

**Mat:** Mold from which relief surface for reproduction is made by pouring or pressing.

**Mechanical:** A piece of finished copy, such as type and artwork, positioned and mounted for offset or other photomechnical reproduction.

**Milline:** A unit of space and circulation equivalent to one agate line appearing in one million copies of a publication.

**Offset:** Surface printing by photomechanical process rather than metal type.

**One-time:** Classified advertising rate for single insertion.

**Open:** Similar to one-time rate.

**Pennysaver:** Controlled-circulation shopping guide, with readership usually confined to small metropolitan or suburban area.

**Plate:** 1. Sheet of metal or other material (sometimes with relief surface) attached to press for printing; 2. sheet of material, often glass, coated with a light-sensitive photographic emulsion, used in processing photographs; 3. an illustration.

**Platemaker:** Person who operates machine for making printing plates.

**Rate card:** List of advertising rates (based on space, placement, and duration of insert or display) prepared by a publication.

**Release:** News or feature story prepared by a PR/advertising agency, institution, or individual for circulation to media.

# Glossary

**Retail:** Rates for advertisements appearing outside the classified section of a publication.

**ROP (run-of-the-paper):** Advertising placed anywhere in a publication at editor's option.

**Rough dummy:** Preliminary sketch of a layout.

**Rules:** Straight lines for separating text and/or illustrative material.

**Shopper:** Newspaper-format shopping directory; content predominantly advertising.

**"Short" rate:** Extra rate charged to an advertiser who has not earned a previously anticipated discount for media space or time purchased.

**Signature:** Tune or sound effect in radio, picture or symbol in TV, to identify a program, station, or network; also the name or identification of an advertiser.

**Sound-track synchronization:** Making motion-picture sound exactly simultaneous with corresponding action.

**Storyboard:** Panel or series of panels on which are mounted rough drawings illustrating main themes and sequence of films or TV programs.

**Sub-headline, or subhead:** Subordinate headline.

**Transient:** Classified ad rates not based on contract; transient advertisers can run inserts for unspecified periods of time.

**Typeface:** The face of printing type.

**Type style:** The design of a particular typeface.

# Suggested Reading

Aaker, D. A., and Myers, J. G. *Advertising Management.* Englewood Cliffs, NJ: Prentice-Hall, 1975.

Baird, Russell N., and Turnbull, Arthur T. *The Graphics of Communication,* 2d ed. New York: Holt, Rinehart, & Winston, 1968.

Bernays, Edward L., ed. *The Engineering of Consent.* Norman: University of Oklahoma Press, 1955.

Cutlip, Scott, and Center, Allen H. *Effective Public Relations,* 4th ed. Englewood Cliffs, NJ: Prentice-Hall, 1971.

Darrow, Richard W., Forrestal, Dan J., and Cookman, Aubrey O., eds. *Public Relations Handbook.* Chicago: Dartnell Corp., 1968.

*Developmental Psychology Today.* Del Mar, CA: CRM Books, 1971.

Divita, S., ed. *Advertising and the Public Interest.* Chicago: American Marketing Association, 1974.

Frank, R., Massy, W., and Wind, Y. *Market Segmentation.* Englewood Cliffs, NJ: Prentice-Hall, 1972.

Katona, George. *The Powerful Consumer.* New York: McGraw-Hill, 1960.

Nicosia, F. M. *Consumer Decision Processes: Marketing and Advertising Implications.* Englewood Cliffs, NJ: Prentice-Hall, 1966.

Ross, Irwin. *The Image Merchants.* Garden City, NY: Doubleday & Co., 1959.

## Suggested Reading

Schramm, Wilbur. *Men, Messages, and Media: A Look at Human Communications.* New York: Harper & Row, 1973.

Schwartz, Alvin. *Evaluating Your Public Relations.* New York: National Public Relations for Health and Welfare, 1965.

Siegal, Gonnie McClung. *How to Advertise and Promote Your Small Business.* New York: John Wiley & Sons, 1978.

Simon, Martin J. *Public Relations Law.* New York: Appleton-Century-Crofts, 1969.

Whyte, William H., Jr., and the editors of *Fortune. Is Anybody Listening?* New York: Simon & Schuster, 1952.

Wolseley, Roland E. *Understanding Magazines.* Ames: Iowa State University Press, 1969.

# Bibliography

Aaker, D. A., and Day, G. S. *Consumerism: Search for the Consumer Interest.* New York: Free Press, 1974.

Arnold, Edmund C. *Profitable Newspaper Advertising.* New York: Harper & Row, 1960.

Berlo, David K. *The Process of Communication.* New York: Holt, Rinehart & Winston, 1960.

Bloomenthal, Howard. *Promoting Your Cause.* New York: Funk & Wagnalls, 1971.

Boorstin, Daniel J. *The Image: A Guide to Pseudo-Events in America.* New York: Harper & Row, 1962.

Bryan, James E. *Public Relations in Medical Practice.* Baltimore, MD: Williams & Wilkins, 1955.

Caples, John. *Making Ads Pay.* New York: Dover, 1957.

Center, Allen. *Public Relations Practices: Case Studies.* Englewood Cliffs, NJ: Prentice-Hall, 1975.

Cook, Harvey R. *More Profits Through Advertising.* New York: Drake, 1969.

Fehlman, Frank E. *How to Write Advertising Copy That Sells.* New York: Funk & Wagnalls, 1950.

Golden, Hal, and Hanson, Kitty. *The Techniques of Working with the Working Press.* Dobbs Ferry, NY: Oceana Publications, 1962.

257

# Bibliography

Hall, Babette. *The Right Angles: How to Do Successful Publicity.* New York: Ives Washburn, 1965.

Hirshleifer, J. "Where Are We in the Theory of Information?" *American Economic Review,* May 1973.

Jacobs, Herbert. *Practical Publicity.* New York: McGraw-Hill, 1964.

Kahl, Joseph A. *The American Class Structure.* New York: Holt, Rinehart & Winston, 1957.

Karch, R. Randolph and Buber, Edward J. *Graphic Arts Procedures.* Chicago: American Technical Society, 1967.

Lippmann, Walter. *Public Opinion.* New York: Free Press, 1965.

MacDougall, Curtis. *Understanding Public Opinion.* Dubuque, Iowa: William C. Brown, 1966.

Malickson, David L. and Nason, John W. *Advertising—How to Write the Kind that Works.* New York: Charles Scribner's Sons, 1977.

McLuhan, Marshall. *Understanding Media: The Extension of Man.* New York: McGraw-Hill, 1964.

Moran, W. T. "The Law of Conservation of Advertising Energy." In C. W. King and D. J. Tigert (eds.), *Attitude Research Reaches New Heights.* Chicago: American Marketing Association, Marketing Research Techniques, Bibliography Series No. 14, n.d.

Nafziger, Ralph O., and White, David M., eds. *Introduction to Mass Communications Research,* rev. ed. Baton Rouge: Louisiana State University Press, 1963.

Palda, K. *The Measurement of Cumulative Advertising Effects.* Englewood Cliffs, NJ: Prentice-Hall, 1964.

Pinkham, Richard P. *Public Relations for Bar Associations.* Chicago: American Bar Association, 1954.

Read, Hadley. *Communications: Methods for All Media.* Urbana: University of Illinois Press, 1972.

Reeves, Rosser. *Reality in Advertising.* New York: Alfred A. Knopf, 1961.

Schmidt, Frances and Weiner, Harold N., eds. *Public Relations for Health and Welfare.* New York: Columbia University Press, 1966.

Schoenfeld, Clarence A. *Publicity Media and Methods.* New York: Macmillan, 1963.

Smith, Cynthia S. *How to Get Big Results from a Small Advertising Budget.* New York: Hawthorn Books, 1973.

Smith, George H. *Motivation Research in Advertising and Marketing.* New York: McGraw-Hill, 1955.

Stahl, LeRoy. *The Art of Publicity.* Minneapolis, MN: Denison, 1962.

Stevenson, George A. *Graphic Arts Encyclopedia.* New York: McGraw-Hill, 1968.

Weiner, Richard. *Professional's Guide to Publicity,* 2d ed. New York: Richard Weiner, Inc., 1978.

Weiner, Richard. *Professional's Guide to Public Relations Services,* 3d ed. New York: Richard Weiner, Inc., 1975.

Welsh, James J. *The Speech Writing Guide.* New York: John Wiley & Sons, 1968.

# Index

# Index

Index